Archibald Henderson

Palestine : its historical geography

With topographical index and maps

Archibald Henderson

Palestine : its historical geography
With topographical index and maps

ISBN/EAN: 9783337282936

Printed in Europe, USA, Canada, Australia, Japan

Cover: Foto ©Andreas Hilbeck / pixelio.de

More available books at **www.hansebooks.com**

Handbooks for Bible Classes and Private Students.

EDITED BY
REV. MARCUS DODS, D.D.,
AND
REV. ALEXANDER WHYTE, D.D.

IN PREPARATION.

THE SABBATH. By Rev. Professor SALMOND, D.D., Aberdeen.

THE GOSPEL ACCORDING TO ST. JOHN. By Rev. GEORGE REITH, M.A., Glasgow. [*Shortly.*

THE BOOK OF ACTS. By Rev. Professor LINDSAY, D.D., Glasgow. Part II., Chaps. xiii. to xxviii. [*Shortly.*

THE FIRST EPISTLE TO THE CORINTHIANS. By Rev. MARCUS DODS, D.D., Glasgow.

THE EPISTLE TO THE PHILIPPIANS. By Rev. JAMES MELLIS, M.A., Southport.

THE EPISTLE TO THE COLOSSIANS. By Rev. SIMEON R. MACPHAIL, M.A., Liverpool.

CHURCH AND STATE. By A. TAYLOR INNES, Esq., Advocate, Edinburgh.

CHRISTIAN ETHICS. By Rev. Professor LINDSAY, D.D., Glasgow.

THE WORK OF THE SPIRIT. By Rev. Professor CANDLISH, D.D.

APOLOGETICS. By Rev. JAMES IVERACH, M.A., Aberdeen.

THE BOOK OF EXODUS. By JAMES MACGREGOR, D.D., late of New College, Edinburgh.

THE DOCTRINE OF SIN. By Rev. Professor CANDLISH, D.D.

ISAIAH. By Rev. Professor EMSLIE, M.A., London.

[*For Volumes already issued see next page.*

HANDBOOKS FOR BIBLE CLASSES.

NOW READY.

THE EPISTLE TO THE GALATIANS. By JAMES MACGREGOR, D.D., late of New College, Edinburgh. *Price 1s. 6d.*

THE POST-EXILIAN PROPHETS. With Introductions and Notes. By Rev. MARCUS DODS, D.D., Glasgow. *Price 2s.*

A LIFE OF CHRIST. By Rev. JAMES STALKER, M.A. *Price 1s. 6d.*

THE SACRAMENTS. By Rev. Professor CANDLISH, D.D. *Price 1s. 6d.*

THE BOOKS OF CHRONICLES. By Rev. Professor MURPHY, LL.D., Belfast. *Price 1s. 6d.*

THE CONFESSION OF FAITH. By Rev. JOHN MACPHERSON, M.A., Findhorn. *Price 2s.*

THE BOOK OF JUDGES. By Rev. Principal DOUGLAS, D.D. *Price 1s. 3d.*

THE BOOK OF JOSHUA. By Rev. Principal DOUGLAS, D.D. *Price 1s. 6d.*

THE EPISTLE TO THE HEBREWS. By Rev. Professor DAVIDSON, D.D., Edinburgh. *Price 2s. 6d.*

SCOTTISH CHURCH HISTORY. By Rev. N. L. WALKER. *Price 1s. 6d.*

THE CHURCH. By Rev. Prof. BINNIE, D.D., Aberdeen. *Price 1s. 6d.*

THE REFORMATION. By Rev. Professor LINDSAY, D.D. *Price 2s.*

THE BOOK OF GENESIS. By Rev. MARCUS DODS, D.D. *Price 2s.*

THE EPISTLE TO THE ROMANS. By Rev. Principal BROWN, D.D., Aberdeen. *Price 2s.*

PRESBYTERIANISM. By Rev. JOHN MACPHERSON, M.A. *Price 1s. 6d.*

LESSONS ON THE LIFE OF CHRIST. By Rev. WM. SCRYMGEOUR, Glasgow. *Price 2s. 6d.*

THE SHORTER CATECHISM. By Rev. ALEXANDER WHYTE, D.D., Edinburgh. *Price 2s. 6d.*

THE GOSPEL ACCORDING TO ST. MARK. By Rev. Professor LINDSAY, D.D., Glasgow. *Price 2s. 6d.*

A SHORT HISTORY OF CHRISTIAN MISSIONS. By GEORGE SMITH, LL.D., F.R.G.S. *Price 2s. 6d.*

A LIFE OF ST. PAUL. By Rev. JAMES STALKER, M.A. *Price 1s. 6d.*

THE BOOK OF ACTS. By Rev. Professor LINDSAY, D.D. Part I., Chaps. i. to xii. *Price 1s. 6d.*

PALESTINE. With Maps. By Rev. ARCH. HENDERSON, M.A., Crieff. *Price 2s. 6d.*

HANDBOOKS

FOR

BIBLE CLASSES

AND PRIVATE STUDENTS.

EDITED BY

REV. MARCUS DODS, D.D.,

AND

REV. ALEXANDER WHYTE, D.D.

PALESTINE.—BY REV. ARCH. HENDERSON, M.A.

EDINBURGH:
T. & T. CLARK, 38 GEORGE STREET

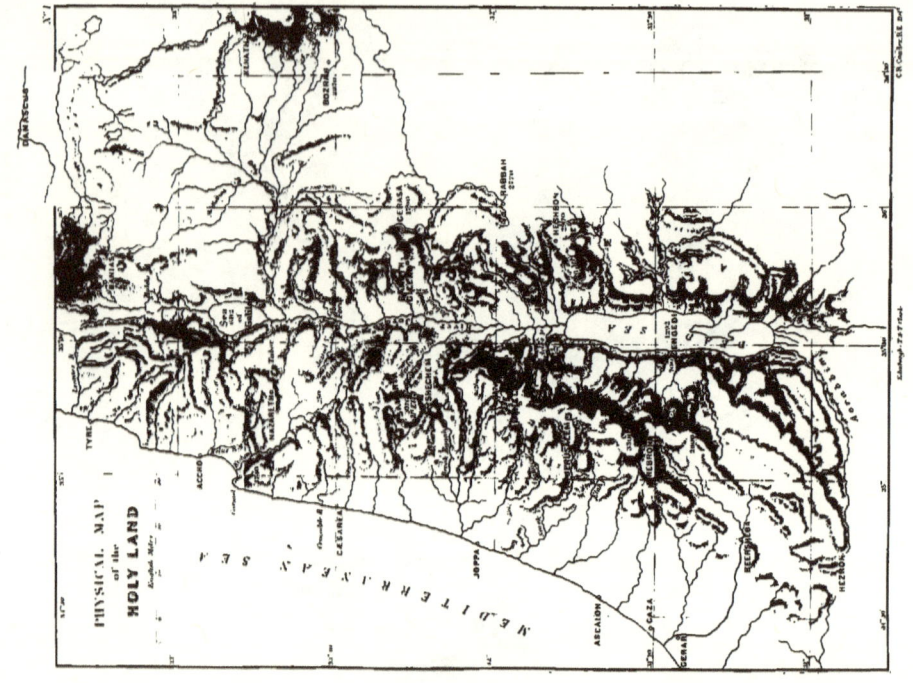

ITS HISTORICAL GEOGRAPHY,
WITH TOPOGRAPHICAL INDEX, AND MAPS.

BY

REV. ARCHIBALD HENDERSON, M.A.

PREFACE.

A *Handbook of Palestine* is of necessity indebted to many to whom only a general acknowledgment of help can be offered. The work of the "Palestine Exploration Fund" is of such exceptional value that express reference to it is required. With the distinguished officers of the Royal Engineers, and others, who have done the work of that Society, Canon Tristram has been associated in preparing the *Survey Memoirs of Western Palestine*, and the reader cannot fail to note how much these pages owe to him. Most special thanks are, however, due to Captain Conder, R.E., for help obtained from his published works and by correspondence, but above all for the Maps, which appeared in his valuable *Handbook to the Bible*, and which he not only generously gave the use of, but most kindly revised for this book. The only point of importance in which the text differs from his Maps is discussed in § 113. The author would add, in Map V., a Bethsaida close to Capernaum.

The survey of Eastern Palestine has been arrested; but a map, complete as far as possible, is in preparation (p. 83), and this Handbook has been designed for use with it. The historical method was chosen, as not only more attractive and useful for Bible classes, but as enhancing the apologetic value of the study of Palestine Geography. Repetition thus caused may be held excused by the importance of the places more frequently mentioned. Bible names are spelt as in the Authorized Version; modern names as in the Survey Map, and the lamented Professor Palmer's *Name Lists*.

CRIEFF, *Dec.* 1884.

[CONTENTS.

CONTENTS.

CHAP.				PAGE
I. POSITION AND IMPORTANCE OF THE LAND OF PALESTINE,				
			§ 1–6,	11
II. PHYSICAL FEATURES OF THE LAND. MAP I.				
	First Longitudinal Division,	Maritime Plain,	§ 8,	15
	Second ,, ,,	Mountains of Israel,	§ 9–12,	17
	Third ,, ,,	Jordan Valley,	§ 13–22,	21
	Fourth ,, ,,	Eastern Palestine,	§ 23–28,	31
III. NATURAL HISTORY OF THE LAND,			§ 29–31,	39
IV. EARLY INHABITANTS,			§ 32–40,	44
V. PALESTINE IN THE DAYS OF THE PATRIARCHS.				
	Abraham,		§ 41–49,	54
	Isaac,		§ 50,	63
	Jacob,		§ 51–54,	63
VI. TERRITORY OF THE TWELVE TRIBES. MAP II.				
	1. Eastern Palestine.			
	Conquests in the East,		§ 55–57,	68
	Nebo,		§ 58,	70
	(1) Lot of Reuben,		§ 59,	72
	(2) ,, Gad,		§ 60,	74
	(3) ,, Manasseh,		§ 61,	75
	2. Western Palestine. MAP III.			
	Joshua's Campaign in South,		§ 62–64,	76
	,, ,, North,		§ 65, 66,	80
	Tribal Boundaries,		§ 67,	82
	(4) Lot of Judah,		§ 68, 69,	83
	(5) ,, Simeon,		§ 70,	87
	(6) ,, Benjamin,		§ 71,	88
	(7) ,, Dan,		§ 72,	90
	(8) ,, Ephraim,		§ 73, 74,	91
	(3) ,, Manasseh, 2nd,		§ 75,	95
	(9) ,, Issachar,		§ 76,	97
	(10) ,, Zebulun,		§ 77,	99
	(11) ,, Asher,		§ 78,	100
	(12) ,, Naphtali,		§ 79,	102
VII. PALESTINE IN THE TIME OF THE JUDGES AND OF DAVID.				
	1. Book of Judges,		§ 80–84,	105
	2. First Book of Samuel,		§ 85–88,	111

CONTENTS. ix

CHAP.		PAGE
VIII. DAYS OF THE KINGDOM. Map IV.		
1. Jerusalem,	§ 89,	119
Surrounding Valleys,	§ 90,	119
Mountain Site. Note on Valley of Hinnom,	§ 91,	120
Water-Supply,	§ 92,	123
Walls and Population,	§ 93,	126
David's Later Years,	§ 94,	129
2. The Divided Kingdom.		
Boundary,	§ 95,	130
Israel,	§ 96, 97,	132
Judah,	§ 98,	135
3. Maccabees,	§ 99,	137
IX. PALESTINE OF THE NEW TESTAMENT. Map V.		
1. The Territorial Divisions,	§ 100,	139
2. The Temple of Herod.		
Site and Retaining Walls,	§ 101, 102,	141
Outer Court,	§ 103,	145
"The House,"	§ 104,	146
3. Other Buildings by Herod,	§ 105,	147
4. Scenes of Our Lord's Life.		
Early Days—Bethlehem, Nazareth, Cana, Nain,	§ 106-108,	149
With the Baptist—Bethabara, Ænon, Sychar, Tiberias, Machærus,	§ 109-111,	153
By the Sea of Galilee—Bethsaida Julias, Gennesareth, Magdala, Capernaum, Bethsaida, Chorazin, Decapolis, Gadara, Gerza, and Dalmanutha,	§ 112-114,	156
Regions beyond—Tyre and Sidon, Cæsarea-Philippi, Ephraim, and Perea,	§ 115,	160
At the Close—Olivet, Bethany, Gethsemane, Calvary, Emmaus,	§ 116-118,	161
5. Palestine in the Book of Acts.		
Gaza to Sidon,	§ 119, 120,	167
APPENDIX,		171
TOPOGRAPHICAL INDEX,		175

PALESTINE.

CHAPTER I.

POSITION AND IMPORTANCE OF PALESTINE RELATIVELY TO OTHER LANDS.

"When the Most High divided to the nations their inheritance, when He separated the sons of Adam, He set the bounds of the people according to the number of the children of Israel."—DEUT. XXXII. 8.

1. Paradise, which was the home of our race before men were divided, lay in the fertile plain watered by the Tigris and Euphrates.[1] Eden was the ancient name of the "field" of Babylonia; and "Babel" is a translation of the primitive name, which was *Ca-dimira*, the "gate of God."[2] From thence the sons of Noah were dispersed over the earth. An account of their geographical distribution is preserved in Gen. x. There will be found the origin of all the nations with whom we meet throughout the Bible history. Every statement in that very ancient record has been attested by recent discoveries.

2. In those early times, as in all times, the strong served themselves at the expense of the weak. The tribes which could do so seized the richer, warmer, and more luxuriant valleys, thrusting others back into the deserts or the mountains. But retribution followed. The easy-living dwellers in the plains gradually grew softer and weaker, while

---

[1] The Tigris was called by the earliest dwellers on its banks *id Idikla;* Pishon means a *canal;* Gihon is probably *Gukhan*, the stream on which Babylon afterwards stood. See Gen. ii. 10–14.

[2] Lenormant states that the most ancient name of Babylon in the idiom of the ante-Semitic population was *Tin-tir-ki*, which signifies "the place of the tree of life."

the hardened mountaineers and desert rangers grew stronger, and at last swept over and conquered for themselves the coveted lands, and dwelt in them. As in our day, so then also overcrowding of the population led to migration. Men journeyed till they found other valleys and plains as rich as those they had left, or pressed on till they reached the shores of the sea. In the Scripture narratives we have to do chiefly, almost exclusively, with those who journeyed westward. Whether they took to the sea and landed in Cush, or edged round by the Arabian sea-coast, or from the banks of the Euphrates struck across for the Mediterranean ("the sea" of the Bible), and felt their way along its shores southward, they very early, by one of these routes or by them all, found the great river of Egypt and the valley of which it is the life. Here was a soil more than rivalling Eden itself, for which, no doubt, many a fierce war was waged long before the times of which we have any record.

3. By the time of Abraham, great nations with vast armies had come into existence, and not content with possessing their own lands, sought to conquer and enslave other peoples. The possession of the two great valleys of the Euphrates and the Nile was the ambition of conquerors during the whole period of Old Testament history, as to this day it is the cause of jealousy and strife among the nations of Europe. But not only did armies march century after century between the Nile and Euphrates, the caravans of commerce thronged the roads in times of peace. *All these roads passed through or close by Palestine.* The great waterless desert lay in the direct line; hence armies and caravans journeying westwards, kept by the Euphrates banks till at its nearest point to the oasis of Damascus and its famous streams; from Damascus they either journeyed southward, keeping on the eastern boundary of Palestine and crossing the desert on the south, or they crossed Palestine in the north and went down to Egypt by the coast-line. They must go the one way or the other to avoid the mountains which occupy the centre of Palestine. These mountains thus became a fortress commanding the roads between the much-coveted lands of Babylonia and Egypt. Their possessors held a position of the highest influence in the world's history, the third with Egypt and with Assyria (Isa. xxiii. 25).

4. The importance of Palestine was in no way due to its size. It is a very small country; its size, when first realized, creating a feeling of surprise and disappointment. The territory included in the promise to Abraham, Gen. xv. 18-21, was not possessed by Israel until the time of David: it includes much more than *Palestine*. Originally Palestine designated the land of the Philistine, or Philistia; now it is used as equivalent to "all the land of Israel" allotted by Joshua to the twelve tribes, though, not unfrequently, of that part only of Israel's territory which lay on the west of the Jordan, the land on the east never having become exclusively the possession of the Israelites, and occupying comparatively an unimportant place in Scripture history. As first assigned by Moses (Num. xxxiv.), the more limited boundaries on the west of Jordan were described; and although at their own request the tribes of Gad and Reuben and Manasseh obtained their inheritance on the east, the names of the earlier possessors still clung to their lands, which have never been known but as "Moab" and "Ammon" and "Gilead" and "Bashan."

5. **Western Palestine** may be roughly described as a truncated triangle, of which the eastern side is formed by the Jordan, the western by the Mediterranean. The base is formed by a line joining the south-east corner of the Mediterranean and the south end of the Dead Sea. Dan lies at the north in the Jordan valley, Beersheba about the centre of the base line; hence the proverbial phrase, "from Dan to Beersheba," as we speak of "from Land's End to John O'Groat's." *The distance between Dan and Beersheba is just* 144 *miles*, or exactly one-half the length of Scotland. The *breadth* is about 90 miles at the line of Beersheba; at a line drawn westwards from the north end of the Salt Sea and passing through Jerusalem, it is 55 miles; at the south end of the Sea of Galilee, it is 40 miles; and at the extreme north, it is only 25 miles. *The whole area is* 6000 *square miles*, or as much as is included in the two Scotch counties of Inverness and Sutherland, or in the principality of Wales.

6. **This country has been known by many names.** The most ancient which has come down to us is *Taneter*, by which it is spoken of in the records of Thothmes III. of Egypt, B.C. 1450. Some translate this by "Holy Land," and infer thence that there was some sacred associa-

tion with it earlier even than the time of Abraham. From very early times it was known as *the Land of Canaan.* Just as the name of Philistia, applied at first to a part, was often given to the whole; so Canaan, which originally applied only to Phœnicia, was also given to the whole land between the Jordan and the Mediterranean (Gen v. 15–19). Canaan means "lowlands," and it is used in its earliest and strictest application in Isa. xxiii. 11, though translated there "merchant city." In Josh. i. 4, Judg. i. 26, the country is spoken of as "the Land of the Hittites," a great people whose empire, rivalling Egypt, extended over Syria to the Euphrates, and who in Abraham's time held possession as far south as Hebron (Gen. xxiii.). Other familiar names, as "the Land of Israel," "the Land of Promise," etc., need no explanation.

CHAPTER II.

PHYSICAL FEATURES OF THE LAND.

(*See* MAP I., *Frontispiece*.)

7. Palestine is a land of mountains. On the map of Europe and Asia, a long range may be traced more or less distinctly from the Pyrenees in Western Europe through Asia to China. Part of this long girdle about the globe is known as the Caucasus. From the Caucasus a branch runs southward, dividing the western sources of the Euphrates from Asia Minor, and forking at its lower end into the Lebanon and the Antilebanon. The Lebanon range—broken up somewhat at the plain of Esdraelon—runs through the whole of Western Palestine, forming the mountains of Galilee, Ephraim, and Judah, as far as Beersheba, where it falls away by easy steps to the desert level, suddenly to rise into the heights of Sinai, 250 *miles beyond Beersheba*. The eastern branch, of Antilebanon, better known as Hermon, runs on as the hills of Bashan and Gilead and Moab to Mount Hor in Edom, which is just 250 *miles from Dan*. Looking at the Physical Map at the beginning of the volume, it will be at once seen that the land is divided by these mountain ranges into four strips lying north and south. There is the coast-line of level sandy soil; then the Lebanon mountain range; next the great Jordan valley, deepening as it descends to the Dead Sea; and fourthly, the Antilebanon range beyond Jordan, spreading out into a great table-land eastwards.

FIRST LONGITUDINAL SECTION—THE MARITIME PLAIN.

8. The western division is the plain which forms the coast-line. In the north, where it is called the plain of *Phœnicia*, it is very narrow.

From earliest times its inhabitants were driven to seek their livelihood from the harvest of the sea and from its commerce. The Leontes or *Litâny* bounded the land on the north. Rising in the neighbourhood of Baalbeck, it drains the rich plain between Lebanon and Antilebanon, flowing south-eastward for some 60 miles; then turning sharply to the west, through a deep narrow chasm it reaches the Mediterranean about 5 miles north of Tyre. In earlier times it poured its waters into the Jordan valley (§ 13). Tyre was originally situated on two islands joined, it is said, by Hiram, and afterwards by Alexander the Great connected with the mainland (see § 115). Ten miles north of the Litâny was Sarepta, while Zidon lay other 8 miles beyond. For about 100 miles north of the Litâny the coast runs almost in a straight course north-east, keeping parallel to the Lebanon range with an average distance between the sea and the ridge of the mountains of but 15 miles. This district lying beyond the Leontes was never possessed by Israel, for even in the days of Solomon the Phœnicians were allies, never subjects. It is not therefore properly reckoned as within Palestine.

The narrow plain of Phœnicia is bounded on the south by *the ladder of Tyre*, a sharp spur from the Lebanon which thrusts itself into the sea, and over which the coast road passes 16 miles south of Tyre. South of this the maritime plain widens (its average width being about 5 miles), till at Acre it is again interrupted by the southern range of the hills of Upper Galilee, which here approach the sea. The Bay of Acre is the most important bay along the coast, and the only natural harbour of Palestine. It sweeps round the base of Carmel, which closes it on the south. The Belus[1] flows into it at the north, and the Kishon at the south, the former coming from the fertile district of the Buttauf, which lies to the north of the Nazareth range, and the latter from the great plain of Esdraelon.

Beyond Carmel the plain broadens out as it extends southward and merges into the plain of Sharon opposite Joppa, south of which it is confined by a protrusion of the Judæan mountains; but

---

[1] The Belus, called *Shihor Libnath*, Josh. xix. 26, is the traditional place of the discovery of glass-making; the name signifies "the river of glass."

again widening, it forms the plain of Philistia, which south of Gaza melts away into the desert, southward and westward.

"Philistia consists of an undulating plain from 50 to 100 feet above the level of the sea, reaching 32 miles from Ekron to Gaza, with a breadth of from 9 to 16 miles. To the east of this the hills commence, not the hill country, but a series of low spurs and undulating ground, culminating in hogs' backs running nearly north and south, and rising in places to 1200 feet above the ocean; to the east of these there is a steep descent of 500 feet or so to valleys which break through the barriers much in the same manner as we find the rivers forming passes through the chalk hills between Aldershot and Chatham. To the east of these again the hill country commences, and in 2 or 3 miles we rise to altitudes of 1700 to 2000 feet—the backbone of the country being at an elevation of 2400 to 3000 feet. In the hill country the spurs, not more than 1 mile or so apart, are often separated by narrow ravines 1500 to 2000 feet deep, at the bottom of which in the rainy season rapid torrents roll. Follow them into the plain and see what becomes of them; . . . The fact is, the bulk of the water reaches the ocean underground; on arising into the plain it forms marshes and pools, and quietly sinks away, while the bed of the stream itself in the plain is merely a narrow ditch some 6 feet wide and 4 feet deep. You may leave the water at the commencement of the wâdy mouth, ride over the plain without seeing any of it, and meet it again welling out of the ground close to the sea-shore, forming wide lagoons there. Now if proper precautions were taken, were the people industrious, and the country cultivated and clothed again with trees, the waters flowing in the ravines might be conducted over the plains in the early summer months, and induce the rich soil to yield a second crop" (Sir C. Warren, "The Plain of Philistia," *Survey Memoirs*, Jerusalem vol., p. 436).

SECOND LONGITUDINAL SECTION—THE MOUNTAINS OF ISRAEL.

9. **The second longitudinal division of the land** lying immediately on the east of the plain now described is formed by the southern portion of the Lebanon.

In Num. xxxiv., Hor-ha-har is named as upon the northern boundary. This Mount Hor (not to be confounded with the mountain of the same name in Edom mentioned § 7) must have been part of the Lebanon range, and is identified by some with Mount Sannîn northeast of Beyrout: it may have been so called as the mountain of the Phœnicians whose name among the early Egyptians was *Khar* or *Har*. Sannîn (8500 feet) is the highest point of the Lebanon.

Farther south the mountains occupying the district of Upper Galilee have an average height of 2800. The *Jebel Jermûk*, 3934 feet, is the highest point, and from it the most of the ranges radiate; it lies 12 miles west of the Jordan at a point in its course half-way between the Lake Huleh and the Sea of Galilee. South of the Jebel Jermûk the hills average half its height, and when due west of the Sea of Galilee we are on a plateau but 900 feet above sea-level.

"These hills ... partake of the jagged outline, of the varied vegetation, and of the high upland hollows which characterize in a greater or less degree the whole mass of the Lebanon range, in contrast to the monotonous aspect of the more southern scenery. So few travellers visit the interior of the Galilean mountains, that their beauty and richness is almost unknown. M. Van de Velde, who, contrary to the usual course, entered Palestine from the north, contrasts them favourably even with the rich valley of Samaria. 'It suffered,' he says, 'in my case from my having entered the rocky mountains of Ephraim from the much finer and truly noble Galilee.' Tabor ... is in fact the farthermost southern and eastern outpost of the peculiar mixture of greensward and forest, which, like a long stretch of English park-scenery, extends the whole way from the plain of Acre to Nazareth, through the tribe of Zebulun. And a similar tract, although in a more mountainous district, characterizes the hills of Naphtali, which bound the plain of Merom" (Stanley's *Sinai and Palestine*, p. 362 f.).

"The reconnaissance survey along the watershed from Hûnin led across a succession of mountain peaks from the great western vale of the Jordan. The highlands—in the tribe of Naphtali—form a series of valleys with which the country is intersected, the ridges between them being described as somewhat of the character of open glades, gently sloping towards the sea (of Galilee). The hills are well wooded. ... At the last peak the hill slopes to the southward, overlooking a little plain 1 mile wide and 2 long, lying sheltered among the surrounding hills. This is the plain of Zaanim" (*Our Work in Palestine*, p. 174. For description of the valley *west* of Nazareth, see § 107).

10. The mountain range is interrupted by the **Plain of Esdraelon** (or *Jezreel*), which runs from the Jordan valley in a north-westerly direction to the Bay of Acre. It is about 9 miles broad at the centre. Its northern boundary at the east is the *Jebel Duhy* range,—the hill *Moreh* of Judg. vii. 1, called also the *Little Hermon* range,—which rises abruptly from the Jordan valley, and encloses the south-western corner of the Sea of Galilee. About the middle of the country the mountains retire suddenly northward, forming a bay into which the

plain extends, and from which rises the conical mountain *Tabor*, 1850 feet. At the west the northern boundary of the plain is formed by the Nazareth range, which rises from it in precipitous steps, but slopes back gently to the north and west. The southern boundary of the plain is formed on the east by the *Mountains of Gilboa*, which bend out sickle-shaped from the hills of Samaria, contracting the eastern end of the plain into the Wâdy Jâlûd. The long stretch of *Carmel* reaching north-westward to the sea, forms the remainder of its southern boundary. The appearance of the map suggests that here the Lebanon range had been broken and bent away westwards, the solitary fragment of Tabor standing as a memorial of the disaster. The watershed of the plain is about 25 miles from the sea. The eastern portion is drained by the *Jâlûd*, which passes l'ethshean (*Beisan*) and empties into the Jordan. By the Wâdy Jâlûd the great highway ran between the east and west, and opposite it the ford of Jordan was called pre-eminently *Abarah, i.e.* the ford. The western part of the plain is drained by the *Kishon*, which springs up about the roots of Tabor, and falls into the Bay of Acre.

11. **Immediately south of the plain the country again rises into mountain heights.** The highest point of *Gilboa* is 1698 feet, and of *Carmel* 1742 feet; the west point of the latter, where it thrusts itself into the sea, being 500 feet. The hill of *Samaria*, 15 miles south of the plain, stands out solitarily amid the mountain ranges round it. Six miles farther south rises *Ebal*, 3076 feet, which is divided by the *vale of Shechem* from *Gerizim*, 2848 feet. After this the mountain watershed of the land becomes more consolidated and maintains a greater, as well as steadier, altitude. About 20 miles south of Ebal, *Tell 'Azûr* (Baal Hazor, 2 Sam. xiii. 23) raises its barren, grey summit 3318 feet. Five miles to north of it lies *Shiloh*, and as far to south lies *Bethel*. From Bethel a journey of 10 miles brings us to *Jerusalem*, 2500 feet above sea-level; the whole distance between Samaria and Jerusalem, the capitals of the northern and southern kingdoms, being, as the crow flies, not over 35 miles, less than the distance between Edinburgh and Glasgow, and about half the distance between York and Lancaster. Five miles south of Jerusalem, *Râs Sherifeh* rises above *Bethlehem* 3260 feet; and immediately north

of *Hebron*, which is 20 miles from Jerusalem, the height of 3500 is attained. Beyond Hebron the height falls again to about the level of Jerusalem, and gradually sinks down towards the southern desert plateau. By the parting of the hills as they descend a great valley is formed, which widens as it goes south-westwards to *Beersheba*, 30 miles from Hebron. The drainage of the southern hills feeds this valley with an abundant supply of water, which can easily be obtained by sinking wells in it. This district is often mentioned in Scripture as the *Negeb*, or Southland (Gen. xiii. 3, xxi. 1; Num. xiii. 17, 22, 29; Deut. i. 7; Josh. xi. 16).

12. From the watershed which we have traced, the valleys run westwards to the Mediterranean and eastwards to the Jordan. The more important on the west are those which form the courses of the streams of the *Kanah*; the valley of *Ajalon*, famed in the conquest of Joshua; the valley of *Sorek*, scene of the exploits of Samson; and the valley of *Elah*, where David smote Goliath. On the east are the *Wâdy Farah*, which carries the waters of Shechem and Ænon to the Jordan; the valley of *Achor*, which runs from Ai to Jericho; the steep pass from Bethany down to Jericho; and the *Wâdy Malâki*, in which David hid from Saul. The hills of Judah are much steeper on the east than on the west, where they fall towards Philistia in long-rolling hills, forming what is known as the Shephelah. Not only do they descend suddenly on the east into the Dead Sea, but on that side the land is barren, being known as the *Jeshimon*, or wilderness of Judea. It is a waste and isolate region, the people who now sparsely occupy it having a dialect of their own. Its isolation is caused by its character, not its distance from the capital; for from its northern part at least the snowy dome of Hermon may be seen—another forcible reminder of the smallness of "the Holy Land."

"The view" from Er Rueikbeh, 9 miles south-west of Bethlehem, writes Conder, "was most extraordinary: on every side were other ridges equally white, steep, and narrow; their sides were seamed by innumerable torrent-beds; their summits were sharp and rugged in outline. These ridges stood almost isolated between broad flat valleys of soft white marl scattered with flints, and with a pebbly torrent-course in the middle. There was not a tree visible, scarcely even a thorny shrub; the whole was like the dry basin of a former sea, scoured by the rains, and washed down in places to the hard foundation of metamorphic limestone which underlies the whole district, and forms precipices 2000 feet high over the shores of the Dead Sea" (*Tent Work in Palestine*, vol. ii. p. 127).

Writing of the ascent from the Wâdy Zuweirah (§ 21), Tristram thus describes his journey over the desert, fully 30 miles south of Captain Conder's point of view :—

" For two hours the ascent was rocky and slippery, and generally we had to lead our horses till we entered upon the south wilderness of Judea. Our course lay north-west, and for another hour nothing could surpass the mountain range in repulsive desolation. Rocks there were, great and small, stones loose and sharp, but no other existing thing. Occasionally, in the depression of a small ravine, a few plants of salsola or retem struggled up, but this was all; and we only saw one rock-chat and two desert larks. Almost sudden was the transition to the upland wilderness, the 'Negeb' or south country —a series of rolling hills clad with scanty herbage here and there, especially on their northern faces. . . . Nothing can be barer than the south country of Judah. It is neither grand, desolate, nor wild, but utter barrenness—not a tree nor a shrub, but scant, stunted herbage, covered with myriads of white snails, of five or six species, which afford abundant sustenance to the thousands of birds which inhabit it. It is the very country for camel browsing, quite unlike any we had hitherto traversed, but sometimes reminding one of the best parts of the Sahara. We were perplexed at first to account for the sharp transition from the sharp rocky peaks, without a blade of green, to the verdure of the smooth rounded hills, till we noticed that we had come upon the soft limestone which here covers the hard crystalline, as it does near Sidon" (*Land of Israel*, pp. 360-362).

THIRD LONGITUDINAL SECTION—THE JORDAN VALLEY.

13. **The third longitudinal section is the Jordan valley**, which is not only the most remarkable feature of the land of Palestine, but one of the most remarkable on the earth's surface. The name Jordan is generally traced from the root *Jahrad*, to descend or flow down. Probably this is correct, though it may be doubted if the origin is not rather from the natural imitation of the sound of a river. This is favoured by the occurrence of similar words as river names. There was in ancient times more than one which bore this name, as the Jordanus in Elis. Farther west still were the Eridanus, now the Po, and the Rhodanus, now the Rhone. But whatever the meaning of

the name as first uttered by those who gave it, undoubtedly the Jordan does "descend" as no other river does. The valley through which it flows was formerly a continuation of the plain which lies between the Lebanon and the Antilebanon, known as *Cœle Syria*, or El-Bukâa, and in Scripture usually called "the entrance of Hamath" (Num. xxxiv. 8). Some 50 miles north of *Hermon* is the watershed of that plain in the neighbourhood of Baalbeck. The *Orontes*, gathering the waters of the northern part, flows far northward till it reaches the valley in which Antioch lies, and there gains an outlet to the Mediterranean; while the Leontes or *Litâny*, draining the southern part of the plain, skirts the eastern base of the Lebanon range, till it is south of Hermon, and then suddenly turns westward and falls into the sea, 6 miles to the north of Tyre. Before it turns westward it flows a little way parallel to the Hashbâny, one of the branches of the Jordan, and at Hashbeiya the two rivers are quite close. Once, indeed, the Leontes flowed into the Jordan valley; but, in what geologists call "a late period," it was driven back, and shut out by a volcanic eruption, and so forced to cut for itself the channel through which it now flows. A very slight cutting is needed to return it to its old course, and unite it again with the Jordan.

14. **The source of the Jordan**, just named, at **Hashbeiya**, is its northmost and smallest spring-head. The *Hashbâny* flows out of a large clear pool, and then, through olive groves and oleanders, finds its way down into the wide-spreading plain at the foot of Hermon. The main source of the Jordan is at *Banias*, or Paneas, called in the New Testament Cæsarea-Philippi. Suddenly it bursts into existence as a full-grown stream. It does not now seem to flow out of the famous cave in the mountain-side, but from under accumulated stones some 100 yards from it. It is like a good-sized stream running, not over, but from the foot of a mill-dam, with no visible stream above. Through a rich district alive with water and beautiful with many trees, it makes its way to the site of Dan — now Tel-el-Kady — 5 miles south of Banias. There the **Leddân** rises. It is the third branch of the Jordan, springing also out of a great fountain, a full-grown stream at its beginning. The site of Dan is exceedingly

beautiful, and must have always tempted dwellers to it. The united streams from Banias and Dan are thereafter joined by the Hashbâny already named. The respective sizes of these three streams, the Jordan, Leddân, and Hashbâny, are as 10, 5, and 3.

15. **The Jordan**, thus formed, flows on with a swift current and a much-twisted course, through banks from 12 to 20 feet high, till it nears the **Waters of Merom**, or **Lake Huleh** (Josh. xi. 5, 7). The mountains on the western side of the valley rise abruptly to a great height. Just a little north of the Lake Huleh on the mountains sits Kedesh, from ancient times a strong fortress as well as a sacred city, and some 7 or 8 miles farther north is the Crusaders' Castle of Hûnin, which has every mark of being also an ancient fortress, commanding the road which goes over northward into the plain of Cœle Syria. The view from this side is very striking. The Jordan valley is here wide and comparatively flat, abundantly watered and fertile. On the east the land rises suddenly, and in the north-east corner the noble Hermon rears itself to snowy heights, the isolated hill of Banias lying at its base crowned with the ruins of its once impregnable castle, and the road to Damascus winding up the valley which opens to the south of it. About 6 miles above the Lake Huleh the river loses itself in wide lagoons, and by no less than six different channels empties itself into the lake, through a papyrus-brake. In this part of its course the Jordan has descended nearly 1100 feet. At Banias it is 1080 feet, but at Lake Huleh only 7 feet above sea-level. This is so nearly sea-level it may be conveniently spoken of, for comparison, as sea-level.

16. The whole valley is but 4 miles broad at Lake Huleh, and the surface of the lake is 4 miles long; but marshes, as mentioned, reach several miles northward covered with the most extensive papyrus growths now known. The river leaves the lake also through a waste of islets and papyrus, and after 2 miles plunges into a narrow gorge, sometimes not over 18 feet across, through which as a foaming torrent it roars along for 9 miles to the Sea of Galilee. On its western side the hills rise so abruptly that Safed (supposed to be referred to Matt. v. 14), though but 7 or 8 miles from the river, is 2750 feet *above* sea-level. The high land on the eastern side is known as

the Jaulan. In the 11 miles between the Lake Huleh and Sea of Galilee, the river descends so rapidly, that the level of the Sea of Galilee is 682½ feet *below* sea-level.

17. **The Sea of Galilee** is 12½ miles long, and at its widest point 8 miles across. Precipices of limestone shut it close in on every side, except at its north-western corner, where the plain of Gennesareth lies, and at the north end, where the Jordan flows in, and has formed a small alluvial plain. From the point where the Jordan enters, the appearance of the sea is tame. On the right hand the hills come down close, but not overhanging, much as the slopes of the mountains come down into a Scotch loch. At the middle of the right bank the *Wâdy Hammâm* opens on the sea as a gulley, and down it sudden blasts often burst. Below it again the land rises and spreads backward and westward towards the upland known as *Ard-el-Hamma*. On the east the coast-line is very steep, the tableland approaching close, and dropping suddenly, to the sea. The rocky wall thus formed is cleft by the watercourses which drain the plateau above.

On the west, below *Tiberias*, are the hot springs of Hammâm, the *Hammath* of Josh. xix. 35, and Emmaus of Josephus, one of many signs of the volcanic character of this region. The waters are abundant; and while ordinarily from 130° to 140° Fahr., their temperature rose so much on occasion of the great earthquake of 1837 that the thermometers available were inadequate to register it. At that time Safed, named above, was left in ruins, and 1000 of its inhabitants—about a third of their number—were killed. After an earlier disturbance, about 1710 A.D., there was no water in these hot springs for at least three years. From its low level, and the form of the hills round it, the Sea of Galilee is peculiarly liable to be swept by sudden and violent storms, sometimes of very limited range. One traveller records his experience of a tempest which swept over it about the end of December, " dashing waves against the shore with great violence, while on the land scarcely a breath of wind was to be felt. Five hundred feet higher, on the western bank, a very severe cold wind was experienced, coming from the distant Hauran plateau, which was then covered with snow." He suspected " that the wind struck the surface of the lake at such an angle as to be reflected again and glance off, striking the shore high up the slope of the basin, and literally leaving the city of Tiberias beneath the motion of the atmospheric current."[1]

The shores of the sea, once clad with tropical luxuriance of verdure, are now barren and all but treeless, and except at Tiberias on the west, almost without inhabitants, though in our Lord's time encircled with a dense and busy population. In spring the verdure is splendid, but the great heat scorches up the grass, which a single spark will then ignite. The best view of the lake is obtained, perhaps, from the hills rising to the south of Tiberias. Beyond that city the shore is lost sight of as it curves into the Bay of Magdala; then sweeping out, it runs as a long promontory to the place where Jordan enters, and over which rises in the distance the three-peaked Hermon. On the east, the shore is steep, and to the north-east retires on the level of the plateau in long-sloping lines running up to points like extinct craters in the rugged background.

18. The next and largest portion of the Jordan stretches from the **Sea of Galilee to the Salt Sea**, a distance of some 65 miles, as the crow flies. The fall upon the river is most rapid at both extremities of this portion, the course of the river being somewhat flatter in the middle. Just after it leaves the Sea of Galilee, it falls for some distance at the rate of 40 feet each mile. Its first important affluent is the **Jarmûk**, or Hieromax, which comes from the east with the water of the *Hauran*, and which after passing the ruins of Umm Keis, the ancient Gadara, joins the Jordan 4 miles below its outflow from the sea. Nearly 10 miles below the junction of the Jarmûk, the Jordan receives from the west the waters of the *Jâlûd*, which flows down the eastern half of the plain of Jezreel past Bethshean. When about half-way to the Dead Sea it is joined by the waters of the **Jabbok**, or Zerka, which comes from the east through the mountains of *Gilead;* and almost opposite to it, on the west, the waters which rise about Shechem and Ænon pour down the Wâdy **Fârah**. Instead of running out eastward direct into the Jordan, the Fârah flows some 5 or 6 miles parallel ere uniting with it. Just where the Jabbok enters is the *Damieh* Ford, and about a mile to the north is *Tell-Deir'alla*,

---

[1] See § 17, and Sir C. Wilson's *Recovery of Jerusalem*, p. 340.

which marks the site of Succoth. Near the Salt Sea the Jordan receives considerable affluents from the neighbourhood of Jericho on the west, and Heshbon on the east. Though about 65 miles only is traversed, and though the windings of the river are at no time very far from the straight line, yet these are so numerous that the actual course of the river-bed from the Sea of Galilee to the Salt Sea measures nearly 200 miles.

19. **The width of the valley** varies considerably. Generally speaking it widens as it descends. For the first dozen miles or so, it is scarce 5 miles across, and is confined by steep cliffs. Where the plain of Jezreel, or Esdraelon, joins it, it is about 8 miles wide, and there Abel-meholah, or "meadow of the dance" (?), lies embayed south of the Jâlûd. This was the district of Zartanah. When 25 miles south of the Sea of Galilee, the valley is contracted to but 2 or 3 miles, and again widens to 8 miles where it joins the valley-plain of Succoth (Ps. lx. and Ps. cviii.). Below this the valley broadens out to an average of 14 miles, and this forms "the plain of Jordan" proper, or *Ciccar*, so often spoken of in the Bible (see Index). On the south-western edge of the plain stood Jericho, "the city of palm-trees," and at the south-eastern corner lay **Abel Shittim**, or "the acacia meadow," also called the "plain of Moab."[1] One peculiarity of the valley, or "**Ghor**," through which the Jordan flows is the channel, in the middle of which is the river-bed. When Jordan overflows its banks, it fills this wider channel called the **Zôr**, which is cut out of the soft alluvial soil. Opposite Jericho the Zôr, or "depression," is 1 mile wide and 200 feet deep, but the usual width of the stream there is only 30 yards. The extent of the flood can thus be estimated. The flood is caused by the rapid melting of the snows of Antilebanon. This

---

[1] The eastern plain, now called the Ghor-es-Seisaban, is much warmer than the western: when barley is scarcely ripe at Jericho, it may be nearly thrashed out and to be purchased in good condition in the east. In botanical specimens it is wonderfully rich, and is the largest and most luxuriant oasis in the whole of the Jordan valley. At Engedi there is but a small spot of beauty surrounded by scorched rocks. Safieh, at the south end of the Dead Sea, is possibly as remarkable for its tropical flora and fauna (§ 34), but it is much smaller. Among the tangled wilderness, chiefly near its western edge, still grow many of the acacia-trees. "Shittim" (*Acacia sayal*), from which the district derived its appropriate name of Abel-ha-Shittim, "the meadow, or moist place of the acacias" (Tristram).

Zôr is thickly grown with jungle, and is the natural home of wild beasts. Its wonderful tropical luxuriance earned for it the name "the pride of Jordan" (Zech. ii. 3). In flood-time, that is, in "the swellings of Jordan," lions and other beasts harbouring in it were driven out (Josh. iii. 15; 1 Chron. xi. 15; Lev. xlix. 19, 1. 44). Though lions are not now found alive here, their bones have been found in the gravel-beds.

20. The Jordan loses itself in **the Salt Sea**, of which the other Bible names are *the Sea of the Arabah* (Deut. iii. 11), and *the East Sea*, a name occurring in the later prophets, as Joel, Ezekiel, and Zechariah. It is never called *the Dead Sea* in Scripture; though that is now its most familiar name. It is also called *Bahr Lût, i.e.* "Lot's Sea," by the Arabs, and was known to classical writers as *Lake Asphaltites* (Josephus, *Ant.* i. 9). *Its surface is* 1300 *feet below the level of the Mediterranean;* and as it is in some parts 1300 feet deep, the bottom is, at those parts, 2600 feet below sea-level—or just about as much *below* as Jerusalem is *above* it. From the spring at Banias to its lowest level in the Salt Sea the "descent" of the Jordán is thus 3600 feet, within 100 miles. The Salt Sea is 46 miles long, and in breadth about 10 miles. The grandeur of its scenery is much enhanced by the steep mountains which on both sides descend sheer into it, rising up on either side to a level of 4000 feet above it. It has no outlet. If any connection did exist with the ocean, the waters would, of course, flow in till they had raised it to sea-level. Lying so deep down, it is intensely warm, and evaporation from its surface extremely rapid. The level rises when the Jordan empties its swelling waters into it, and gradually subsides as these dry up; the changes on its level thus caused being from 10 to 15 feet. It is intensely salt —hence its name. Three lbs. of its water yield 1 lb. of solid salts. This is caused partly by the evaporating of the pure water—as all inland seas having no outlet to the ocean are salt; and partly by the melting down of the great mountains of rock-salt, known as *Jebel Usdum.* It lies at the south end, is 300 feet high, and covers an area of 7 by 3 miles. It is a deposit upon what was once part of the sea-bottom. Streams constantly trickling from it carry its salt into the sea. The bitumen, from which the name Lake Asphaltites

was given to it, is still found on the shores, and occasionally floating in masses on the surface. This doubtless is the "slime" of Gen. xiv. 10. It is noteworthy that it is found also up at Hashbeiya at the head of the Jordan, where a large mine of it has long been wrought, and where it has long been valued for its antiseptic properties, and its efficacy in cleansing vines of destructive insects and parasites.

21. In olden times the Jordan valley was continuous through the Arabah to the Red Sea. The land to the south of it has risen and shut it in. The ancient channel of the river can, however, be still traced through "the desert of Zin." This extraordinary depression of the Jordan valley was caused by "a fault" or break-down on its eastern side, the western edge consequently falling in. This is told by the formation of the rocks, and explains the greater depth of the Salt Sea along its eastern side. Towards the south the sea becomes shallower, not averaging in depth over 10 or 12 feet. On the eastern side projects the remarkable promontory of El-Lisan, "the tongue." Although the intense saltness of the sea renders life impossible in it, its shores are alive to the water's edge, as well as the streams which enter it. The name Dead Sea is not biblical, and if not given because of exaggerated accounts of the absence of life around it, has certainly led to such. Possibly the language of Ezekiel may have suggested it (Ezek. xlvii.) in contrast with "the river of life." Mythical statements as that birds could not fly over it have, not so long since, been discredited; but the name remains familiar. The Arabic name *Bahr Lût* also originated, doubtless, in the false notion that the cities of the plain lay buried beneath its waters. In fact, the sea once stood 1400 feet above its present level, as its banks witness, and the whole Jordan valley was then one fresh-water lake, 150 miles long. From the changes taking place on the levels of its bed as well as from drying up, the lake shrank, and became divided. What is now the Salt Sea then reached 18 miles farther north than it does now. Another change reduced it till it was but 4 miles longer than it now is; and these 4 miles are yet thoroughly saturated with salt, and utterly barren. The yet earlier times when this valley reached possibly to the great chain of lakes in Eastern Africa will be spoken of afterwards. Changes now going on seem to be in the direction of again deepening

and extending the Salt Sea. (*Palestine Quarterly*, July 1884, p. 160 ff., Report of Expedition under Professor Hull.)

There is on the western shore of the Salt Sea, 23 miles from its northern end, a spot of rare beauty which is often mentioned—Engedi, in early times called Hazezon Tamar. From the name *Tamar* we learn that it was once a place where palm-trees grew. There are none now, though they were there in Josephus' time; and their shade is sorely needed.

Sir C. Warren tells of his finding his thermometer at 95° Fahr. after sunset, while yet 500 feet above the sea, the morning sun by its first rays waking him to find it over 100°; and how he set off for a grotto which Tristram describes. This is the experience of his party: "We soon became quite exhausted, struggling amid the tall bamboos; and we presented a ludicrous spectacle crouching down under the pieces of rock which gave a few inches of shade. Eventually somebody found an overhanging rock near the bed of the torrent, with bamboos making a lattice-work in front, and we here collected our forces, the Bedouins wanting to share the shade with us. It was a charming little retreat, only so very hot." The description of the grotto which the party ultimately reached is, as given in *Land of Israel*, p. 286, certainly very attractive: "A fairy grotto of vast size, under a trickling waterfall, with a great flat ledge of rock overhanging it, dripping with stalactites, and draped with maiden-hair fern. Its luxuriance was wonderful. We gathered many tresses of its fronds a yard long, and yet the species is identical with our own. The sides of the cliff, as well as the edges of the grotto, were clothed with great fig-trees, hanging about and springing forth in every direction covered with luxuriant foliage, and just now budding into fruit. Mingled with these were occasional bushes of retem, with its lovely branches of pendent pink blossoms waving their sweet perfume all around. To reach the grotto we had to force our way through an almost impenetrable cane brake, with bamboos from 20 to 30 feet long and close together. No pen can give an adequate description of the beauties of this hidden grotto, which surpasses anything Claude Lorraine ever dreamt."

22. Beyond Engedi, the ancient roadway from the south led along the sea-shore. At Engedi it turns up the pass, and ascends by the cliff of Ziz, now Tell Husâsah. There are other passes to the south, but ascending by them would entail a longer journey across the desert plateau that stretches away towards Hebron. By the sea-shore and the cliff of Ziz the ancient invaders came (Gen. xiv.), and to this day the salt-laden camel-trains from Jebel Usdum pass the same way.

Ten or twelve miles along the shore south of Engedi is *Sebbeh*, the site of the famous Jewish fortress of Masada (Josephus, *Wars*, vii. 8 and 9). It stands out a solitary block with a flat top girt all round with walls of rock. The top is 350 yards east and west, by 690 yards north and south. A narrow plain lies between the rock and the sea, on the other side of which, right across, is the *Lisan*.

Just in the south-west corner the *Wâdy Zuweirah* descends to the sea, and there stands the Jebel Usdum. Between the Salt Mountain and the sea is the little oasis of Zuweirah, and beyond as the shore turns eastward is the desolate Sebkha, across the south end of the sea-basin. A track over its mud flats leads to the south-eastern corner, where lies the *Ghôr es Safieh* already named (note, p. 2(.), a strip of well-watered and fertile soil running to a point 6 miles south of the sea.

The Wâdy el Teib descends from the 'Arabah on the west, and the Wâdy Gurundul on the east. They form respectively the western and eastern sides of the 'Arabah, which goes due south 112 miles to the Gulf of 'Akabah. Sixty-five miles south is the watershed, 660 feet above sea-level, therefore nearly 2000 feet above the surface of the Salt Sea, which is thus fast shut in.

"The south end of the Dead Sea is formed of extensive mud flats of a very slimy character. The recent rains had doubtless contributed to the soft state of the mud, but the natives told me it was never hard. It was almost impossible to reach the edge of the water of the Dead Sea through the mud. A line of driftwood had been thrown up a considerable distance inland, forming a shore line almost half a mile south of the water's edge. I found it was quite impossible to measure a base line through this slime, and the dense vegetation of the Ghôr left no open space available. After several attempts, I was obliged to relinquish the idea ; this I regretted very much, as I found the portion of the Dead Sea to the south of the Lisan had been very inaccurately delineated on previous maps. . . . The descent to the Ghôr was down a sandy slope of 300 feet, and the change of climate was most marked, from the sandy desert to masses of tangled vegetation with streams of water running in all directions, birds fluttering from every tree, the whole country alive with life: nowhere have I seen so great and sudden a contrast" (Major Kitchener's Report, *Palestine Quarterly*, October 1884).

FOURTH LONGITUDINAL SECTION—EASTERN PALESTINE.

23. The fourth and last longitudinal section of the land is the mountain range and plateau lying beyond the Jordan, and spreading out to the eastwards. It is the prolongation of the Antilebanon. At the north rises *Hermon*, almost attaining the line of perpetual snow; its actual height being 9200 feet. Hermon is by some interpreted as "the lofty," by others as "the sanctuary." The difference will not appear so great when it is remembered that every high mountain was a holy place. This mountain had also the names of Sirion or Shirion among the Phœnicians, apparently from its glittering as a breastplate. The Amorites, impressed by the same appearance, named it "Shenir" (Deut. iii. 9). It is also called Sion "the Elevated," in Deut. iv. 48, and possibly in Ps. cxxxiii. 3—a name not to be confounded with Zion, which means "sunny," or "dry." The name of *Baal-Hermon* is also given to it, though this seems at other times to be distinguished from Hermon (1 Chron. v. 23). The use of the *three* names in the last-quoted passage has been supposed to refer to its three peaks; and to this there is doubtless allusion in Ps. xlii. 6, where the plural—not the dual—is used meaning "Hermons," not *Hermonites*, as in Authorized Version. Its modern Arabic name is *Jebel-esh-Sheikh, i.e.* "the chief mountain." The snow lies usually upon it till the end of August, and may sometimes be seen even in September, while the crevices on which the sun does not directly beat are never clear of it. Hermon is seen from far, even from Eastern Judea, in the descent from Marsaba to the Salt Sea, and is a conspicuous object in all views from hill-tops. At *Damascus* its shape seems quite different; it there towers over the plain with commanding aspect, and indeed almost seems to overhang the city as it rises against the western sky at sunset. Of its three peaks the westmost is the lower, the other two being of the same height. On the southmost of the two greater heights are the ruins of *Kusr-esh-Shabib*,—"a rock-hewn hollow, or trench, and a circular dwarf wall with a temple just below the peak, on the south. On the plateau is a rudely-excavated cave, with a rock-cut pillar supporting the roof, and a flat space levelled above, probably once the floor of a building over the

cave" (*Tent Work in Palestine*, vol. i. p. 265). Here may have been the point specially devoted to Baal's worship, and known more exactly as Baal Hermon.

The view from the summit is described as magnificent. To the east, close by, is Damascus amid its gardens, while beyond stretches afar the desolate plain in which the rivers of Damascus lose themselves, the horizon being broken by the "Hill of Bashan," 70 miles off. To the south-east lies the treeless waterless Lejah, a basin scarred with deep gorges and dotted with extinct craters. Southward the eye rests on the mountains of Bashan and Gilead as far as the line of the Jabbok, beyond which the height of Jebel Osh'a shuts in the view (Conder, *Heth and Moab*, p. 131); and ranges down the Jordan valley, across the Sea of Galilee, over the mountains of Ephraim and the wilderness of Judah. Farther west the Galilean hills and the heights of Carmel are clearly seen. A very notable feature of this mountain, alluded to in the Bible, is the rapidity with which the clouds form about it, and the abundance of dew by night, which drenches everything, even through waterproof coverings (Ps. cxxxiii. 3). This is caused by the extremes of temperature in the Jordan valley and on the mountain-sides.

24. South of Hermon, reaching to the Jabbok, lay **Bashan**, an extensive region, parts of which were early, and, at one time, very densely peopled. It included *El Lejah*, which is named in Scripture Argob, "the Stony"—a characteristic noted by the Greek *Trachonitis* (Deut. iii. 4; Luke iii. 1).

Edrei, the capital of Og, was situated on the edge of this wild district. "Elevated about 20 feet above the plain, it is a labyrinth of clefts and crevasses in the rock, formed by volcanic action; and owing to its impenetrable condition it has become a place of refuge for outlaws and turbulent characters, who make it a sort of cave of Adullam. The Government of the Porte is unable to exercise any authority here, and its inhabitants know no law but their own. It is in fact an impregnable natural fortress, about 20 miles in length by 15 in breadth" (Oliphant, *Land of Gilead*, p. 57. See also *Giant Cities of Bashan* (Porter), p. 91 ff.).

Bashan included also the **Hauran**, afterwards *Auranitis*, beyond which to the south-east lay *Bozrah*, or *Bostra*. The name of Bashan remains in *El-Battein*, applied still to the district south-east from the Sea of Galilee. It seems to have suffered in pronunciation by western lips as Shibboleth did (Judg. xii. 6), becoming in Aramaic Bothenin and in the Samaritan Pentateuch Batanin, whence the Greek Bethania and the Roman Batanea. The modern name of the district, *Ard-el-Bethaniah*, still preserves it. The great ford 'Abarah led over to it from the plain of Jezreel, and this explains John i. 28, where the Authorized Version reads Bethabara, and the Revised Version, Bethany beyond Jordan. Geshur lay in the north of Bashan, **Maachah** on the north-west, and **the land of Tob** in the west, just south of the Sea of Galilee, its name surviving in that of the town, and Wâdy, "Taiyibeh," which has the significance in Arabic, of Tob in Hebrew—*i.e.* "good." The land of Uz is also by some located in Bashan (see Oliphant's *Land of Gilead*, p. 76 ff.).

Bashan has always been famous for its pasturage and cattle, and also for its great oaks, specimens of which are yet to be seen. The ruins, thickly strewn, are those of a great people. Across Bashan lay the routes of armies and caravans, some descending by the river-courses into the Jordan to cross Palestine, and some holding on south on the eastern tableland, like the great Haj road to this day, leading to Edom and Arabia. Jebel Kuleib, "the hill of Bashan," lying out on the eastern boundary of the land of Israel, is 5600 feet high.

25. Gilead joined on to Bashan and reached some 25 miles southward. The beauty and fertility of Gilead have always been proverbial. Its general level is about 2000 feet above the sea. The highest point is Jebel Osh'a (3597 feet), in the north-western corner of the land just south of the Jabbok. Hereabout Peniel must have been, if that was not the name of the mountain itself (see § 52). Between the Jabbok and Wâdy Heshbon "the horsemen wander by clear mountain brooks, through glades of oak and terebinth, with dark pines above. The valleys green with corn, the streams fringed with oleander, the magnificent screens of yellow green and russet foliage which cover the steep slopes, present a scene of quiet beauty, of chequered light and shade of un-eastern aspect which makes Mount Gilead

a veritable land of promise" (*Heth and Moab*, p. 187. See also *The Land of Gilead*, by Oliphant, and *East of Jordan*, by Merrill, chap. xxi.).

The course of the Jabbok forms three-fourths of a circle. It rises in the south-eastern part of Gilead, and sweeps round with a wide bend northward, and then passes westwards to the Jordan about the base of Mount Gilead. In this course it embraces a circular basin, called El-Beja, round which are hills covered with oak forests. If "the Wood of Ephraim" was on the east of Jordan, as it certainly seems to have been, it may well have been here.

"No one can fairly judge of Israel's heritage who has not seen the luxuriant exuberance of Gilead, as well as the hard rocks of Judea, which only yield their abundance to reward constant toil and care. To compare the two is to contrast nakedness and luxuriance. Yet the present state of Gilead is just what Western Palestine was in the days of Abraham. Subsequently the Canaanites must have extensively cleared it. Even before the conquest, and while the slopes and terraces were clad with olive groves, the amount of rainfall was not affected. The terraces have crumbled away; wars and neglect have destroyed the groves until it would be difficult to find any two neighbouring districts more strangely contrasted than the east and west of Jordan. But this is simply caused by the greater amount of rainfall on the east side, attracted by the forests, which have perished off the opposite hills. The area of drainage is about the same on each side. The ravines or wâdys are numerous; but few of the streams are perennial on the west—*all* are so on the east. Every stream draining from Moab and Gilead is filled with fishes and fresh-water shells. I never found living fresh-water shells but in two streams on the west side. In other words, the brooks there are now but winter torrents" (Tristram).

The southern part of Gilead lying just north of the Wâdy Heshbon was the land of the Ammonites, their capital, or *Rabbath-Ammon* lying at the southern spring of the Jabbok.

26. South of Wâdy Heshbon the land of Moab stretched along the eastern side of the Salt Sea. The portion between Heshbon and Arnon became the territory of Reuben, and the Moabites dwelt to the south of the Arnon, as they did originally (Deut. ii. 36). The mountains, which go down in great steps to the edge of the Sea, form on the west a sure wall of defence, for they are practically unassailable. From these, which bear the name of *Abarim*, the tableland or

'Mishor" spreads eastward in rolling downs. The great wall of the Abarim range is seen even from Jerusalem, forming a conspicuous object in its scenery beyond the south shoulder of Olivet. At its north end the deep cleft of the Wâdy Heshbon leads down to Abel-Shittim (§ 19), and the Jordan passage, over against Jericho. Immediately south of this are the "Springs of Pisgah," now Ayun Musa, the last camp of Israel before descending to the Jordan (Deut. iii. 17, etc.).

Captain Conder gives this account of these springs:—"The northern spring, rising in a shallow valley, pours its stream over a cliff some 30 feet high, down which hang long trailing creepers beside the water. The hollow below the fall is full of maidenhair fern, and a large wild fig grows up against the cliff. There are two cascades again lower down, and the rushing brook disappears in a narrow gorge, between tall canes and various shrubs. The contrast of this vegetation with the great blocks of limestone in the valley, the tawny hill above, glaring against the blue sky, without a tree or a blade of grass, is very effective. The southern spring, some hundred yards away, issues from a cave at the foot of a cliff, forming a fine clear pool with a pebbly bed, flanked by two aged wild figs, curiously gnarled and twisted, but with rich foliage. The stream breaks down hence in a rapid shoot to join the northern brook in the gorge. To the south a high mountain, quite bare, and of a drab-coloured limestone, rises steep from the valley with a ruined site on the sky-line. This is the town and ridge of Siâghah, the Pisgah of Moses" (*Heth and Moab*, p. 128).

Nebo still preserves its name, which seems to have applied to the actual point of the mountain. The *Talat-es-Sufa*, discovered by Captain Conder in his late expedition to the east of Jordan, preserves the name of Zophim, Num. xxiii. 14, and possibly is the Mizpeh-Moab of 1 Sam. xxii. 3. It leads up to the ridge of *Siâghah*, or Pisgah, the flat top of which is *Nebo* (§ 67).

27. Ten miles south of Nebo the edge of the plateau is divided by the deep ravine of the Zerka M'ain, the ancient Callirhoe. This is now identified with Nahaliel, Num. xxi. 19, "the valley of God," which may signify no more than "the great valley," or may be connected with the Baal-worship of this district. The lofty mountain of *Jebel Attarus* stands on the south of the valley. Its height and imposing aspect have led some to mistake it for Mount Nebo. From its summit,

Bethlehem and Jerusalem, Gerizim and Gilboa on the western side, may be seen. It rivals Jebel Osh'a in height.

Tristram, in his *Land of Moab*, has given a striking account of the gorge of the Callirhoe. The following vivid description is from Captain Conder's *Heth and Moab*, pp. 145-147 : "On the 30th September we rode from Minyeh through white desert slopes, growing only sage and the retem broom, and caught glimpses from time to time of the calm blue waters of the salt sea reflecting the western precipices. At length we reached the brink of the gorge—here some 1700 feet deep— the stream being, near the springs, still 1600 feet above the Dead Sea. Tawny cliffs of limestone capped with chalk rise on the north, and are seamed with gullies, where the marl has been washed down like snow streaks left in summer, beneath the cliffs. On the south is a steep brown precipice with an under-cliff of marl and a plateau stretching thence to another and yet another ridge ; beyond and above this plateau (on which are the stone heaps of Machærus), appeared the shining waters of the lake of its western cliffs, fading away into a blue mist on the south. But the central feature of this ghastly scene of utterly barren wilderness, was the great black bastion projecting from the southern cliff, and almost blocking the gorge—an outbreak of basalt which shows like a dark river in the valley of Callirhoe, as seen from the west side of the Dead Sea. It resembles the high spoil-heaps of an English coal mine, and bears witness to the volcanic action which has made the springs in this gorge of boiling heat, and which no doubt accompanied the sudden depression of the enormous fault now known as the Jordan valley. It took a full hour to reach the bottom of the gorge, and the scene beneath was wonderful beyond description. On the south, black basalt, brown limestone, gleaming marl. On the north, sandstone cliffs of all colours, from pale yellow to pinkish purple. In the valley itself the brilliant green of palm clumps, rejoicing in the heat and in the sandy soil. The streams, bursting from the cliffs, poured down in rivulets between banks of crusted orange sulphur deposits. The black grackle soared above, with gold-tipped wings, his mellow note being the one sound re-echoed by the great red cliffs in their utter solitude. The brooks (which run from ten springs in all) vary from 110° to 140° Fahr. in temperature, and fall in little cascades amid luxuriant foliage, to join the main course of the stream, which is far colder and fresher, flowing from the shingly springs higher up the valley, and forming pools beneath white rocks of chalk, which we found full of fish, and hidden in a luxuriant brake of tamarisk and cane. The weather being very hot, the thermal springs were not smoking, but a strong smell of sulphur was very perceptible at times. Crossing three rivulets, from each of which our horses, apparently aware of the heat of the water, shrank back in fear, we reached the principal hot spring, which has formed a ledge of breccia-like deposit in the valley, just north of the basalt cliff. Here the chasm is narrowest, and the main stream below could be seen winding among black boulders, which impede its course, with the dark precipice frowning as though about to fall, like Sinai in the *Pilgrim's Progress*. The stream has bored through the sulphurous breccia, and runs in a tunnel of its own making, issuing from this hot shaft about 100 feet lower, in the gorge itself . . . Of all scenes in Syria, even after standing on Hermon, or among the groves of Banias, or at Engedi, or among the crags of the Antilebanon, there is none which so dwells in my memory as does this awful gorge, 'the valley of God,' by Beth Peor, where perhaps the body of Moses was laid—the fair flowing stream which Herod sought below the gloomy prison of John the Baptist at Machærus— the dead chasm where the Bedawin still offer sacrifices to the desert spirits, and still bathe with full faith in the healing powers of the spring."

28. Twelve miles south of the Callirhoe flows the **Arnon**, now Wâdy Mojib, falling into the Salt Sea just half-way down its eastern shore. This gorge is also of great depth, "the river absolutely splits by its narrow channel the great Moab range to its very base for several thousand feet, yet its channel is not more than one hundred feet wide" (Tristram).

About 15 miles up from the mouth of the Arnon stands Aroer, now Ar'air, and at that distance from the Salt Sea the ravine on the edge of which it stands is 1500 feet deep. Yet 15 miles farther to the south the Wâdy Kerak similarly cleaves the plateau opening into the sea close to the northern side of *El Lisan*. This valley is named from Kerak, the "nest in the rock" of Moab, which stands on a solitary height 2700 feet above the sea. At the south-eastern corner of the Salt Sea is the *Ghôr es Safieh*, § 22. Allusion is made to it in "the book of the wars of the Lord," quoted Num. xxi. 14: "Wherefore it is said, What He did in Suphah" (see margin, A.V.). This was the extreme south of Moab. From the western edge now described, the "Mishor," Moab stretched far out eastward, a land singularly adapted to the pasturing of flocks—a rolling, treeless plain with hillocks rising over it which are crowned with the ruins of former cities. A notable feature of the landscape is the frequent occurrence of two such hillocks close together, which were of old surrounded by a wall enclosing a pair of towns as one. The familiar dual form of Moabite names—ending with *im*—is thus explained. Beyond Kerak the tableland rolls away for five-and-twenty miles to a barren ridge of limestone which forms the natural boundary between the pastures of Moab and the Arabian desert. Farther north, however, the width of the pasturage is greater. Many ruins and extensive remains of cisterns and vineyards, testify to the density of its population in ancient times.

CHAPTER III.

NATURAL HISTORY OF THE LAND.

29. The feature of the land which most impresses the student of the Physical Geography of Palestine, is its **extraordinary range of levels, and therefore of climates.** Over the whole land, indeed, great changes of temperature are experienced throughout the year; but apart from such uncertainties of climate, there is always the contrast between the extremes at the top of Hermon and in the basin of the Salt Sea. The summit of Hermon is all but at the line of perpetual snow, and for little more than a fortnight in any year is the top entirely clear of it; though it lingers in the crevices and gullies. Down the valley of Jordan the Dead Sea lies 10,500 feet lower, in its intensely hot tropical basin 1300 feet below the sea-level, shut in and sheltered by mountains rising 4000 feet above it east and west. Between these extremes are the coast and hill country of the greater part of the land, and the desert land which surrounds it east and south, and invades the territory of Judea. Each region has its own occupants, plants and animals adapted to its climate.

"I have camped," says Canon Tristram, "under Scotch firs on the top of Mount Gilead, and then descending past Ramoth-Gilead I came to the Turkey oaks and then down to the evergreen oaks, the prickly ilex, then the forests of wild olive, the sycamore, fig, and the splendid Syrian arbutus; then we came to the false balm of Gilead; and finally I camped at night under the date-palms and the shittim in a temperature of 88°, in the plains of Jordan. That is one day's ride. In that day I passed through four different zones, from Scotch fir down to date palm in its native soil. I do not think you could do that in any other country in the world in so short a ride" (*Manchester Science Lectures*, 1879).

Undoubtedly this great variety of plant and animal life has largely contributed to the adaptation of the Bible to all nations. It is full of illustrations from, and of references to the *flora* and *fauna* of the land of the chosen people. The story of them and their surroundings was for all people, and in their country there was a place for the representatives of even the plants and animals of every land. The American *cactus*, which cannot have been introduced beyond three or four centuries, is now so abundant and so manifestly at home that most travellers take it for a native of Palestine.

30. This adaptation has been brought about by means which **the geological history** of the lands explains. Far back in ages long before man lived, while the habitable places of the earth were being prepared and furnished for him, there was a hot tropical period in which the Salt Sea existed—but not then *salt*. The hills about it had the climate and vegetation of tropical lands, and it must itself have been the hottest of hot places. Geologists say that then the land stretched continuously from India to Africa, westward to the Azores, and the waters of the Mediterranean (?) rolled over the Sahara and washed the base of the Atlas Mountains, while a chain of lakes extended from the Jordan valley southward as far as the great lakes of Eastern Africa to the Zambesi. In that time plants and animals would migrate freely within the limit of congenial climates.

But this hot period was followed by a Glacial Age which gradually crept southward till it reigned in Palestine. As in our country it has left its marks and remains in deeply-scored rocks over which glaciers ground their path, and in boulders and moraines, so on the rocks of Hermon its history is engraved. Before its cold, the plants and animals of the warmer age perished, some hardier specimens, more capable of adapting themselves to change, alone surviving. Then Alpine plants grew, and reindeer fed on them. In course of time there came a change to warmth again, and the general climate became temperate. On the heights the survivors of the Arctic Age remained, while in the depths of the Jordan valley those hardier specimens of the tropical period which had outlived the cold, flourished once more. The land now contains these selected remains of its former flora and fauna. As regards plants, the botanical life of the Lebanon reminds us of that of Northern Europe, that at the level of Jerusalem and Carmel of Southern Europe, and that found in the neighbourhood of Jericho (and yet more tropical Abel-Shittim) of the botany of Western India. This last point of resemblance, between the botany of the Jericho plain and Western India, was noticed by Dr. Wilson of Bombay forty years ago, and is commented on in his *Lands of the Bible*.

31. In illustration of the more remarkable affinity of Palestine flora with tropical lands, and more specially with Eastern and South-eastern Africa, may be noticed the *papyrus*, which has disappeared from the Nile valley, and yet covers many acres about the Lake Hûleh. Canon Tristram mentions that in one little valley at the south-western corner of the Salt Sea, he found 160 species of plants. Of these, 27 are common and widespread species, found from Europe in the west to Northern India eastward. One hundred and thirty-five are *African*, of which 17 are found in Arabia in the neighbourhood of Aden on the Red Sea, and not fewer than 23 are found distributed over Africa and westwards as far as the Canary Islands.

As regards the fauna, or animal life, the following facts are interesting in themselves, and will more fully establish and illustrate what has been stated.

In one ascent of Hermon, Tristram mentions finding on the sides and top two English winter birds, with the horned lark of Persia, the chough of the Alps, a finch related to the Himalayan birds, and a warbler whose relatives are in Central Africa.[1] The ostrich has been found even recently in the eastern desert, while around the warm Jordan valley Tristram found "fifteen new species of birds, and seven or eight that are not found nearer than Southern India, and as many more that are only found in the hotter parts of Abyssinia and the Zambesi." He found also a sunbird, the only one found in the Mediterranean basin, whose nearest cousins are found in Southern India and Central Africa; a kingfisher, only to be found also at Madras; a grackle, whose relations are to be sought in South Africa; and a partridge, for whose kindred one must go to Southern India.

The great Behemoth (Job xl.) may be the hippopotamus, which is a

[1] On the western coast, near the ladder of Tyre, he shot the "eagle owl," a bird "never before found west of Southern India, though its range extends to China."

native of Africa; possibly it survived for some time in the warm waters of the Jordan. It has there left behind its near kindred, the small "coney;" two other species are found, one in Abyssinia and one at the Cape. The crocodile—leviathan (?)—has even survived to this day, giving its name to a stream south of Carmel, and having been seen and also caught in the Kishon.

Most curious of all, perhaps, are the fishes of the Sea of Galilee, whose kindred are also African. One remarkable species is found there, of which we are told that after the ova has been spawned, it is taken by the male fish into his mouth and hatched there, his jaws swelling to a tremendous size as the young grow, ere they at last swim off from their strange nest,—such of them as their nursing father has not swallowed while feeding! The same extraordinary process was observed by Livingstone in Lake Tanganyika. From the Zambesi, Nyanza, and the salt lakes of the Sahara, fish have been brought of the same peculiar *genus* with fish of the Sea of Galilee. It cannot certainly be said that all the plants and animals named in the Bible have been identified, though in this, as in other departments, much has been done. The fallow-deer of Deut. xiv. 5, etc., has been found in the "roebuck" on Carmel still bearing the same name. It has been said that the "hart" could not be the "red deer," because it is not found in the land, but its teeth have been found in cave remains. Of course "the unicorn" has not been found in Palestine; but the word so rendered has been found on an Assyrian sculpture written over a wild ox, or bison, and its remains have been also found in the Lebanon. No wonder our translators stumbled at the idea of "the horn*s* of an *uni*-corn," Deut. xxxiii. 17, text and margin!

It is thus seen how wide are the affinities of Palestine in the vegetable and animal kingdoms, and how wonderfully unique and exceptional has been the history of its forming and furnishing to be the home of that people chosen as the medium of revelation and instruction for all peoples of the earth.

Note.—As the limits of a class handbook do not admit of fuller treatment of the natural history of Palestine, those who desire to study the subject may consult *Flora and Fauna of Palestine*, published by the Palestine Exploration Society, or the other interesting works of Canon Tristram, the author of that splendid volume, *Land of Israel*, and *Natural History of the Bible;* or the well-known *Bible Animals* by the Rev. J. G. Wood. A most useful summary of information will be found in Conder's *Handbook to the Bible*, and also in *Aids to Bible Students* (Eyre & Spottiswoode, in Sabbath School Teacher's Bible).

CHAPTER IV.

EARLY INHABITANTS OF THE LAND.

32. From the scattered statements of Scripture, a good deal may be gathered as to the earliest dwellers in the land, and those who invaded and possessed it before the Israelitish conquest under Joshua. In very early times the spreading tribes must have found homes by its shores and in its valleys. The oldest Scripture scenes represent well-organized tribes who had attained to no mean state of civilization—their cities and customs indicating long previous settlement. But those who met the patriarchs coming into the land were not the aborigines. The **Philistines**, for example, were in the land; they had come from Caphtor=Keft-ur, or the "greater Phœnicia"—that is, the Nile delta. Yet, as late as the time of David, there were tribes whom they had overawed, though not exterminated, and whom they so despised that they never thought of quarrelling with David for spoiling them if he could (1 Sam. xxvii. 8-10). There were also the dwellers in Edom, and among the caves of Mount Seir the **Horites**= cave-dwellers (Gen. xiv. 6; Deut. ii. 12, 22). Ewald supposes Job in chap. xxiv. 4-8, and xxx. 3-8, to refer to the sufferings of such when driven to the rocks for shelter by the Edomites. They seem also to have dwelt in caves about *Beitgibrin* in Philistia, and their flints have been found with the bones of wild oxen and reindeer in the Lebanon. It is possible that they made their homes in caves not of necessity, but in the indifference, or poverty, or sloth of primitive savages.

The aboriginal tribes alluded to in the country of the Philistines were known as **Geshuri**, and apparently also as **Avim** (Josh. xiii. 3). Singularly, they seem to have done exactly what the tribe of Dan did afterwards, when it sent part of its population from the south-west to the far north-east of the land. Geshurites were also found in the extreme north of Bashan, § 24. (Compare 1 Sam. xxvii. 8, and 2 Sam. xv. 8, with other references in Index.)

33. Very frequent mention is made of a primitive race of "giants." **Rephaim** they are called. To them Bashan specially belonged. Their capital was Ashteroth Karnaim, the two-horned Ashteroth, a name which reveals their religion. The **Zuzims** dwelt at Ham, apparently south of Ashteroth in the line of Chedorlaomer's march (Gen. xiv.), and when the Israelites came northward from Moab they encountered the Rephaim whom the Ammonites called Zam-zummims, which most probably means the Ham-zuzims, the Zuzims dwelling in Ham. If, as some think, Ham was the ancient name of Rabbath Ammon, its first builders may have left their name there as the children of Ham. If the **Zam-zummim** of Ammon and the **Emim** of Moab were of the same stock, they (Rephaim) may be said to have held all Eastern Palestine. But their name is found also in the plain of Rephaim, beside Jerusalem, and in the north (Josh. xvii. 15); and as **Anakim** they dwelt in the south, where Arba built Kirjath Arba, afterwards Hebron, and where his three sons Ahiman, Sheshai, and Talmai, and their families, divided the land among them. Most probably the change of the name of Kirjath Arba to "Hebron" marks the proceeding of a conqueror. If so, we may conjecture that the conquerors were those who seven years afterwards built Zoan in Egypt (Num. xiii. 22). From Egyptian history we know that the invaders known as the Hyksos came from Canaan and Arabia and established themselves at Zoan or Tanis. Most probably the same invasion from the East brought the Phœnicians to Tyre and Zidon. The Philistines probably came into this land at a later time; possibly when the Hyksos were driven from Egypt. It is significant that the power of Egypt was firmly established in Philistia at the time of, and long prior to, the exodus.

Chaldean records tell of the invasion of Palestine by Sargon I. of Accad, and by his son. Sargon, whose date is given as 3750 B.C. (?), left his image carved on the shores of the Mediterranean. Two similar invasions occurred long after in Abraham's time (Gen. xiv.) at intervals of fourteen years; and the father of Arioch, who figures in that story, is entitled, on the cuneiform monuments, "the Father of Palestine," implying his lordship over the land. No wonder if the primitive nationalities cannot now be clearly described, after being so often trodden down by invading armies. It must not be forgotten that the nations of Gen. x. 6-14, as well as the descendants of Canaan named in the six verses which follow, were all children of Ham. The Israelites were the children of Shem : the remains of the primitive inhabitants of Palestine suggest that they were of the same origin.

34. **Seven nations of Canaan** are named in Gen. x. 15-18. Their names seem to be rather descriptive of their habits than of their origin or appearance, and could only become distinctive after some generations. The name **Canaanite** means "lowlander;" but it also indicates descent from Canaan; whose sons had most probably seized and held the *lowlands*, the best parts of the soil, and given their name to them (§ 6). Singularly the name Canaan remains yet in one place in the far south. To the south-west of Hebron the ruined site of *Kan'ân* has been found where the roads to Hebron from Gaza and from Beersheba join, guarding the approach to the valley of Eshcol. It was taken by Seti I. of Egypt some forty years before the exodus (*Quarterly Statement of Palest. Explor. Society*, 1883, p. 175, and 1884, p. 59). According to some authorities, the name Canaan is found in Assyrian records applied to the whole coast lands of the Mediterranean down to the Egyptian territory. The name Canaanite seems in later times to have acquired a special significance from the trading habits of the Phœnicians, see Hos. xii. 7.

35. **The Amorites**, as their name implies, were the highlanders, or mountaineers (Num. xiii. 29). On the Egyptian monuments they are called *Amaru*. They are mentioned (Gen. xiv. 7) as dwelling at Engedi, but they possessed, it would seem, the whole of the mountain fastnesses in the south-east (Judg. i. 36). Mamre, from whom the place of Abraham's dwelling was named, was an Amorite, and his brother Eshcol, who similarly gave his name to the neighbouring valley (Gen. xiv. 13).

They afterwards conquered and possessed, under Sihon and Og, the northern part of Moab and Mount Gilead, not long before the

Israelitish conquest (Num. xxi. 26; Deut. xxxi. 4; Judg. x. 8, xi. 12, 23). They had also firm possessions in Mount Ephraim (Judg. i. 35), where they had come into conflict with the patriarch Jacob to their loss (Gen. xlviii. 22); and they even forced the Danites to live in the mountains, not suffering them to come down into the corn-bearing valleys (Judg. i. 35). As the five confederate kings of Jerusalem, Hebron, Jarmuth, Lachish, and Eglon are also called Amorites (Josh. x. 5), it is obvious that the word is used in a pretty wide application.

36. **Perizzites** were dwellers in the plains, frequently named in patriarchal times along with, yet as distinct from, Canaanites, Amorites, Hittites, and (Josh. xvii. 15) Rephaim. It is impossible to decide from all that is said whether they were a different race from the Canaanites, or merely a separate class, as the peasantry of the time. But it is most probable that they had some distinct history as well as habit of life, though not named in Gen. x. as a distinct people.

The **Hivite** lived in villages or towns. He is named expressly in Gen. x. 17. And the remarkable league of towns of which we read, Josh. ix., and the separate action which it took, with the enmity of the Amorites thereby incurred (Josh. x.), all testify to a distinct nationality. Their towns were Gibeon, Chephirah, Beeroth, and Kirjath-Jearim, which had earlier the name Baalah, and was therefore, probably, conquered by them. Shechem also belonged to their confederacy (Gen. xxxiv. 2). From Gen. xxxvi. we also learn that Esau married a grand-daughter of Zibeon the Hivite, who must have been a man of some distinction in those days from the manner in which he is mentioned. From Josh. xi. 3, Judg. iii. 3, it appears that Hivites lived also in the north, under Hermon, and by the entering in of Hamath. Possibly at Abel, famed afterwards for its wily counsels as was Gibeon in the south (2 Sam. xx. 14-18), some of the inhabitants of Beeroth journeying north had founded the colony of the Berites. Their cities were ruled by "elders," and they do not appear to have had kings; but, as Ewald suggests, to have adopted thus early a pure republican constitution not unlike the German free cities.

The **Jebusite**, best known in connection with Jerusalem, is named in Gen. x. 16 and Josh. xi. 3. From so long holding the fortress of

Jerusalem in the midst of the land, he became more memorable in Scripture history than his actual strength of numbers could otherwise have made him. Of the Girgasites so little is known that some have located them in the west of Phœnicia, and others on the east of the Sea of Galilee! Their name occurs but seven times, and never with an indication of locality.

The **Giblites**, or men of Gebal, were Phœnicians, Josh. xiii. 5, and 1 Kings v. 18, marg. Gebal is now Jibeil, 40 miles north of Zidon: its inhabitants from early times were distinguished as craftsmen. Their city was also called Byblos, and was sacred to Adonis. Gebal Afka (§ 78), and Baalbeck, "are almost in one line in the direction of the summer sunset and the winter sunrise."

37. The great nation of the **Hittites**, or "children of Heth," deserves some notice, Gen. x. 15. It was a mighty empire when God promised to give its land to the seed of Abraham, Gen. xv. 21, covering the region afterwards known as Syria. One capital was in Cœle Syria, Kadesh on the Orontes, and another at Carchemish on the Euphrates, Josh. i. 4.[1] As far south as Hebron they had possession in Abraham's time (Gen. xxiii.) under Ephron; and probably held one at least of the mountains on which Jerusalem stood (Ezek. xvi. 23), dividing possession with the Jebusite-Amorite. Their name has been traced in Hatta in Philistia, and Kefr Hatta above Lydda, also in Hattin west of the Sea of Galilee, "the Caphar Hittai of the Talmud." It is not yet ascertained whether the Hittites formed one empire, or were a confederate state under the supremacy or suzerainty of the Hittite kings. They came from the north, having their earlier dwelling between the Black Sea and the Mediterranean, in what is now known as Asia Minor. Their features and dress as depicted in the Egyptian records are distinctive, and exhibit them as inhabitants of cold regions. In appearance they are like Caucasians, and they have "pigtails" like the Chinese. About the time Moses was born, Thothmes III. of Egypt invaded Palestine and broke the power of the Hittites at Megiddo, attacking Kedesh and apparently making good his hold of the shores of Palestine as far north as the Lebanon.

[1] Sir C. W. Wilson proposes instead of Jerablûs on the Euphrates, usually identified with Carchemish, Membij, the ancient Hierapolis, west of the Euphrates.

Raamses II., Pharaoh of the oppression, captured Kadesh, his exploits being celebrated in a poem, and depicted on the walls at Thebes and Abu-Simbel. The pictures exhibit Kadesh as a strong fortress surrounded by water. Captain Conder in an exploring expedition, of which an account is given in his *Heth and Moab*, has identified the site as the great mound of Tell Neby Mendeh on the Orontes,—a mound 50 to 100 feet high, and 400 yards long. On the Egyptian monuments Raamses II. is said "to have broken the back of the Hittites for ever and ever." But he had to make a treaty with them, which is preserved. It includes extradition clauses, which bind the "Kheta" to return any inhabitants from the territories of Raamses, or any slaves of his who should flee to their land (see Judg. i. 26). The treaty was cemented by the marriage of Raamses to a daughter of the Hittite king. The Hittites were a people of some considerable culture. Kirjath-Sepher (the book-town) was one of their cities in Southern Palestine, and many of their engraved tablets have been recovered, though not yet deciphered. They appear in the confederacy of the northern princes of Syria again and again (Josh. xi., and 2 Kings vii. 6), as a strong people, but never as when they met Raamses with 2500 chariots. The presence of Ahimelech with David while a fugitive, 1 Sam. xxvi. 6, and of Uriah among his "mighties," as well as of a Hittite princess in Solomon's harem, proves that they lived afterwards on terms of friendliness with the Israelites. Riblah, the extreme north point ever included in the bounds of Israel's land, lay a little south of Kadesh. By it Joab went numbering the people, "as far as Gilead and the land of the Hittites of Kadesh" (2 Sam. xxiv. 6, LXX.). Whether or not their power was waning, and that of the Amorite increasing, before Israel came to take possession, as some think, it is certain that both the Hittite power and the Egyptian were much enfeebled by their conflicts. While they were thus engaged in their fiercest wars, and Palestine was a continual battle-field, the young nation of Israel was practically sheltered under the strong wing of Egypt, till the time when those who would have imperilled its life were powerless, and then God "called His son out of Egypt," and led him about and brought him to possess the inheritance of these divided and broken peoples.

38. The land of the **Amalekites** lay outside of Palestine proper. They had one strong possession in the heart of the country known as the "Mount of the Amalekite," Judg. xii. 15, within the territory of Ephraim. They suffered from the raid of Chedorlaomer, Gen. xiv. 7, and tried issues with the Israelites at Rephidim, in defence of the wells and pasturages of the Sinaitic peninsula into which Israel was entering (Exod. xvii.). The **Kenites** were a sub-tribe of Amalek. Part of them, at least, joined the Israelites, attracted to Moses doubtless because of his relation to Hobab (Judg. i. 16). They had "cities" in the south of Judah, and some afterwards camped in tents in the north (Judg. iv. 11). The town of "Cain," which was planted on the edge of the mountains above Engedi, is thought by some to be "the nest of the Kenite," spoken of by Balaam (§ 57, 58).

Kenizzites mentioned with Kenites, Gen. xv. 19, hardly appear as a distinct nation; yet curiously, Caleb, of the tribe of Judah, is called a Kenezite, Num. xxxii. 12, and Josh. xiv. 6, 14, perhaps by descent from them on the mother's side. It may be that the less honourable birth-rank of Amalek as compared with Kenaz led to their alienation (Gen. xxxvi. 11, 12). The vigorous Amalekite race, however, survived to the time of Hezekiah, notwithstanding what it suffered from Saul and David (1 Chron. iv. 39–43).

The movement of small bands from place to place is very clearly proved to have taken place all through the history of the land. Hivites, Jebusites, Geshuri, Kenites, are thus found distributed in scattered groups as well as the Danites and Ephraimites. This helps us to understand the mingling of Israelites and Canaanites even in the same town in earlier times, and the treaty arrangements for the facilitating of such settlements of which we have an instance in 1 Kings xx. 34. Mons. Clermont Ganneau discovered an example of it at Siloam by the very gate of Jerusalem, which he thus relates: "The constant communications which I have with the Silwan (Siloam) people have brought to my knowledge a curious fact. Among the inhabitants of the village there are a hundred or so, domiciled for the most part in the lower quarter, and forming a group apart from the rest, called Dhiàbiyé, *i.e.* men of Dhiban. It appears that at some remote period a colony from the capital of King Mesha (Dibon-Moab) crossed the Jordan, and fixed itself at the gates of Jerusalem at Silwan. The memory of this migration is still preserved, and I am assured by the people themselves that many of their number are installed in other villages round Jerusalem." (For another illustration scarcely less interesting and more recent, see *Land of Gilead*, pp. 251–255.) There seems little reason to doubt that the same writer is sound in his conclusion as regards the fellaheen or native peasantry of Palestine, that taken as a whole they are the modern representatives of those old tribes which the Israelites found settled in the country (*Survey of Western Palestine, Special Papers*, p. 313).

39. It is not possible to judge of the influence of all those nations on Israel without some knowledge of their religion. From very early times there seem to have been sacred associations with the land (§ 6). Not only was the name of "Taneter," or Holy Land, the known designation of the country as early as the time of Thothmes III. of Egypt, but the names of its cities and mountains and valleys and wells are suggestive of the nature-worship which prevailed. Generally speaking, the worship of all those primitive nations from the Egyptians to the Hittites was substantially the same; and in this there was a bond of union among them in resisting not only the invasion of a new people but of a new and pure religion. This appears in the way the Moabites under Balak sought to defeat Israel, and it explains the real motive of Balaam's shrewd but vile advice for defeating God's people. The Hittites do not appear to have been Shemites but Hamites, as were also the Amorites and the Egyptians with the Philistines and Phœnicians. Their worship was originally like that of the Accadians of Babylonia, from among whom Abraham at God's call came out. But the Shemitic people dwelling among these Canaanite peoples too readily adopted their faith, as is seen in the case of the Moabites, Midianites, Ammonites, and others in earlier, as of the Israelites themselves in later times. The separation of Kenites and Kenizzites from their kindred, as that of the Moabite Ruth and others, may have been more decidedly an act of religious repentance and return to Jehovah than we commonly suppose. Though the worship of these nations was originally nature-worship,—worship of the sun and moon and stars, and the forces of nature,—it rapidly degenerated, for it required no morality, and did not even recognise it. On an old rock-hewn monument of the Hittites, there is a representation of a thanksgiving to the god who gives fertility to the earth. "The god is a husbandman, marked as giver of corn and wine by his attributes, and the gorgeous raiment of the suppliant priest, praying for a blessing on the country

and people, is purposely contrasted with the plain garments of the god" (quoted by Sir C. W. Wilson, *Palest. Q. S.*, 1884, p. 84. Compare Hos. ii. 8, 9). But their gods were also professedly worshipped in all nature, till every natural desire was consecrated in indulgence. The fairest spots of the land thus became the haunts of foulest lusts. The great dread of death still demanded other sacrifices, and men were ready to give the fruit of their body for the sin of their soul. The Tyrians, when besieged by Alexander the Great, did just as the king of Moab did, as recorded in 2 Kings iii. 27.

40. Baal was their god—called also "El." He had many local suffixes to his name, as Baal-Hermon, Baal-Gad, etc., and was worshipped often as Baal-Shemaim = lord of the heavens; Baal-Hammâm = lord of fierce summer heats and of destructive droughts; Baal-Zephon = Baal of the north, the dread of sailors, as sending storms; and so on. He was called also Melech, or Moloch, or Milcom—that is, simply king—among the Ammonites and the sons of Hinnom; also Adoni or Lord, familiar in its compounds, Adonibezek, Adoni-Zedek, and in the Greek form of Adonis. Beside Baal was Baaltis, the female deity, called Pene-Baal, the face of Baal, but by Bible writers more commonly spoken of as Ashteroth, and Ashêrah (mistranslated "groves" in Authorized Version), the former representing the goddess of love and war, the Istar of the Assyrians; and the latter the goddess of birth and growth. Over the whole land the remains of primitive idolatry are found. *Menhirs*, or rude obelisks, sometimes solitary and often in groups; *circles* and *dolmens*, which latter word is rendered by some "table-stone," and by others "holed-stone," were all connected with their worship—though they may have at the same time marked places of burial. While great numbers of these have been found in Moab, and Ammon, and Bashan, none have been discovered found in Judea, a fact no doubt attributable to the zeal of Jewish kings. One doubtful circle survives in Samaria, while in Galilee, at Tell-el-Kady, in the north of the Jordan valley, and between Tyre and Zidon, altogether some six dolmens, one circle, and an enclosure of menhirs have been discovered; one being on Mount Gilboa, which may be a remnant of the days of Jezebel of Jezreel. Over in Moab 700 specimens were found, which is no marvel,

seeing Balaam required the erection of seven on each of three neighbouring holy heights. It should be kept in remembrance that such "stones" are found all over the world, even in our own country. Signs, as cups and rings, are sometimes cut on them, but no words of inscription, which does not, however, signify much as regards their age, as long habit might consecrate the practice of erecting a stone on which no tool had been used (Exod. xx. 25). It is not possible to look at many of the "trilithons" (*i.e.* three stones) forming dolmens, such especially as stand like gateways to "circles," and have charms attached to the passing through them, without having the suggestion presented that we have here a dim remembrance of the first altar by the gate of Paradise—at Babel toward the sunrising (Gen. xxviii. 17). That they should be found by waters, and in spots of special beauty, is in keeping with the thought, as is also their undoubted use in some cases as places to receive the dead.

CHAPTER V.

PALESTINE IN THE DAYS OF THE PATRIARCHS.

41. Abraham with his father and brethren came from Ur, then the capital and chief seaport of the Chaldees, a fortified town, which boasted its great temple to the "moon god." By that time civilization was far advanced. "The civilization," says Professor Sayce, "which existed on the banks of the Euphrates more than 4000 years ago almost startles us by the modernness of its details." From Ur they came to Kharran on the Euphrates, and thence by Damascus to Canaan (Gen. xii.).

Abraham's first encampment was at Shechem. Shechem lies in a beautifully-watered vale which runs east and west between Ebal on the north and Gerizim on the south. The vale opens eastward upon a broad level plain, and it was there by an "oak" that he built his first altar, and that Jehovah first appeared to him in Canaan. From that time the spot was a "sacred" one. To it Jacob returned (Gen. xxxiii. 18-20), settling first in Shalem, or Salim, on the east of the plain, and afterwards purchasing the land where his grandfather had worshipped, and building an altar upon it (Gen. xxxv. 4; Josh. xxiv. 6). To this same place Joshua led Israel by Divine instructions to make the covenant that was sanctioned by the blessings of Gerizim and the curses of Ebal (Josh. xxiv.). Here too the first "king" was anointed in Israel (Judg. ix. 6); and hither also, in hope of conciliating Israel, came Rehoboam to be made king (1 Kings xii. § 73).

But Jacob left a more permanent memorial than his pillar there. He sank the *well* that bears his name to this day, and is the most certainly identified spot in all the land. There was water there, though the vale of Shechem drains mainly westwards; but water was a precious possession not to be shared with a stranger who had many retainers and great flocks and herds. Jacob therefore sank a well to a great depth. Robinson's measurement in 1838 made it 105 feet. The upper part was built, as it passed through alluvial soil and broken limestone, till the compact limestone rock was reached. The mouth is contracted, so that a man can descend with his hands uplifted, as holding by a rope, but immediately widens to a diameter of 7 feet 6 inches. Now it is often dry, and cannot be depended on for any water. No spot has such memories as this, where Abraham built his first altar and Jacob acquired his first possession in the land, and most significant of all, where Jesus offered the water of life to the woman of Sychar (§ 109, 110). The Shalem of Jacob (some think, though it is unlikely, of Melchizedek also) lay 2 miles east of Jacob's well, now *Salim*. It is well supplied with water, which might be the reason Jacob had for first settling there.

42. Abraham's second encampment was between **Bethel and Hai**, where also he built an altar. At that time Bethel was called Luz, though the narrative in Gen. xii. adopts the later, and to the readers the more familiar name. Bethel, now *Beitîn*, has always been known. It stands upon the great watershed and great high-road through the land, and from it a steep valley descends to Jericho, some 8 miles off. To this, on returning from Egypt, Abraham came back, and there he and Lot parted. Hai is most probably to be placed at *Haiyan*, just 2 miles east from Bethel—it is called, from Joshua's time onward, as by Josephus, Aina.

"It is built on the side of a flat spur which rises slightly on the north. On the south-east is a flat dell, with good fig and pomegranate gardens, and there are other fig-trees round the village and among the houses. . . . The ground is very open, and the slopes gentle; the village slopes down gradually south-east. The surrounding ground is quite bare of trees, of white chalk, very barren and stony on the south; of hard limestone cropping up on the north; the fields divided off by low dry-stone walls. . . . The place is supplied from a fine perennial spring on the south, which wells up in a circular basin. The spring is double, and was surrounded with a large reservoir of massive stones. Three other good springs are found in the neighbourhood. One of the most peculiar features about Bethel is the group of rocks covering two or three acres north of the town. Although these seem to have been hewn in some places, there is no reason to suppose them to be other than natural features. A similar group occurs farther east, and the country round the village is exceptionally stony and barren. In the valley by the reservoir of the spring there are several rock-cut tombs, as also farther west (2 Kings xxiii.). About half a mile eastwards are the ruins of *Burj Beitin*, on a little plateau, stony, but fertile, which is probably the site of Abraham's altar east of Bethel (Gen. xii. 8). The Jordan valley is plainly visible from this spot. Standing just here, Lot could see the *ciccar*, or plain of Jordan, which allured him by its luxuriant and well-watered [1] pasturages away from Abraham. It lay at his feet temptingly" (*Survey Memoirs*, ii. 295, 307).

To Bethel Jacob came when he left his father's house, and there he slept and dreamed of heaven (Gen. xxviii.). It has been suggested that the peculiar stepped formation of the rocks may have shaped the imagery of his half-waking thoughts as he dreamed, but this is over-fanciful. On a special Divine summons he returned there to pay the vow which that night he made (Gen. xxxv.). That it maintained a reputation as a sacred place, is proved by the narrative of Judg. xx. 18 (where "the house of God" should be rendered Bethel); while from vers. 26–28 of the same chapter it appears that "the ark of the covenant was there in those days." It was one of Samuel's circuit towns (1 Sam. vii. 16), became one of the "sacred places" where Jeroboam instituted calf-worship, and frequently reappears in Old Testament history, as if a lingering remnant of true Israelites always adhered to it (2 Kings ii. 3, xvii. 28). It seems strange that it is never once named in the New Testament. Ai seems to have been always coupled with Bethel as its dependency (Ezra ii. 28).

43. **The third encampment of Abraham** was at the "plain" or "oak," or rather "terebinth," of **Mamre** the Amorite, near Hebron. He had thus moved along the main watershed southward, passing "Jebusi" and "Ephratah." The place where his tent then stood, and where Jehovah came to him once and again, we do not know with any certainty; but the tradition which locates the oak of Mamre at Er Râmeh, 2 miles north of Hebron, has, to say the least, much in its favour. There most likely, as it is said, his famous "*Terebinth*" stood. The great "oak," a mile and a half west of Hebron, is a noble tree;

---

[1] In Gen. xiii. 10, for Zoar we should read *Zar*, that is, the fortress Zar at the entrance of Egypt, where Joseph met his father Jacob.

but it cannot be even a descendant of that which sheltered Abraham's tent. The remains of a large church built by Constantine fix what was in his time the traditional site; and a well, still containing water, determines for us almost the spot. It is an upland plain at a level of 3346 feet. Looking eastward, the hills seem to slope gently down into its meadow-like fields, shutting it in as a quiet resting-place, and a holy dwelling for one whose fellowship was with heaven. Here, we may allow ourselves to believe, the scenes of Gen. xv.–xix. were enacted. Its associations may have been Sarah's attraction to it, drawing her thither again when she felt that death was near, though apparently she did not reach it (Gen. xxiii. 2).

44. How long Abraham dwelt there we cannot say, but it would appear he had not done so very long before Lot's captivity summoned him to war. **The story of Gen. xiv. 1–24** is in many respects a most remarkable one, and the narrative as there preserved must have been taken from some very ancient document. Fourteen years before, while Abraham was in Haran, Chedorlaomer (or Kudur Lagamar, *i.e.* servant of Lagamar) had invaded the land and put the cities of the plain under tribute (§ 33). He now came to punish their rebellion and take them captive. With him was his son Arioch, whose name as Eri-aku—servant of the moon god—has been found on bricks with which he built at Larsa (Ellasar of Gen.). With Chedorlaomer came his vassals, the king of Shinar or Babylonia, and Turgal, king of Gutium, the northern land, afterwards known as Assyria; both which countries were at that time subject to Elam. The route taken by the invaders is easily traced; they came over by Damascus, doubtless, for they smote first the Rephaim in Bashan at *Ashteroth Karnaim, i.e.* Asheroth of the two horns, indicating a place sacred to the worship of the moon. This is most probably Tel 'Asherah, about 20 miles east of the Sea of Galilee. The Yarmûk rises here, and its most interesting features have yet to be surveyed. Within some 7 or 8 miles it falls at least 2000 feet. Mr. Lawrence Oliphant reports on the authority of a friend who has seen it, that the *Rukad*, one of the tributaries of the Jarmûk, has a fall of 300 feet in an unbroken sheet of water. It is very likely that amid the watercourses and pools the worship of Ashteroth was observed as it was

amid the similar scenery of Afka in Phœnicia (§ 78). From Ashteroth Karnaim, the kings of the east advanced southwards to the land of Ammon, where the *Zuzims* were yet in possession (Deut. ii. 10–12) of Ham or Rabbath, their capital. The *Emims* who lived in the "Shaveh," or plain of Kiriathaim, now Kureiyât, in Moab, just north of Dibon, and the Horites of Mount Seir, next succumbed to them. Having thus reached the wilderness, they turned north again by Kadesh, ascending into the mountains in the south of Canaan, overrunning the land of *Amalekites*, and *Amorites* (which may be understood as the land afterwards possessed by Amalekites and Amorites), and finally spoiling the Amorites who dwelt down at Engedi (Hazezon Tamar) in the warm, sheltered oasis beneath the sharp cliff of Ziz, still called *Hasâsah*. They had thus swept round the Salt Sea and came last to *the cities of the plain*, whose rebellion had provoked the expedition. The men of the plain, of luxurious and loose habits of life, were easily smitten, and with their families and goods fell a prey to the victors. Lot being taken also, Abraham summoned all his retainers and his allies, and pursued the returning kings up the Jordan valley to Laish (afterwards Dan), where he suddenly fell on them and chased them to Hobah, north of Damascus. He returned towards Mamre by *Shaveh*, or "the king's dale," the place where Absalom's pillar afterwards stood, 2 furlongs from Jerusalem (Josephus, *Ant.* vii. 10, 3). There he was met by Melchizedek, king of Salem.

45. Not long after this the Lord appeared to Abraham and intimated the coming judgment upon these five cities of the plain. It was most probably upon the hill lying on the north side of Mamre that the memorable interview took place, recorded in Gen. xviii. 23, 33. On the same spot Abraham stood next morning (Gen. xix. 27), and from there, though he could not see down into the plain, he could see *toward it* and could see the smoke ascending. One standing there can see the hills of Gilead over and beyond the steaming haze that floats above the Salt Sea.

Captain Conder, however, thinks that the oak of Mamre was in Hebron, and that the spot whence he saw the smoke of Sodom was at the traditional site *Beni N'aim*, 3 miles east of Hebron, "whence the cliffs of Engedi are clearly seen at the eastern slopes from Kerak to Nebo, although the waters of the Dead Sea and the Valley of the Jordan are hidden by the western precipices." Beni N'aim was formerly known as Kefr Bareka—the village of blessing, and he suggests this may be a remembrance of Abraham's intercession on the spot. But the language of Josh. xv. 19 suggests another origin.

There is no doubt that the cities which were overthrown lay in the plain of Jordan, north of the Salt Sea, and just under Hai, whence Lot saw them. Some consider that the name of *Admah* still lingers in that of the Damieh ford, and may have been the Adam of Josh. iii. 16 (but see notes in Index). *Zoar* is with probability placed at Zell-Saghûr, close to the ascent leading up from Abel-Shittim to the eastern mountains (§ 25). "It is a whitish mound, about 40 feet high, and 170 paces north and south, by 55 paces east and west, stony, and quarried on the east. A little spring rises on the north, and on the east a larger spring is surrounded with grass and rushes" (*Heth and Moab*). Zoar was in existence till a late period (Isa. xv. 5 and Jer. xlviii. 34). *Zeboim* seems to have left its name on the west of Jordan in the valley mentioned 1 Sam. xiii. 18, Neh. xi. 34, and may be the modern Wâdy Shakh-ed-Dub'a, north of Jericho, or it may be traced in "Zeeb," at whose wine-press the Midianite prince Zeeb was slain (Judg. vii. 25. See § 91). Much cannot, however, be made of the recurrence of such a name; it is found even as far north as Tel edh Dhiabeh on the Jordan right down from Bethshean. Zeboim (or the two Zeebs ?) is apparently derived from the name of the "wolf." *Gomorrah* or *'Amorah* has not been identified, though possibly the echo of the name lingers in the rocky cliffs and valley of 'Amrîyeh, at the north-west corner of the Salt Sea. In this region doubtless the cities lay. *Sodom* may have been near Jericho, but more probably lay within the bounds of the tempting acacia-meadow Abel-Shittim, towards which Lot gradually approached going eastward (§ 19 and 57). When he left Zoar, Lot doubtless went up to Heshbon by the ascent of Luhith (Isa. xv. 5). The land of his sons spread thence on his right hand and his left—that of Moab to the south, and that of Ammon to the north, of the Wâdy Heshbon.

46. **Abraham's fourth encampment** lay yet farther south, in "*the*

south" or "Negeb," "between Kadesh and Shur" (Gen. xx. 1), which he had already twice traversed (Gen. xii. 9, xiii. 3), though he had not before dwelt in it. A fine pastoral land reaches westward from Beersheba towards the south of the land of the Philistines and to the "river of Egypt," usually identified with the Wâdy el Arish, beyond which it is absolute desert as far as the border of Egypt. "Shur," meaning "wall," marked no doubt a physical feature of the desert. This desert lay between Egypt and Philistia. It is not clear which Kadesh is meant. "Ain Kadeis," or the well Kadesh, lies south of Beersheba; but this may mean the Holy Well, and Kadesh, the Holy City, may lie farther east in the ascent to Tel Arad, where Kadesh-barnea is marked on the map. The frequent recurrence of the name "Kadesh" makes it difficult to fix the site (see Index). The locality in which Abraham encamped was near Gerar, which is well known; it lies 10 or 12 miles south of Gaza, in a valley running westwards from Beersheba, which lies some 25 miles to the east. Here Abraham met with the Philistine king Abimelech, in contrast to whom even the father of the faithful appears at a disadvantage. Here Isaac was born and in this country lived with his father. Gerar is now to be recognised in the ruin Umm el Jerrâr. Shur, on the strength of rabbinical authority, is fixed at Khalasah, 25 miles south of Beersheba, and is by some identified with Bered of Gen. xvi. 14.

47. The next event in Abraham's life after Isaac's birth was the sending forth of Hagar and her son Ishmael. Hagar's name is connected with the well Beer-lahai-roi, which may pretty confidently be identified with 'Ain Muweileh placed on Mr. Holland's map about 10 miles west of 'Ain Kadeis. There is a Jebel Muweileh, along the eastern base of which runs a wâdy of the same name in which the well is. Mr. Rowlands (in *Palestine Quarterly*, 1884, p. 177) says it is pronounced Moilahhi by the Arabs there, and this, as it has been pointed out, if written Mâ-lehayy-rái, would in Arabic mean the "water of the living one seeing."

The house of Hagar (Beit Hagar) is shown by the Arabs, "not a cave, but cut square out of a rock in the side of a precipice at some height from the ground, with a staircase leading up to it, and two smaller interior chambers for dormitories,"

48. Two other places next named in the Patriarch's history are of much interest. The one is Beersheba (Gen. xxi. 31), said to have got its name from the covenant made there between Abraham and Abimelech the Philistine. It has always been known and to this day is much frequented. There are "seven wells" at the spot, now unprotected openings. The largest is 13 feet in diameter, and though its edges are worn with the ropes of the shepherds watering their flocks, the stones now there have not been built into their present position over 700 years. No remains of Abraham's planting are to be seen, the neighbourhood being destitute of trees, and after summer heat becoming scorched so that the flocks desert it. The other memorable place is Moriah, to which at God's command Abraham went to offer Isaac (Gen. xxii. 2). There are two claimants to represent this sacred spot—the site of Solomon's temple, which *seems* supported by 2 Chron. iii. 1; and Mount Gerizim, in support of which the Samaritans quote their version, which here they say reads Moreh for Moriah—the plain of Moreh being beside Gerizim. It will be observed that the expression is the "*land* of" Moriah, where was an *unnamed* mountain. The name Moriah was given to the temple site not in connection with the Lord's appearing to Abraham, but to David (2 Chron. iii. 1), and no reference is made to any earlier use of the name to designate it before David's time, which might have been expected if the "appearing" were so old and memorable as that to Abraham when he offered Isaac. There is reason to believe (§ 44) that the Salem of Melchizedek was Jerusalem, and if so the temple hill would, if not actually occupied, be in sight of the city. The narrative of Gen. xxii. certainly suggests that on Moriah Abraham was in a thicket and alone with Isaac. The land already known to Abraham by the name "Moriah," was most probably near Shechem, Gen. xii. 7; or Bethel, xiii. 14; or Mamre, xvii. 1, xviii. 1. That the scene of chap. xvii. should be also that of xxii. is not improbable. No doubt Josephus preserves a Jewish tradition at least as good as the Samaritan one (*Ant.* i. 13), though some may attach no value to either, as Scripture is silent. Dean Stanley (*Sinai and Palestine*, p. 248) has pled the cause of Gerizim most ingeniously, and yet perhaps few will be satisfied with his arguments : and though naturally one would incline to suppose that the act of Abraham

giving his well-beloved son *ought to be placed* at Jerusalem, the studied silence of Scripture and its avoidance of such definite statements as would lead to the consecration of localities warn us not to be confident as to this. From the land of Moriah, Abraham and Isaac returned to Beersheba, where after this Abraham dwelt (Gen. xxii. 19).

49. "Sarah died at Kirjath Arba—the same is Hebron." There is every reason to accept the traditional site of the **cave of Machpelah** there. It was on the *east* of Hebron, and cannot be sought at the Kabr Habrûn (the grave of Hebron) on the west, as some have suggested. Besides, the building which surrounds the famous site (now a mosque) is undoubtedly very old and of Jewish workmanship, corresponding so entirely with Herodian building at Jerusalem as to fix its age with certainty. As at Jerusalem, many of the stones are of great size, nearly 40 feet long by 3 to 4 feet deep. There are pilasters all round 2½ feet broad and 5 feet apart, and traces of similar work have been found at the north-west corner of the Haram wall at Jerusalem. The height of the wall is 40 feet, and the enclosed space is 197 feet long by about 111 feet wide. From the levels of the ground outside the walls, it is inferred that the rock within must be an isolated knoll. The approach to this sacred place is fiercely guarded by the fanatical Moslems of the town, but it has more than once been visited by British Royalty, to which even Mohammedan fury has had to bow. There is no reason to doubt, that when the way is open, and access gained to the rock beneath, the cave in which Abraham laid Sarah when he had purchased it from the Hittite will be found, though it is not possible to imagine that the bodies of the patriarchs should yet be where they were laid, as the cave was not closed in ancient times.

Beside Dean Stanley's accounts in *Sinai and Palestine*, a full account of a visit by the two sons of the Prince of Wales (1881), in which they were accompanied by Sir C. Wilson, Captain Conder, Consul Moore, and other most competent observers, will be found in the *Memoirs*, vol. iii. p. 333, and in *Palestine Quarterly* for October 1882. The sheikh of the mosque described the cave as double, and this is undoubtedly the testimony of tradition, and may be suggested by the name itself. It is not known to have been entered for 700 years.

50. Abraham's own wanderings were at an end, and it is well worth noticing **the line and length of his travels in the land** promised him. He entered it most likely, as Jacob on his return, by Gilead, and settled in Shechem. Some 20 miles south he pitched his tent in Bethel, and other 30 miles southward along the watershed rested for a while at Hebron, 25 miles south of which lay Beersheba, west of which again by the Wâdy Sheba he went to Gerar. At Beersheba, his last camp, he was but 75 miles from his first at the oak of Moreh, by Shechem. He had visited Egypt, and once "on the war path," made a rapid journey to Dan. How far we may infer from Gen. xiii. 17 that he traversed the whole land, we cannot tell; but apart from that he went, as we know, from Dan to Beersheba, a distance which in our day seems of no account. An express train, if it could travel at the speed daily maintained over the greater distance between London and York, would traverse it within three hours. By the way he had come from Kharran, Abraham sent Eleazar of Damascus to seek a wife for his son Isaac; and he brought Rebekah to the south, where he dwelt by the well Lahai-roi. The life of Isaac was apparently very stationary. Between the well of Hagar and Beersheba there is " a long line of ruined cities and of old wells," and within this neighbourhood his wanderings were confined. Once he went to Gerar in time of famine, and leaving it went to the valley of Gerar and dwelt there (Gen. xxvi. 1-17). This is the Wâdy Jerûr, some 10 miles south of Hagar's well, where are great rolling plains of pasturage. The position of Ezek has not been recovered, but Sitnah (Gen. xxvi. 21), his next well, has been placed by Professor Palmer at Shutneh, just west of Ruheibeh or Rehoboth, his next well, where he found "room," and which lies 20 miles south of Beersheba, whither he next removed. At the close of his life, Isaac, like his mother Sarah, came to Hebron, where he died (Gen. xxxv. 27, 29).

51. Jacob's adventures open with the memorable scene at Bethel, or Luz (Gen. xxviii. 10, 11), 50 to 60 miles distant from Beersheba. It is on his return journey that we find ourselves in localities before unnamed. He came to the **mountains of Gilead**, and was there overtaken by Laban (Gen. xxxi. 21, 23), when a covenant was made on a spot on which they raised "a heap." The Arabs still raise up such

heaps or cairns, and call them "Meshâhed," or witnesses, just as Laban called the heap "Jegar-sahadutha," while Jacob called it "Galeed." But he gave it also the name of Mizpeh, or watch-tower, a name very frequently met with. This Mizpeh may be supposed the same as that known in Jephthah's time, and where his house was. Probably we may safely place it at "Sûf," about 10 miles north of the Jabbok. Sûf is from the same root as Mizpeh, and doubtless preserves the site of the old watch-tower or outlook. It lies 3 miles north of Reimûn, which is most likely the ancient Ramoth-Gilead. "A fine group of rude stone monuments exists near Sûf, showing in all probability that there was once a sacred centre here" (*Heth and Moab*).

The next place mentioned in Jacob's return is *Mahanaim* (Gen. xxxii.); its position is yet undetermined. It lay in the tribe of Gad. Maneh and Birket-Maneh, which have been suggested, lie too far north; for to put Mahanaim there would require the placing of Mizpeh still farther north. Its position cannot be gathered from the history of later times, as *the wood of Ephraim*, where the battle was between David's men and Absalom's, is unknown (2 Sam. xviii. 6). From Josh. xiii. 25, 26, and 1 Kings iv. 13, 14, we may infer it lay south of Gilead, and all its cities. Future exploration may recover this interesting site. See Index for notices of it in Scripture.

52. The site of Peniel or Penuel cannot have been far from *Succoth* (Gen. xxxiii. 17 and Judg. viii. 4–11). It lay west of the road which led to Nobah and Jogbehah in the east. Nobah, as we learn from Num. xxxii. 42, is Kenath, now Kanawat, in the wild district of the Lejah or Argob, 60 miles eastwards from the south end of the Sea of Galilee. Jogbehah, now Jubcihah, will be seen on the map in the centre of the circle surrounded by the southern branch of the river Jabbok (§ 24), east of Jebel Osh'a. Gideon probably pursued the Midianites up the Jabbok valley. The position of Succoth has been, on the strength of the testimony of the Talmud that its later name was Terala, fixed at Tell Deir 'Alla by the Jordan, north of the Jabbok, and it is quite possible Jacob turned back thither on parting with Esau; the site of Peniel and its tower must have been near Jebel Osh'a. From it a Wâdy Fâneh runs down to the Jabbok, in which it possibly stood.

Note.—The suggestion (Smith's *Bible Dict.*) "that Jebel Osh'a may be Peniel is ingenious. Pene-el certainly suggests Pene-Baal, or 'the face of God,' a name given to the promontory of Râs Shakka near Tripoli, called by the Greeks 'Theoprosopon,' which has the same meaning—'the face of God.' Pene-Baal was also the name of a Phœnician goddess, and along with this we may notice that the name Succoth or Sekut reappears in Egypt in Succoth (Ex. i. 11), built by the Israelites for Pharaoh, the site of which has been recently recovered, and where was also Pi-Tum, *i.e.* the sanctuary of Tum. Siccuth or Sakkut was originally a deity of the Babylonian Hamites, early adopted by the Shemitic people, and even worshipped in the wilderness by Israel. In Amos v. 26, 'He is called Sakkuth your king;' and in 2 Kings xvii. 20, we read that the men of Babylon settled in Samaria worshipped Succoth Benoth. The confusion of this name with the word for 'booths,' may have arisen from a mistranslation of the Babylonian title of *Zit-banit*, the wife of Belmerodach (Rawlinson's *Herod I.*, p. 630), *Zirat* = 'supreme,' having been mistaken for *Zerat* = 'tents.' But the connection of Succoth and Peniel as sacred places of early heathen worship, and their existence as such before Jacob's time, can hardly be doubted. For this and other reasons they must be sought close together. That Peniel was a height is plainly indicated by the expression, 'As Jacob passed over Penuel the sun rose upon him, and he halted upon his thigh.'

"The Talmud states definitely that in its time Succoth was called 'Ter'alah;' and in the great plain north of the Jabbok, about 1 mile from the stream, and about 3 miles from where the river leaves the hills, there is a large mound or Tell which bears the name Der'ala. . . . There is a ford or crossing of the Jabbok, some distance to the east of Tell Der'ala, but before the hills are reached, which bears the name of 'Mashra'a Canaan,' *i.e.* 'Canaan's Crossing.' . . . I have alluded to the Jabbok as being the main thoroughfare from the eastern plains to the Land of Canaan." "From a thorough personal examination of the country, I think I can say with truth that neither to the north nor to the south of the Jabbok is there any other feasible route by which to enter Canaan from the plains and deserts of Arabia." . . . "It is on this great thoroughfare that I suppose Penuel, a frontier tower or fortress, to have been built in the earliest times in order to repel invasions from the east." "About say 4 miles above Canaan's Crossing, following the course of the stream, there is one of the most singular formations in Syria. At this point the valley is quite narrow, and its walls are precipitous. In a line with the valley, the course of which is from east to west, there spring from its lowest level and rise to a height of 250 feet, *two conical hills*. One of these sugar-loaf hills is on one side of the stream, and the other is on the other side. . . . The sides of these mounds are steep, and it took me fifteen minutes to reach the summit of one of them." . . . "On both these hills there are extensive and ancient ruins. The one to the west is larger than the other, and has upon it more ruins; but the ruins upon the one to the east are remarkable. Whatever the nature of the structures once standing here may have been, they could have been built, considering the nature of the ground and the size of the stones, only at enormous expense." "This, if anywhere on the Jabbok, would be the most suitable place for a frontier fortress, and such we have reason to believe was Penuel" (Rev. S. Merrill).

53. Like Abraham, Jacob moved from Shalem (see § 41) southward first to **Bethel**, and then to Mamre at **Hebron**. On the way Rachel died, when there was but a little way to come to **Ephrath**, which is Bethlehem. The position of Bethlehem-Judah is undisputed, so that the traditional sepulchre of Rachel and birthplace of Benjamin can hardly be matter of doubt. It forms one of the landmarks of the country, and stood on the border of Benjamin (1 Sam. x. 2). The position of the little domed building which now is known as Rachel's sepulchre exactly suits the description in Gen. xxxv. It is a little way from, and over against and higher than Bethlehem, which lies on a spur of the hills jutting abruptly eastward from the watershed (§ 106). The sepulchre is 4 miles south from Jerusalem, on the main road to Hebron, to which Jacob now journeyed. From Hebron he sent Joseph to inquire as to his brethren's welfare. He came to Shechem, whither they had first gone, and there learning that they had gone on to **Dothan** to feed their flock in the little plain of choice pasture there, he followed, passing through the valley of Shechem some 6 miles to Samaria (*i.e.* to the hill on which Samaria afterwards stood), and then to Dothan 12 miles beyond. Tell-Dothân still retains its old name; it lies on the road of caravans, crossing from the east by the plain of Esdraelon and passing westward of the hills which encompass Samaria, among the valleys and upland plains of what was afterwards the rich territory of Manasseh. Dothan is not named in Joshua. Here a spring yet bursts at the foot of a smooth hill. Round this spring Joseph's brethren probably sat as he drew near. They cast him into a cistern that was empty, for the season must have been advanced, and possibly had been one of drought when they took their flocks from Shechem to Dothan. The town remained till the time of the kings, when it was the scene of Elisha's deliverance (2 Kings vi.).

54. From another incident in the history of Jacob's family, we learn that they spread themselves over the land and did not dwell together. Judah went down to Adullam, now 'Aîd-el-Mâ, where dwelt a Canaanite named Hirah. It was afterwards a royal city; and if it was so at this time, Hirah would be its king. In that neighbourhood Judah pastured his flocks. The *open place* of Gen. xxxviii. 14 is rendered by the LXX. " by the gates of Ainam," which is probably the Enam of Josh. xv. 34. Close to Timnah, on the road from Adullam, is 'Allin. (The interchange of *l* and *n* is familiar in all tongues.) Here, then, we are undoubtedly in the country afterwards familiar in the stories of Samson and David. For here was the cave in which David, Judah's son, gathered about him the mighty men by whom he was surrounded and helped to his kingdom. Judah would easily pass from Hebron to Adullam. From the probable site of Mamre, a 10-mile walk down a valley brought him to Adullam, from which he went to Timnath in the valley of Sorek. The straits of famine naturally took him and his brethren back to the tents of Jacob at Hebron to consult and act together to save their households (Gen. xlii. 1, 2). From Hebron, Jacob went by Beersheba into Egypt.

CHAPTER VI.

TERRITORY OF THE TWELVE TRIBES.

(*See* MAP II.)

1. EASTERN PALESTINE—CONQUESTS IN THE EAST.

55. The twelve families and their retainers who went down to Egypt came up about 400 years afterwards a nation of **twelve tribes**. They came through the wilderness to *Kadesh*, and sent their spies to view the land. And they went up and searched the land to the far north at Rehob, which probably is now represented by the castle of Hunin commanding the road from Hamath into the plain of Cœle Syria, between Lebanon and Antilebanon. From Eshcol they fetched grapes, to show the fertility of the good land. Eshcol was brother of Mamre, and son of Arba the founder of Hebron. It may be identified with 'Ain Kash Kaleh, which is close to Hebron on the north, and is usually pronounced by the natives as Askali. There are rock-cut tombs and caves, marking ancient dwellings near it, and a fine spring rising among the vineyards, the origin of "the brook" (Num. xiii. 24).

When the Israelites, after wandering forty years, again approached their inheritance, they did so from the east, and crossed *the Arnon, the border of Moab*. From this point onwards their journeyings can be traced. Their next camp was at *Beer*, Num. xxi. 16, or Dibon-Gad, Num. xxxiii. 45. Beer, "the well," was dug because there was no water. Dibon, still called Dhibân, lay just north of the Arnon, an easy march for a great host of men, women, and children, such as Israel was. The next stage was *Mattanah*, which must have been at the Wâdy Wâleh as they journeyed thence to *Nahaliel*, already described (§ 26). The next encampment was at *Bamoth Baal*, or the high places of Baal, and must have been the ridge now called "El Mashîbîyeh," on which is still a group of more

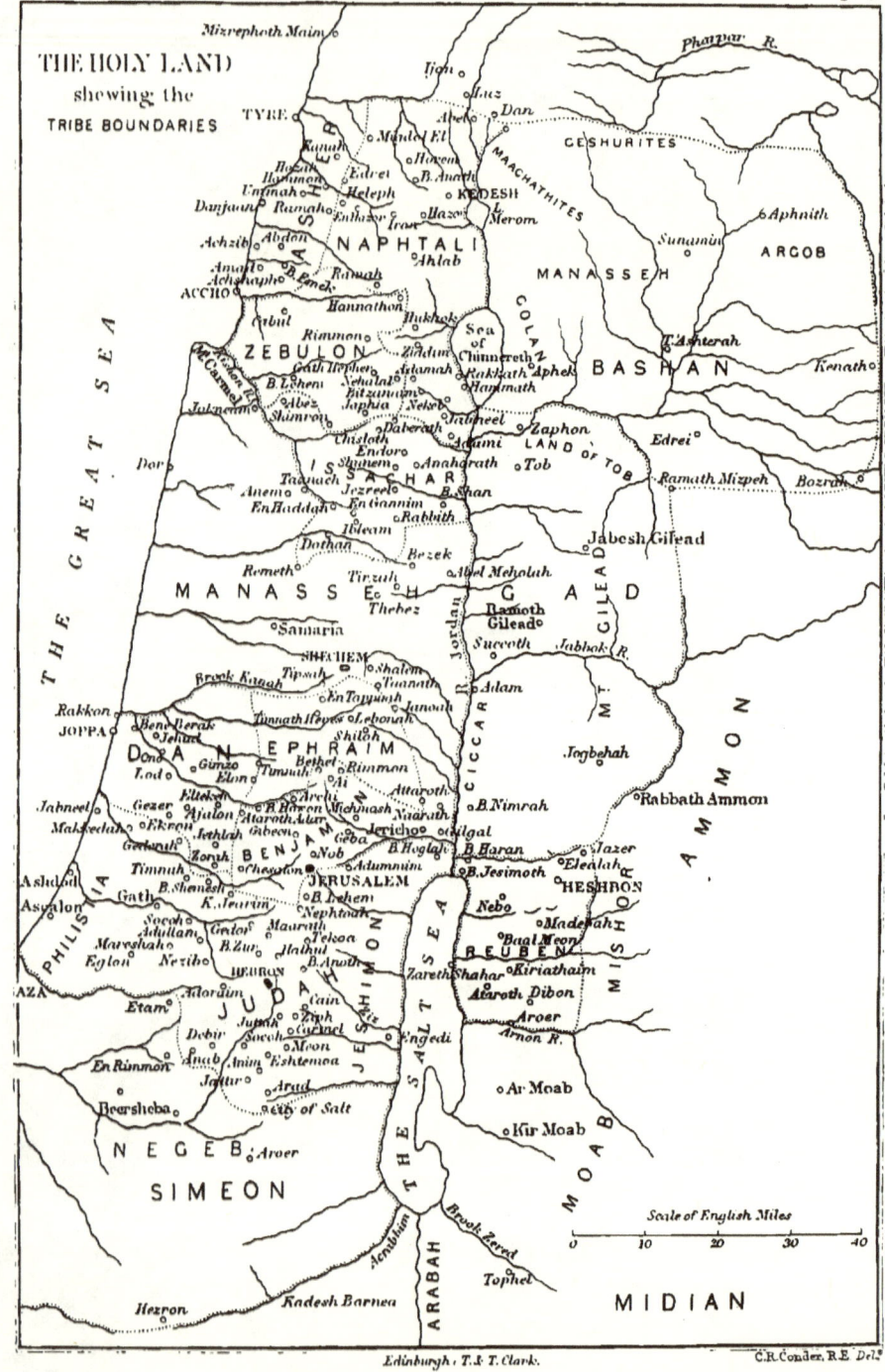

than a hundred rude stone monuments. Thence they moved to *the top of Pisgah* (§ 25).

56. At **Jahaz**, the Israelites overthrew in battle **Sihon, king of the Amorites**. Its position is uncertain, though it existed in the time of Isaiah (xv. 4) and Jeremiah (xlviii. 34); and from the manner in which it is in these places spoken of, it must have been at one extremity of the district, most probably to the north-east of Heshbon. It was given from among the cities of Reuben to the Levites of the family of Merari. The victory there, often celebrated in song, gave Israel possession of all the land between the Arnon and the Jabbok. Y'azer, or Jazer, next captured, with its villages, is usually supposed to be Sâr, or Beit Zer'ah, near Elealeh, 4 miles north-east of Heshbon. Twelve miles north of Heshbon, a valley of the same name descends to Abel Shittim, which may have been included in "the land of Jazer" (Num. xxxii. 1). The tempting "land" which Reuben and Gad desired, may well have been the rich hollow plain, or round basin, "possessing a fine extent of arable land," in the neighbourhood of which it has been suggested that Mahanaim must be sought (§ 60). Alarmed by the Israelites' conquests, **Og, king of Bashan**, came to oppose them at **Edrei**, now Edr'a, where he fell. It is placed on a rocky promontory on the south-west of the Lejah (§ 23), the Argob of the Old Testament, and Trachonitis of the New—a wild inaccessible region, whose inhabitants have always felt safe as in a stronghold, and who are so jealous of strangers that they will scarcely guide them through its intricate and secret passes. The situation of Edrei was chosen for strength alone, "without a single spring of living water; without river or stream; without access except over rocks and through defiles all but impassable; without tree or garden."[1] It rises 20 or 30 feet above the plain on which Og marshalled his armies against Israel. It does not appear again in Scripture history, though in the time of the Romans it was a great city. Possibly the Israelites did not keep possession, but allowed it to become the stronghold of banditti and outlaws who fled thither. The remains of the Roman city cover an extent of 3 miles (Tristram). In Christian times it became the Episcopal city of Adraa. By these victories over Sihon and Og, the strength of the Amorites

---

[1] Porter's *Giant Cities of Bashan*.

was broken, and Eastern Palestine lay entirely in the power of Israel.

57. The next camp of Israel proved a sadly memorable one; it was down in the Jordan valley amid the enervating influences of the acacia-meadow **Abel Shittim**.

When they were there, Balak summoned Balaam from Pethor by the Euphrates to curse Israel. He took him from Kirjath-huzoth, probably *Kureiyat* immediately south of Jebel Attarus, first to Bamoth Baal, then to the field of Zophim on the top of Pisgah, and finally to the top of Peor. Bamoth Baal lay south of Nebo, whence he could see but little of Israel's camp in the plain below. From Nebo he could see more, yet not quite down into the valley. The site of Peor has been recovered by the recent survey by the Palestine Exploration Society, at a line of "seven large stones," on the edge of the cliff from which a complete view is had of the plains of Abel Shittim (*Heth and Moab*). At each of these places undoubted remains of ancient shrines have been found. It is also suggestive that the first shrine was sacred to Baal, the second to Nebo, and the third to Peor ("the Priapus of Moab"), as explaining how Balak hoped that where one deity would not curse, another might. The view from these heights accords with the words of the seer. At his suggestion, a snare was set for Israel, to entice them to sin so that Jehovah would forsake them, when they should immediately fall a prey to Moab and Midian. The temptation was too successful: they were seduced to take part in the licentious worship of Baal-Peor, and there fell of them in one day four-and-twenty thousand, till Phinehas stayed the plague by executing judgment. They were even then encamped on the scene of Jehovah's judgment upon Sodom, when they repeated its iniquities.

58. The site of **Nebo** is for ever memorable as the view-point not of Balaam, but of Moses. From the plain beneath, he ascended by the Wâdy Heshbon, by the Tal'at es Sufa, to Nebo or Pisgah, as Aaron had ascended Mount Hor in Edom. The position, not the height, of Nebo afforded him the promised view of the land of Israel's inheritance. It is only 2643 feet high, but standing out as it does, it commands a view over the whole of Western Palestine. The projecting ranges of

Abarim running out on the south, parallel to Nebo, shut in the view on the left, so that the Lisan in the Dead Sea is hid, while on the right the height of Jebel Osh'a intercepts the view of Hermon; yet the view, as it has been described by all who have stood there, as Moses did, is magnificent. On the near right are the mountains of Gilead beyond the Wâdy Heshbon and Elealeh; close below, under the mountain, lies the plain of Moab, on which Israel's tents were spread when Balaam and Moses looked on them, the streams of Moab rushing over it towards Jordan, amid tamarisks and oleanders and acacias; Jordan winding itself about within its broader channel, or Zor, dark and tortuous, comes from out the deep haze that rests upon its valley northward; just across the plain is the steep mountain of Quarantania, and at its foot the green spots which mark the springs of Jericho, and the lands they water; right up behind Jericho goes the deep cleft of the valley of Achor, and the ascent over the southern shoulder of Olivet, which is clearly seen to its summit, with Jerusalem lying beyond amid its mountains; up the Jordan valley from Jericho the peak of *Sartabeh* guards the Wâdy Far'ah; while southward the Salt Sea lies heavy and slumberous "like a long strip of molten lead," the steep wall of its farther shore being broken where beneath the cliff of Ziz is the descent to Engedi, the well where the wild goat still has pasturage and a refuge, and where, farther south, towers the boldly projecting rock of Masada, the last foothold of the Jews in the land which God gave to their fathers. The centre ridge of the western mountains stands clear against the sky behind, from Cain, "the nest of the Kenite," over Hebron, northward by the mountains behind Bethlehem, and Jerusalem, along the highway to Bethel and the crown of Baal Hazor, thence to Gerizim and Ebal, which Moses might well have pointed out to Joshua (Deut. xxvii. 4), and beyond, still northward, the heights of Tabor and the ranges which enclose the eastern end of the valley of Jezreel are seen, though Carmel is hid by the higher and nearer ranges. The utmost sea cannot be visible. Dr. Tristram describes the appearance beyond Gerizim "of a faint and distant bluish haze which suggested the sea, the utmost sea. It seemed as if but a whiff were needed to brush off the haze and reveal it clearly, but the haze was that of distance rather than of water."

In the account of Deut. xxxiv. 1–3, if only we read *towards* instead of *unto* as applied to Dan and the Western Sea, the accuracy of the description is perfect.

59. The territory conquered on the east of Jordan was at their request divided between the tribes of Reuben and Gad (Num. xxxii.). Half of Manasseh afterwards removed to the east. The assignment of the land was that suggested by its natural divisions. To **Reuben** was allotted the *Mishor*, now called *Belka*, between the Arnon on the south and Heshbon on the north. The Salt Sea shut in his territory on the west, save at the extreme north, where it descended to the plain and afforded, by Beth Jesimoth, an access to the fords of Jordan.

Going up by the Wâdy Heshbon towards Nebo is *Sûmieh*, the ancient Sibmah, where rock-cut wine-presses explain the prophetic words of Isaiah and Jeremiah. The ruins of Heshbon are very considerable, "old great stones with the Jewish or Phœnician bevel, Roman arches, Doric pillars, and Saracenic work all strangely mingled in their overthrow." To the north of it, close by, lies Elealeh, so often mentioned with it, similar to Heshbon with a great central mound, now called El 'Al. To the south, on the great road through Moab, lies Madiyabah, or Medeba, in the centre of the Mishor, a flourishing city down to the days of the Romans, and even in Christian times. Roads and streets, gateways and Christian churches, can be traced. It had a great reservoir, 120 yards square, like Solomon's pools, still perfect, though now dry and tilled as a field (Tristram). The position of Jazer has been described (§ 65). South of Nebo is *Tal'at el Heith*, in which we can trace the ascent of Luhith. *Beth Meon*, from the mound of its great citadel, commands a splendid view, from Gilead in the north to Dibon in the south; it lies 4 miles south-west of Medeba, and its name Tell M'ain is given to the Zerka M'ain or Callirhoe, on the edge of which it stands. For a description of the Callirhoe, see § 26. Some 3 miles along the shore of the Salt Sea, southward from the mouth of that river, is a little recess, and in the oasis thus formed are the ruins of *Zâra*, named in Josh. xiii. 19, Zareth Shahar. On the south side of the Callirhoe valley rises Jebel Attarus, and on its southern slopes stand the remains of Kiriathaim, now called *Kureiyat*. Here Balak met Balaam (§ 66). Its high place would doubtless be on Attarus, which may have been the Shophan or Atroth-Shophan of Num. xxxii. 35. North of the Arnon, between 3 and 4 miles, stands Dhibân, representing the famous Dibon whose extensive ruins covering two rounded hills, once enclosed by one city wall, have in recent times become famous from the discovery there of the " Moabite stone," in 1868.[1] " Some clue to the position of Minnith, and certainly a most interesting illustration of the persistency of topographical nomenclature, as well as an illustration of the minute accuracy of the Bible narrative, may be found in the fact that a valley, or rather a gentle depression with sloping sides, running for about 4 miles east of Dhibân, is still called *Kurm Dhiban*, or 'the vineyards of Dibon.' They are the old dykes, or grass-grown ridges which mark the sites of the vines; but for centuries not a vine has grown here. When we turn to Judg. xi. 33, we read that Jephthah, after his defeat of the Ammonites, ' smote them from Aroer, even till they came to Minnith, even twenty cities, and unto the plain of the vineyards, with a very great slaughter' " (Tristram).

The southmost of the three cities of refuge east of Jordan was Bezer, afterwards Bosor, in the Midbar or downs of Moab; it was discovered by Palmer some 2 miles south of Dibon, on a knoll with ruins of some extent called Kasur el Besheir. Aroer, which lay on the south boundary of Reuben, is now called 'Ar'aîr; it is on the brink of the Arnon valley, which is 1500 feet deep, though not over 100 feet wide: such a ravine was a definite boundary for Israel. Beyond the Arnon in the land of Moab, are Rabbath or Ar, the ancient capital; and 8 miles farther south, Kerak, the Kir or Kir Haraseh of Isaiah, or Kirheres of Jeremiah, and the Kirkha of the Moabite stone (see Appendix), set on an almost isolated peak, 2700 feet above the sea, a little higher than Nebo. No wonder it could stand against combined hosts (2 Kings iii.). In the oasis of Ghôr es Safieh there was a Nimrim or Beth Nimrah—*i.e.* " house of leopards " —as in the Ghôr es Seisebân at the north end; but this was not a town of Reuben, but of Moab.

These are the principal places named in the square of pasture-land allotted to Reuben beyond the Salt Sea, which enclosed only some

[1] See Appendix II.

400 square miles, the same in extent as the lot afterwards assigned to Benjamin.

60. From about 5 miles north of the Salt Sea to the south of the Sea of Galilee, stretched the land of Gad. Its general features have been already described. It was bounded on the west by the Jordan, on the south by the Wâdy Heshbon, on the north by the Jarmûk. The eastern boundary in the south ran for a good way by the course of the Jabbok, as shown on the Map, and in the north by a branch of the Jarmûk. From Ramoth Mizpeh a line was drawn to the Jabbok, the position of which cannot be exactly fixed, and probably was often altered as the power of the Gadites waxed or waned. The places in Gad mentioned in the Old Testament, besides those already described in the patriarchal history, are very few. The chief are —(1) Jabesh Gilead, whose site is on the Wâdy el Yâbis, opposite Bethshean, and 6 miles south of Pella. From this place wives were taken for Benjamin after that tribe had been nearly exterminated, and hence there was a blood-tie to Saul's tribe of Benjamin prompting the appeal to him for help and the care of his dishonoured bones (1 Sam. xi. 31). (2) Ramoth Gilead, or Ramoth, must from the incidents connected in Scripture with its name, have been a strong city situated on or near a plain. The Argob was also under the care of Solomon's officer who dwelt here (1 Kings iv. 13). It was a city of refuge. All indications favour its identification with Remun (marked by Kiepert), 5 miles west of Jerâsh on the northern slopes of the Jabbok. Jerâsh or Gerasa, one of the chief cities of Decapolis, is described by Tristram as probably the most perfect Roman city left above ground; he places it 10 miles north of the Jabbok. (3) In the Jordan valley lay Beth Nimrah and Beth Haran, still to be found with names scarcely changed in the Ghôr es Scisebân. The territory of Gad included 1300 square miles.

"It would seem as if the boundary-line between the tribes of Gad and Manasseh had been determined upon with relation to the character of the country and to the tastes and habits of the tribes; for while to Manasseh was reserved the vast arable plains and luxuriant pastures of Batanea, Iturea, and Golan, with only a margin of Gilead, Gad had almost a monopoly of its forests and mountains; and that the character and tendencies of the two tribes must have differed as widely as those of highlanders and lowlanders do elsewhere. The Gadites were apparently a wild, turbulent set of mountaineers, and their country, in consequence of its inaccessible and easily defensible character, often became the home of the outlaw and the refugee. Exposed to the attacks of the Assyrians and the tribes of the deserts, the Ammonites, Midianites, Hagarites, and others who were contiguous to their eastern frontier, they lived in a state of perpetual warfare, and were doubtless much given to raiding themselves—indeed, Jacob predicted of them, 'A troop shall plunder him, but he shall plunder at the last.' In all the records of their warfare, however, they seem to have been actuated by a certain chivalrous instinct" (*Land of Gilead*, p. 155). See story of Jephthah, of Barzillai, of the heroes who joined David in the hold (1 Chron. xii. 8, 37), and that also of Elijah, who was of the inhabitants of Gilead.

61. Beyond the Hieromax and to the east of the Sea of Galilee, lay the great territory allotted to the half-tribe of **Manasseh**. It has already been described (§ 23). Jair had his stony cities here in the wild, rocky district of Argob on the east, while Geshurites and Maachathites shared with Manasseh in the north; so that the 2500 square miles assigned to this half-tribe were never really in his possession. Most probably in this region we should seek the brook Cherith which was east of Jordan. Possibly it was the Jermûk itself, which has also the name *Sheriat el Mandhur*. Elijah "of the inhabitants of Gilead" would be familiar with its hiding-places. *Golan*, the appointed city of refuge in Manasseh, is unknown, though it gave its name to the province of Gaulonitis, now "the Jaulan," and was known in the time of Josephus. It is undoubtedly owing to the separation of these eastern tribes from the rest of Israel that we read so little of them in Scripture; that far from help, not always as willingly given as it was by Saul to Jabesh Gilead, they were overborne and dispossessed of their inheritance, and what was worse for them, lost their interest in the history of redemption as transacted in the west. Yet we should remember that its remoteness from Israel made their land a place of refuge not only for David, but for David's son (2 Sam. xvii. 22 ; John i. 28 and x. 40).

2. WESTERN PALESTINE.

(*See* MAP III.)

Joshua's Campaigns in the South.

62. After the death of Moses, **Israel crossed the Jordan** as he had crossed the Red Sea, dry-shod (Josh. iii.), the river being arrested from the district of Zaretan, or Zarthan, which is beyond Succoth (1 Kings vii. 46). The city Adam is most likely represented by the Damieh ford at Succoth, 18 miles up from Jericho; a great length of the river being thus dried to allow the far-spreading host to cross rapidly.

Their first camp on the west of Jordan was at **Gilgal.** Some derive the name from the rounded hills, or rollings of the plain; but with more probability others suggest that the name arose from the erection of stone circles, in connection with heathen worship. That Joshua gave a new meaning to the name (v. 9) is in accordance with a familiar practice, and was probably intended to mark the erection of his twelve stones; so consecrating the spot that had been devoted to ignorant superstitions, by a memorial of Jehovah's miraculous interposition in favour of His covenant people. But faint traces of ruin mark the spot now known as *Jiljûlia*, 4 miles from the Jordan, by the river Kelt; and some 3 miles from the *Ain es Sultan*, where it is generally agreed Jericho then stood.

Jericho was not only a walled city, it was wealthy, as its spoils show; being visited doubtless by caravans as well as armies from Babylonia (Gen. xiv.). The salt waters of the Ain Sultan, which Elisha healed, were favourable to the growth of palms, from which it was also named (Judg. xvi. 3, 13). The capture of the fortress of Jericho did not obliterate its name. Even before the rebuilding of its walls by Hiel of Bethel in the evil, God-defying days of Ahab (1 Kings xvi. 34), we frequently read of it in Scripture. The modern village of *Eriha*, which bears the name, is much farther east, and the Roman Jericho beautified by Herod and rebuilt by Archelaus lay at the point where the road down from Jerusalem emerges suddenly from the hills. Around another fountain, *Ain ed Duk*, 2 miles up from the *Tell es Sultan*, are ruins marking an ancient site. The plain was too fertile and valuable to be deserted. Possibly the different sites may explain

SOUTHERN PALESTINE

the apparent contradiction in the Gospel narratives regarding the healing of Bartimeus, as at "the entering" and at "the leaving" Jericho.

63. After the capture of Jericho, *the fixed camp of Israel remained at Gilgal* till the conquest of the land was achieved. The site was a good one for defence, and convenient for attack upon the land. The next step was to strike at the heart of the country. This was attempted in the assault on **Ai**. There is no reason to question the identification of the Wâdy Kelt with the *valley of Achor*, where Achan was stoned to death. On the identification of Ai, which is disputed, see § 42 and Index. The region in which it must have lain is narrowly circumscribed; it was close to Bethel, on the east. The uncertainty arises from the recurrence of the name on more than one spot, and of *Tell* or "*heap*," such as Joshua made Ai (Josh. viii. 28). Without question it lay up the **Wâdy Suweinit**, which goes down from Bethel to join the Wâdy Kelt above Jericho. Up that rugged valley the ambush made its way by night, and hid in the deep hollow on the north of Ai, while the army under Joshua, advancing so as to reach Ai in the morning and engage the attention of the defenders, drew them down the valley by feigned flight, till the ambush had taken possession of their city and set it on fire. The Wâdy Suweinit is a steep, almost impassable valley, cleaving the land from the Jordan valley up to Bethel on the watershed, and compelling traffic to keep to the one central main-road. It was the scene of Jonathan's exploit when he crossed from *Seneh*, its southern cliff, to *Bozez* on the north (1 Sam. xiv. 4). Seneh had its name, as the valley itself has at this part, from the thorns which grew in it (Josephus, *Wars*, v. 2, 1). Bozez was called "the shining," from its white sunlit brow, in contrast with the darkly-shadowed Seneh over against it. At *Michmash*, now *Mûkhmâs*, on the northern edge of the ravine, some 3 miles below Ai, the march of Sennacherib was arrested (Isa. x. 28), and his heavy ordnance and baggage left, ere he could advance on Jerusalem.

When Ai was captured, and Bethel, on the central main-road, was consequently in Joshua's hand, he held a position from which he could turn to deal with his enemies one by one. The inhabitants of Gibeon therefore quickly sought to make peace.

64. **Southern Campaign.**—Gibeon, El Jîb, lies on the northern slope of the outstanding hill known as *Neby Samwil*. It is but 6 or 7 miles south of Bethel, and between 2 and 3 miles to the west of the central main-road. There yet remains the famous "pool of Gibeon" at which the forces of Abner and Joab met (2 Sam. ii. 13). The other cities of the Hivite confederacy (§ 36) were not, apparently, consulted by the Gibeonites; on the contrary, the Hivites are named among those who now combined to oppose Israel (Josh. ix. 1). On hearing that the Gibeonites had deserted to the enemy, and thus opened his way into the very heart of the land, Adonizedek, king of Jerusalem; Hoham, king of Hebron; Piram, king of Jarmuth; Japhia, king of Lachish; and Debir, king of Eglon, gathered suddenly against Gibeon, both to chastise it for its perfidy and secure its strong position. Summoned to help his new allies, Joshua went up by night from Gilgal—by no means an extraordinary march, as appears from that of Abner on the occasion just referred to, 2 Sam. ii. 29. Falling on the besiegers, Joshua drove them westward and southward before him by upper Bethhoron, 5 miles west of Gibeon, down the **valley of Ajalon**, even into the land of the Philistines. The fugitive kings passing *Gezer*, a Canaanite stronghold, hid themselves in the cave of **Makkedah**; whence they were brought out, slain, and hanged. If the Azekah, named Josh. x. 11, is the Deir el 'Ashek on the south side of the Wâdy Surar, 8 or 9 miles east from Makkedah, it would appear that part of the Canaanite forces fled down that valley of Surar or Sorek, while others fled over Bethhoron. This is, of course, likely enough, as Joshua's attack was delivered from the north-east, and the fugitives would be almost at once parted, as they fled by the east or the west of Neby Samwil, towards which they were driven. The valleys of Sorek and Ajalon may be easily traced on the Physical Map of the land, rising respectively on the east and west of the isolated hill of Neby Samwil. The victory was followed up by the capture of the cities of **Libnah** (not identified), of **Lachish**, probably Um Lâkis, 14 miles north-east of Gaza, which offered a stout resistance, being a place of strength, as its after history proves.

Note.—The map as drawn by Captain Conder places Lachish at Tell el Hesy, south of Eglon; but the difference between it and the identification in the text is but a mile or two, and does not alter the general direction of Joshua's march. The reader may well take note of the important and most significant fact that the cases are very few in which rival identifications are at any distance from one another; the requirements of Scripture narratives, found always so wonderfully exact, circumscribe very narrowly the area within which lost sites must be sought. Another thing also to be learned from this instance, is how entirely ruins of great cities may disappear. The ruins at Um Lâkis cover very nearly a mile in circumference. They are situated partly on a hillock and partly in the midst of fields either cultivated or bristling with thistles and brambles. A multitude of excavations show that stones, the materials of ancient buildings, have been taken from the place. There remains, however, a good quantity of materials scattered on the ground. Fifteen ancient *silos* (§ 75) continue to serve the Arabs of the neighbourhood (Guérin,. *Judea,* ii. 299; *Memoirs,* iii. 293). As late as the days of Hezekiah, Lachish was a city strong enough to detain the great Sennacherib before its walls. On Assyrian slabs, now in the British Museum, it is depicted with towers and battlements crowded with armed defenders. Underneath the sculptured representation are inscribed the words, "Sennacherib, the king of Multitudes. The king of Assyria sat on an upright throne, and the spoil of the city of Lachish passed before him." An engraving of this will be found in Professor Sayce's *Fresh Light from the Ancient Monuments,* p. 144.

A diversion, attempted by Horam, king of Gezer, only led to Joshua's turning back to his town, which lay more than 20 miles north of Lachish. Its site has been recovered at *Tell Jezer,* which commands the entrance to the hills some 4 or 5 miles west of Emmaus Nicopolis. Though now conquered and assigned to the Levites, it was a stronghold of the Canaanites till Pharaoh captured it and gave it to King Solomon as his daughter's dowry (1 Kings ix. 16). One of the stones which marked its suburbs as a Levitical city was found with its name in its original site by Clermont Ganneau in 1874.

Eglon, next captured, is now 'Ajlan, between 2 and 3 miles eastward from Lachish. After its allotment to Judah, it is not named in Scripture. **Hebron,** 25 miles east of Eglon, next fell before Israel, and then **Debir,** fully 12 miles to the south-west of Hebron. This last had been a Hittite town, and bore the names of Kirjah Sepher and Kirjath Sannah. Like Gezer, and apparently all the cities named, it was, immediately on Joshua's retiring, re-occupied by the Amorites (Judg. i. 11-13). Indeed, the only one of all these cities possessed by Israel from this time was Hebron; the most of them lay in the country of the Philistines, which Israel never occupied. This may be explained, in part at least, by the strong influence of Egypt, which held Philistia in the days of its power both before, and at the time of, the Exodus, and which of necessity always regarded with jealousy its occupation by any rival. Philistia commanded the way down to Egypt from the east. The conquest of all the land "from Kadesh-barnea to Goshen, and from Gaza to Gibeon" (Josh. x. 44), must, from the accounts of after conflicts and conquests in the same territory, be understood in a general sense. This southern campaign of Joshua's practically gave to Israel dominion in all the land south of Gibeon from the Dead Sea to the Mediterranean.

65. **Joshua's Campaign in the North.**—Alarmed by the triumphant career of Israel in the south, the kings of the north gathered at the summons of Jabin of **Hazor**, by the waters of Merom. The extent and formidable power of the combined armies was great. They were "as the sand that is upon the seashore in multitude, with horses and chariots very many." As this takes us into a part of the land regarding which we have not, as yet, learned much, it may be well to go carefully over the localities from which these multitudes were gathered.

Hazor was their rallying-point, or rather the plains below it by the waters of Merom, or Lake Hûleh; for Hazor itself was set on the western mountains above the plain, and was no place for chariots; (Hazor is a common name, meaning simply an enclosure). Its site is now marked by Jebel Hadîreh and Merj Hadîreh, 6 miles west of Hûleh, and 4 miles south of Kadesh.

The king of **Madon** was his next neighbour, dwelling 20 miles south at **Hattin**, where the name Madîn is still found. From the horns of Hattin, its two summits between which his fortress lay, the king of Madon looked down on the fertile valley of Lubieh, and the sea of Galilee to the east. Here, in 1187, the Crusaders were utterly overthrown by the Turks, to whom the victory gave the land to be trodden down and desolated, as it is until this day. The fiery cross from Hazor was passed westwards to **Shimron**, now known by the name given it in the Talmud,—*Simûnieh*, on the northern edge of the plain of Esdraelon, 5 miles due west of Nazareth. From thence it was sent on to *Achzaph*, Kefr Yâsif, 20 miles north-west of Shimron, and 6 north-east of Accho. These cities, as will be observed, are named as they stand in a semicircle enclosing Galilee (Josh. xi. 1). In the next verse the historian's description encloses a wider circle, naming the kings of the more northern mountains, and of the plains south of Chinneroth, *i.e.* Gennesareth, and in the great valley of Esdraelon, westward to Dor, upon the seashore, some 12 miles south of Carmel, where its old tower is yet a conspicuous landmark, and its extensive ruins projecting into the sea testify to its former importance as a seaport. It lay close to the present village of Tantûra. Then as the summons went far and near, there gathered Canaanites from the east (Phœnicians) and from the west (Amorites), and Hittites with their multitude of trained hosts and chariots from Cœle-Syria; Perizzites and Hivites from the plains and cities, with the Jebusite from the mountains, joined the host. The whole strength of Israel's foes was thus gathered to be destroyed at one blow. Joshua came on them by surprise, his victories, humanly speaking, being due, as those of most great conquerors, to the swiftness of his action and the concentrated force of his stroke. A special assurance of victory, such as he must have sorely needed, was given him the day before he joined issues in a battle on whose result so much depended (Josh. xi. 6). The smitten host parting before his assault fled, some westward over the hills to Sidon and Sarepta (called here Miz-rephoth-maim), and some eastwards and northwards to "the land of Mizpeh," whence they had come.

66. As he had done in the south, so in the north he followed up his victory, promptly appearing before and overthrowing the cities whence his foes had mustered to the battle against him. Practically his work was done, though there remained much land to be possessed. A young man when he led Israel against Amalek at Rephidim, full forty years past, he was now "old and stricken in years" (Josh. xiii. 1). The lot of each tribe was now to be assigned, that each might make good a possession in the land conquered by their united strength. Joshua's faithful companion, Caleb, put in his claim for fulfil-

ment of the promise to him of an inheritance, not because he desired to have preference, or because he feared that as a Kenezite his right might be questioned, but because he desired still to set an example to all Israel of the fearless courage and unchanging youthfulness of faith. And so Joshua gave him Hebron, the city of the Anakim. From Hebron, already smitten, Caleb drove out the Anakim. Debir he smote also a second time (§ 64), and gave to Achsah his daughter as her portion, with the blessing which she sought, the upper and the nether springs (Josh. xv. 13-19). The advance to Shechem and the pitching of the tabernacle at Shiloh, where the lots for the inheritance were cast, prove that the conquest of Central Palestine had also been accomplished, though we have no record of it.

DIVISION OF WESTERN PALESTINE AMONG THE TRIBES.

67. The careful survey of the land which we owe to the Royal Engineers who have so ably served the Palestine Exploration Fund Society, and through them, all Bible students, enables us now to follow the boundary lines drawn and described in the Book of Joshua. We read that the allotments of the chief tribes of Judah and Joseph were first determined; the others being ranked under them. Discontent and grumbling seem to have early broken out; and there are too manifest signs of the selfishness of the tribes, each in its several lot. The national spirit quickly declined, and all through the time of the Judges, was with difficulty and with but partial success aroused from time to time to repel the common foes, who from north and south, east and west, attacked the land of Israel. There is evidence also that the land with its various advantages was apportioned to the different tribes, with due regard to their habits, and their several abilities to make the most of it. No doubt the bent of each tribe, thus recognised and provided for, was developed, and in great measure fixed, by the apportionment thus made.

One very notable result of the new survey is the discovery that the boundary lines followed the natural features of the country. No doubt this might have been expected; but owing to deficient knowledge, the tribal divisions had before been but vaguely ascertained, and had been made on the maps but not on the ground, with the results which might have been anticipated. The recovery of frontier towns, not before known, also guides us more surely in drawing the tribal boundaries.

North of Benjamin, the boundaries are but imperfectly described, save in the case of Zebulun, which is exceptionally exact. The position of the towns assigned to each tribe is in the other cases our only guide. But these are so named as to enable us to perceive the general outline of the territory indicated, and to fix the natural line of valley or mountain-ridge to be followed. In the following notes on the several tribes, exact distances are given as far as possible, to aid the student in finding the places upon the map. In studying a map, covered with names as full as is the map of the Palestine Exploration Society, it will be found useful to make a small scale of tape, or of a slip of paper, marked to 20 miles: it saves adjusting compasses or calculating from the measurements by foot-rule. Students of Scripture should supply themselves with the maps now announced as in preparation by the Palestine Exploration Fund Committee, including Eastern and Western Palestine, and find for themselves the places named and designated. By no other means can an accurate idea be formed of the relative positions and distances of the scenes of Bible story; and though a tedious, it will prove a most suggestive study. The distances given are for reference to the map; in calculating distance for a traveller, considerable allowance must necessarily be made for the windings, as well as the "ups and downs," and the roughness of the roads.

JUDAH.

JOSH. xv. 1–63.

68. The territory assigned to **Judah** was the largest portion west of Jordan; and as first marked out, included 2300 square miles, little short of the great territory given to Manasseh in Bashan. But from this, 1000 square miles were given to Simeon in the south. The Jeshimon, or wilderness on the east, along by the Salt Sea, was but of small value; while the fertile plains of Philistia and the rounded hills above it were never actually in the possession of Judah, though nominally within his boundaries. The *southern boundary* started from the end of the Salt Sea at the east, following the ascent of Acrabbim and the great mountain wall above the desert to the south of Rehoboth, and thence by the Wâdy el 'Arîsh to the Mediterranean.

The Mediterranean formed the *west* boundary, as the Salt Sea did the *eastern*. The *northern* boundary alone remains to be determined.

Two accounts are given of it, the one from east to west (Josh. xv. 5-11), and the other from west to east (Josh. xviii. 15-20); the first describing it as the northern boundary of Judah, the second as the southern boundary of Benjamin. At the two extremities there is no uncertainty in following the narrative; difficulties meet us only in the centre, at and to the west of Jerusalem. There was difficulty in drawing the line, as well as in describing it by a written narrative, caused not so much by the form of the land, as by the presence here of the great stronghold of the Jebusite, and that jealousy as to its possession, which ultimately led to its division, so that it in part belonged to Judah, and in part to Benjamin.

The boundary of Judah began at the north-west of the Salt Sea, passing from the Jordan through Beth Hogla, now 'Ain Hajlah. It went up by the Wâdy Kelt, the valley of Achor, keeping south of Jericho, which belonged to Benjamin. Thence by "the going up of Adummim," recognised in Talat ed Dumm, it reached Enrogel at Jerusalem. What is known, or plausibly conjectured, as to the less important points of the line, will be found in the topographical index at the end of the volume.

The position of **Enrogel** is the first point to be fixed.

It has been proposed to identify it with the Fountain of the Virgin, *'Ain Umm ed Deraj*, which lies close under the eastern cliff of Ophel, and also with the *Bir Eyub*, farther down the Kidron valley. But the one, "the Fountain of the Virgin," like Rogel, is a "spring" or Ain, so called to this day, and is the only Ain at Jerusalem. The other, Bir Eyub, on the contrary, is a well, but not a natural spring-head. The distinction between these, which is in Scripture always observed, seems conclusive in favour of the Fountain of the Virgin under Ophel. It is, moreover, by *the stone of Zoheleth*, still known as *Zahweileh*, a cliff on the east side of the Kidron valley, on which the village of Siloam stands (1 Kings i. 9), just opposite the Pool of Siloam, which is supplied from the Virgin's fountain. The next part of the boundary which is described as passing to the other side of Jerusalem, to the north end of the valley of

Rephaim, belongs to the much-disputed topography of Jerusalem, and may be considered in connection with it (§ 91).

69. From the head of the *Emek* Rephaim, the fertile "plain" running south-westwards from Jerusalem, and skirting the road to Bethlehem, the boundary went out to the waters of Nephtoah, by the Sepulchre of Rachel (1 Sam. x. 2), running, that is, exactly along the watershed. Nephtoah seems to be the same with Netophah, the former being the name in the earlier, and the latter in the later books of Scripture. It is always joined with Bethlehem (see Index), so that there need be little difficulty in accepting the express assertion of the Talmud that it was at Etam where were the waters which fed Solomon's pools and supplied the temple. Perhaps we should rather say Etam was in Netophah, which seems to have been a district with villages (1 Chron. iv. 16; Neh. xii. 28). From thence the boundary passed by the cities of Mount Ephron (not Ephraim) to Kirjath Jearim. Possibly the mountains of Ephron are alluded to in the Song of Solomon under the phrase, "as *a young hart* on the mountains of Bether." There need be no difficulty in identifying Bether (perhaps so named as the dividing mountain between Judah and Benjamin), where the Ephron, or young hart, skipped, for the Wâdy Bittîr to the west of Bethlehem is memorable in Jewish story, and still bears the name. Out due westward, along the watershed on the south of the Wâdy Bittîr, the boundary ran to Khurbet 'Erma, which represents 'Arim, the later form of the name Jearim, as we find it in Ezra ii. 25. Four miles down to the west, just off the mountains in the valley of Sorek (Surâr), lies 'Ain Shems, "the well of the Sun," marking the site of the well-known Bethshemesh, by which the boundary passed to Timnah (Tibneh), 3 miles farther west, thence to Ekron ('Akir) and Jabneel, afterwards Jamnia, now Yebnah, which lies but 4 miles from the Mediterranean. Thus the line may be said to have run down the valley of Surâr, following that branch which drains the country west of Bethlehem. But some of the towns named (as Naamah and Makkedah), Josh. xv. 41, lay off the line of the river; and there are other indications that the line thus described was not strictly kept. The most serious deviation was west of Jerusalem, probably; for in the Septuagint, or Greek version of

the Old Testament (usually written LXX.), there are several towns not named in our Hebrew Bibles. These would be included if we suppose the boundary in after times to have been shifted so as to follow the northern branch of the *Wâdy Surâr* till it came within 2 miles of Jerusalem on the north-west. Such a change might take place, either through the diminishing of Benjamin (Judg. xx. 21) or the increase of Judah; and in later times, when they formed one kingdom of Judah, it could not be a matter of much importance.

The towns inserted in the LXX., after Josh. xv. 60, are :—(1) *Theco*, or Tekoa (2 Sam. xiv. 2; 2 Chron. xi. 6), the home of the prophet Amos. It is now Tekû'a, 5 miles south of Bethlehem. (2) *Ephrata*, which is Bethlehem. (3) *Phagor*, now Faghûr, 4 miles south of Bethlehem. (4) *Ætan*, now 'Ain 'Atân, 2½ miles south of Bethlehem. (5) *Culon*, generally placed at Kolonia, which seems, however, a name not older than the time of the Romans; possibly K. Umm Kûlâh, 5 miles west of Bethlehem. (6) *Tatam*, unknown, perhaps Hamdân, 1 mile north of preceding. (7) *Soris*, usually placed at Sâris, 10 miles north-west of Bethlehem. (8) *Carem*, most likely 'Ain Karim, 5 miles north-west of Bethlehem (see Index). Some identify this with Rekem of Benjamin; they may, however, be inverted forms of the same name. (9) *Galem*, Beita Jâla, 1½ mile west from Bethlehem. (10) Bether, Bittîr, 5 miles west of Bethlehem. (11) Manocho, placed by some at Mâlhah, 4 miles north-west of Bethlehem. It is thus evident that the group of towns really represents "Bethlehem and her villages," and may have been inserted from a public register, though not originally in Joshua. The imputation of deliberate omission of the name of Bethlehem from the Book of Joshua as an antichristian act of the Jews, though seriously made and argued, is on the face of it absurd, considering the frequent mention of Bethlehem with honour, from the Book of Ruth to that of Micah.

The position thus assigned to Judah was one of great natural strength. From but a few points could it be assailed, and the valleys by which it could alone be approached from the west were well fitted to be defended by a few against a host. This will appear as we trace the after history. The principal towns in Judah will be described as occasion arises, the others will be found in the Index.

Hebron was the southern city of refuge for Western Palestine.

SIMEON.

JOSH. xix. 1–9.

70. The part assigned to Simeon is nowhere exactly defined. In Josh. xix. 1–9 there is a mere enumeration of the towns which were assigned, out of Judah, to Simeon in the south. They are Beersheba (Bîr es Seb'a); Sheba (Tell es Sebâ, 2 miles from Beersheba); Moladah (Malatha, LXX., now El Milh); Hazar-Shual (S'aweh?); Balah (Zubâlah? or Khurbet Umm Bagleh, half-way between Beersheba and Hebron, but more probably the former); Azem (possibly Iim, see Index); Eltolad (not identified); Bethul, or Chesil (Khelasa); Hormah, or Zephath (Judg. i. 17, probably Sebaita, but uncertain); Ziglag Zuheilikah (?); Beth-Marcoboth (see Index); Hazarsusah (Susîn); Bethlebaoth (not recovered, most probably the same as Bethbirei in 1 Chron. iv. 31, and may be El Berein, "the wells," 15 miles north-east of Hagar's Well); Sharuhen (Tell esh Sheriah); Ain, probably to be joined with Remmon (Umm er Rumâmîn); Ether, possibly Khurbet Attir, 16 miles north-east of Beersheba; and Ashan, which is not identified satisfactorily.

From the indications afforded by the positions of these towns, so far as recovered, it will be seen that Beersheba was the central point of Simeon's lot, and that it lay out from the hills which, south of Hebron, fall to the desert; it is now untilled, but covered in many parts with ruins and wells, which tell of a once dense population. Very little is known of the history of the inhabitants of the "South," or Negeb; they fall very much out of sight in the after history of Israel. One almost forgets that there was a tribe of Simeon, it is so absorbed in Judah even from the earliest time.

The land was in fact divided as it was naturally adapted to the habits of a settled or a wandering people. Simeon's territory lay in the desert lands which lie round the base of the soft limestone hills on the west and south, where still the Bedawin tribes pitch their tents. To Judah was assigned the arable land for corn and vineyards. Around Beersheba, which was the centre of Simeon's lot, the pasturage is beautiful in the spring; by the end of autumn it is scorched, and the treeless expanse of grey mud is a desolation.

"To Simeon the fierce and lawless tribe, the dry 'south' was given, for out of the portion of Judah was the inheritance of the children of Simeon; for the part of the children of Judah was too much for them; therefore the children of Simeon had their inheritance of them (Josh. xix. 9). In the prophecy of Jacob he is 'divided and scattered;' in that of Moses, he is omitted altogether. Amongst these Bedouin villages his lot was cast; and as time rolled on, the tribe gradually crossed the imperceptible boundary between civilization and barbarism, between Palestine and the desert; and in 'the days of Hezekiah,' they wandered forth to the east to seek pasture for their flocks, and 'smote the tents' of the pastoral tribes who 'had dwelt there of old;' and roved along across the 'Arabah till they arrived at the 'Mount Seir'—the range of Petra—and 'smote the rest of the Amalekites, and dwelt there unto this day' (1 Chron. iv. 39-43)."—Stanley's *Sinai and Palestine*, p. 160. From the Book of Judith it would seem as if a colony of the Simeonites had settled at Bethulia, possibly they went from Bethul (Josh. xix. 4) taking the name with them.

BENJAMIN.

JOSH. xviii. 11-28.

71. The southern boundary of Benjamin was the same as the northern boundary of Judah from the Jordan westwards to Kirjath Jearim (compare Josh. xv. 5-9 with xviii. 15-19 and § 58). The Jordan was for 5 miles the east boundary. The *northern* boundary line was traced from Jordan, probably from the point where the Aujeh flows into it, passing westwards by Tuweil edh Dhiab and Wâdy Shukh-ed Dubâ, in which the Zeboim of 1 Sam. xiii. 18 and Neh. xi. 34 may be recognised (§ 45), and upwards thence by the wilderness of Bethaven (Josh. xviii. 12) to Bethel—that is, up in a north-westerly direction to Tell 'Azûr, or Baal Hazor, a notable landmark (§ 11). It will be at once recognised on the Physical Map, marked 3318 feet in height. Though after the division of the kingdoms the boundary was removed so far south as to include Bethel in the northern kingdoms, we see from Neh. xi. 33 that in the "registers" Hazor was counted to Benjamin. In 2 Sam. xiii. it is named as the sheep-farm of Absalom, and the scene of his brother Amnon's murder. If this ancient Baal

Hazor (enclosure of Baal) be Bethaven, the references of Hosea to it become more intelligible (Hos. iv. 15, v. 8, x. 5, 8, 15, where for "your great wickedness" we should read as margin," evil of your evil").

Baal Hazor was a chief place of Baal-worship; hence the emphatic witness of Abraham to Jehovah in setting up a distinct altar at Bethel and worshipping there; and hence "the wickedness of Jeroboam's wickedness" in setting up at Bethel worship fit for Bethaven.

The boundary ran southward to Bethel along the height of the watershed. Placed at this point, where the central road runs on a narrow ridge breaking rapidly down to the Wâdy Suweinit eastwards, and also falling off quickly on the west, Bethel held an important position, and was a place of strength (Judg. i. 22–25; § 95). For 4 or 5 miles farther south, the boundary kept by the central watershed, and then turned westwards to Archi, which is now recognised in 'Ain 'Arîk, Josh. xvi. 2 (see Index). Thence it went to Ataroth Adar, now represented by Khurbet Dâriah, 4 miles still farther to the west, lying on the hillside about a mile south of the Lower Bethhoron, exactly as described in Josh. xviii. 13. Passing Japhleti, which is unknown, it went to Gezer, the royal city of the Canaanites, already described (§ 73).

The western boundary of Benjamin ran up the watershed from Gezer in a south-easterly direction for 5 or 6 miles, and then turning southward, met the southern boundary at Kirjath Jearim.

The territory assigned to Benjamin was cut out of that at first assigned to Ephraim and the tribes reckoned with it; it was in area one of the smallest, containing only some 400 square miles. Though in area small, it was in importance one of the first. It included part of Jerusalem, and the natural line of defence of Jerusalem upon the north, the wealthy and luxuriant plain of Jericho, and the sacred cities also of Bethel, and Gibeon which was so long the resting-place of the ark and the scene of Solomon's coronation. From the rugged neighbourhood of its greatest eastern valley, running down from Bethel to Jericho, came Saul, Israel's first king; and from its great western valley of Ajalon came Israel's last great military leader and deliverer, Judas Maccabæus. Holding the fortress of the land, fierce in war and skilful too (Judg. xx. 14–16), the tribe fulfilled the prediction of

Jacob, "Benjamin shall ravin as a wolf; in the morning he shall devour the prey, and at night he shall divide the spoil" (Gen. xlix. 27).

The towns of Benjamin named in Josh. xviii. 21-28, but not occurring again in the history, will be found as far as known in the Index.

DAN.
JOSH. xix. 40-48.

72. The tribe of **Dan** was in the first instance allotted a small territory to the west of Benjamin's lot. It spread along the sea-shore, including the lower part of the valley of Sorek, now Wâdy Surâr, on the south, and the plain of Sharon northward as far as Joppa. It is described Josh. xix. 40-48, by the cities which were included in its borders. In area it was probably much the same as the tribe territory of Benjamin, or about 400 square miles.

Beginning in the south, Zorah and Eshtaol and Irshemesh are first named. These lie in the Wâdy Surâr, due west of Kirjath Jearim. Irshemesh, "the city of the sun," is probably represented in 'Ain Shems, "the fountain of the sun." In Scripture we read oftener of Bethshemesh. Zorah is now Sura'h, and Eshtaol is Eshua, close to it. These three form a triangular group just where the stream breaks out into the Shephelah from the mountains of Judah. Of the towns named in the next verse, Ajalon is now Yalo, 4 or 5 miles north of Eshtaol; Shaalabbin is most probably Selbît, 3 miles to the north of Yalo; and Jethlah, called Silatha by LXX., is identified with Shilta, fully 4 miles still farther north. These lay immediately to the west of the territory of Benjamin in the valley of Ajalon. Elon next named is without question Beit Ello, which lies 7 miles north-east from Shilta; and Thimnathah (Josh. xix. 43) is Tibneh close by—not the Timnath of Samson's story, which lay far south of this. Ekron, or 'Aker, was one of the five chief cities of the Philistines. Gibbethon is no doubt Kibbiah, between Tibneh and Lydda, 7 miles from the latter. Baalath has been placed at Bel 'Ain in the plain of Sharon, but it may be Deir Ballût, 6 miles due north from Kibbiah just named. Japho or Joppa, last named in the list, serves as a good guide to the others; its position and history are familiar to all. Jehud, El

Yehûdujeh, is some 8 miles east of it, and Benebcrak, now Ibn Ibrâk, half-way between them. Rakkon, now called Tell er Rekkeit, is on the sea-shore 6 miles north of Joppa, while Mejarkon, "the yellow water," is identified by Conder with the river 'Aujeh, which has the same meaning. These are all the towns save Gath-Rimmon and El Tekeh. The famous Philistine town of Gath lay too far south for the one, and Beit Likia seems too far east for the other, though the identification has been generally received. The territory thus occupied by *Dan* was very small; and the strength of those in possession was too great for that small tribe to dispossess them. Even with the aid of Ephraim, it failed to do so. The position was a very important one, as the approaches to the centre of the land, and more especially to Jerusalem, from the west were in charge of the Danites. The roads by Bethhoron and Amwas-Nicopolis in the valley of Ajalon, and that which ascended the valley of Sorek, were committed to his keeping, and a foe assaulting the capital from the west, as in the days of the Maccabees, discovered the significance of the prophetic description, "Dan shall be a serpent by the way, an adder in the path that biteth the horses' heels so that his rider shall fall backward" (Gen. xlix. 17. Compare § 99). Of the towns in this district not named, the most important are Nicopolis or Amwas of Maccabean fame; Lydda, illustrious in apostolic times; and Ramleh (possibly the lost Rimmon), best known in the days of the Crusaders. The lot of Dan, according to Josephus, reached from the valley of Elah northward to Dor (§ 74), but this is too large to be in accordance with the narrative of Joshua.

EPHRAIM.

JOSH. xvi. 1–10.

73. The southern boundary of **Ephraim** coincided with the northern of Benjamin. The extent of land assigned to this tribe is usually much exaggerated. His valleys were "fat valleys," and his possession was thus most valuable, but it was limited. The northern boundary is described in Josh. xvi. 5–8, and again, as the southern boundary of Manasseh, in Josh. xvii. 7–9. In both places it is stated shortly, and as if the writer, at Shechem, or some such point, were regarding it first as it ran thence eastward to Jordan, and then as it

went out westwards to the Mediterranean. The most important feature in the description is the *Brook Kanah*, which may be traced on the map, as it flows westwards from the south of Mount Gerizim. Another point of the line may be ascertained from the description of Josh. xvii. 7, where we learn that it went from the east of Shechem southward to "Yeshebi ain Tappuah." Yeshebi is translated *inhabitants*, but is more probably, as Captain Conder has pointed out, the proper name of the village *Yeshepheh* of the Samaritan chronicle, and probably Yassûf, 8 miles south of Shechem. En, or 'Ain, Tappuah, "the well of the apple or apricot," cannot be recognised, but it not improbably was one of the springs of which there are several near Yassûf. Shechem, which lay between Ebal and Gerizim, was to the north of this boundary, for it belonged to Manasseh.

Asher ham Michmethah lay to the east of Shechem on the border of Ephraim. Asher may be 'Askar, or Ischar (which is named as Sychar in John iv.), on the north-west corner of the plain of Mukhnah, which is to the east of Shechem, and in which is the well of Jacob and the tomb of Joseph. Following the ridge east of the Mukhnah plain past Salim (or Shalem) in a south-easterly direction, we reach T'ana, the ruins of which, no doubt, mark the site of Taanath-Shiloh. Janoah, the next point of the boundary given, is also easily recognisable in Yânûn, scarcely 3 miles south of T'ana. By Ataroth the border ran to Naarath, which was also on the south boundary. This proves that the description east of Shechem was following what was really the *eastern*, rather than the northern, boundary of Ephraim. Ataroth has not been recovered. It no doubt marks some ancient place of heathen worship; not improbably the prominent height of Kurn Sartabeh, which stands out into the Jordan valley close to the site assigned to Naarath by Eusebius, 5 miles north of Jericho.

The description is at some points obscure, yet there can be little doubt that the line is correctly drawn on the map of tribe-boundaries enclosing but a small area—Conder reckons it at but 300 square miles—a fourth less than that of Benjamin and Dan. As stated, the district was well watered by many and abundant springs, those which feed the river 'Aujeh being the largest in all Palestine, those from which the Jordan springs not excepted. The limited area assigned to Ephraim may have led to an early migration to the woodlands on the east of Jordan.

74. It is singular to find so few cities named as belonging to **Ephraim.** If a list of the cities of Ephraim was once included, it is now awanting. One of its most interesting sites is *Timnah*-Serah, which was specially assigned to Joshua and his family for inheritance. In Judg. ii. 7 it is called Timnath-heres, and may be placed at Kefr Hâris in the very heart of the land, 10 miles south-west of Shechem. There are three holy places shown at the village, those of "Neby Nun," "Neby Lush'a," and "Neby Kifl." Of these, the first two are undoubtedly "Nun" and "Joshua;" the third, "the Prophet of division by lot," may be a confusion arising out of an older Jewish and Samaritan tradition that "Caleb" was buried here. Guérin proposes to identify Joshua's Timnah with Tibneh, 9 miles south of Kefr Hâris. See *Memoirs*, ii. 374. At 'Awertah, 5 miles south of Shechem, are shown the traditional tombs of Eleazar and Phinehas, the former at El 'Azeir on the west, and the latter at El 'Azierat on the east (Josh. xxiv. 33).

Shechem is one of the towns we first meet with in Scripture (§ 41). It kept its name till, in the time of the Romans, it was changed to Flavia Neapolis, "after the Flavian family to which Vespasian belonged." Neapolis has become Nablous, by which it is now known. It is beautifully situated; one would almost take it for an ideal capital for the land. Here the law was read as Moses commanded. "Two questions have been raised in connection with the reading of the law, the possibility of hearing it read, and the possibility of assembling the twelve tribes on the ground at the same time. Of the first there can be no doubt: the valley has no peculiar acoustic properties, but the air in Palestine is so clear that the voice can be easily heard at distances which would seem impossible in England; and as a case in point, it may be mentioned that during the excavations on Mount Gerizim, the Arab workmen were on more than one occasion heard conversing with men passing along the valley below" (Sir C. Wilson, *Memoirs*, ii. p. 193). He points out that it is not necessary to suppose every word was heard; the law was familiar, and the responses would be taken up as the sound of the reader's voice ceased; and as regards the second point, he says: "There are few localities which would afford so large an amount of standing ground on the same area, or give such facilities for the assembly of a great multitude."

Another site within the territory of Ephraim which should be noted is **Shiloh**, 12 miles south of Shechem and 10 miles north of Bethel, on the road between them. Shiloh was the site of the tabernacle (Josh. xviii.), which apparently had been removed to Bethel (Judg. xx.) and then returned to Shiloh in the early times of the Judges. It is most likely it was at Bethel in the time of Deborah (Judg. iv. 5). Nothing of Shiloh remains but the ruins to give emphasis to the warning of Jer. vii. 12–14, and xxvi. 6–9. Though the name Seilun remains (the form from which came Shilonite), the place was only recovered by Robinson. It lies off the main road, and so escaped notice. Its ruins are strewn over a "Tell," or mound, rising at the base of the hills on the north side of a plain where two valleys meet. " Northwards the Tell slopes down to a broad shoulder, across which a sort of level court, 77 feet wide by 412 long, has been cut." Most probably here stood the tabernacle which was, according to rabbinical tradition, a building of low stone walls, with the tent drawn over the top. The spring (Judg. xxi.) is ¾ of a mile north-east, up a narrow valley on the sides of which are rock-cut tombs; in some of these the old high priests of Israel may have been laid. Shiloh was central in situation, but seems otherwise to have no attractions.

Jiljiliah, 4 or 5 miles south-west of Shiloh, and 7 north of Bethel, is the Gilgal of 2 Kings ii. 1, iv. 38, where there was a school of the prophets. This is not to be confounded with the site of the camp of Israel which lay between Jericho and the Jordan; nor with the Gilgal near Dor of Josh. xii. 23, which is now represented by Jiljuleh in the plain of Sharon, about 12 miles up from the mouth of the brook Kanah.

In general character the mountains of Ephraim are quite different from the forbidding and barren hills of Benjamin. Cut off from Ephraim's first allotment, they are more fertile and open. The villages perched on heights for safety looked down on little plains lying between the hills—often, no doubt, as in Gideon's time, looked down helplessly on invaders reaping their harvests.

MANASSEH.

JOSH. xvii. 1–18.

75. "The half-tribe of Manasseh had the land from Jordan to the city Dora (Dor); but its breadth was at Bethshan, which is now called Scythopolis." Such is the brief statement of Josephus, leaving us to ascertain the territory of Manasseh from the list of towns which are named within it. The southern boundary marched with Ephraim, the eastern was the Jordan from Naarath up by the district of Zaretan, to over against Bethshean (now Beisan). The western boundary was the sea. The northern line it is impossible to fix accurately; for, besides Bethshean, Endor, close to Tabor, beyond the plain of Esdraelon, was reckoned to Manasseh (Josh. xvii. 11), although it lay in Issachar. Westwards, no doubt, the line followed that of the range of Carmel, the wood of which Joshua told the children of Ephraim they might cut down and possess, since they were, as they said, "a great people" (Josh. xvii. 14–18). The tortuous line on the map really follows the watershed which, as in other cases, was naturally followed as the obvious and permanent line of demarcation. Carmel, famed for its park-like beauty, for its oliveyards and vineyards, was a valuable possession. Travellers still notice the many remains of olive-presses and traces of vineyards. The following description of *wine-presses*, *cisterns*, and *silos*, by Dr. Tristram, explains several Scripture allusions (see also § 106) :—

"We examined several wine-presses. . . . In all cases, both on Carmel and elsewhere, a flat or gently-sloping rock is made use of for their construction. At the upper end a trough is cut about 3 feet deep, and $4\frac{1}{2}$ by $3\frac{1}{2}$ feet in length and breadth. Just below this, in the same rock, is hewn out a second trough, 14 inches deep and 4 feet by 3 feet in size. The two are connected by two or three small holes bored through the rock close to the bottom of the upper trough, so that on the grapes being put in and pressed down, the juice streamed into the lower vat. Every vineyard seems to have had one of these presses. What a record is here graven in the rock of the old fitness of that name Carmel!" (Others interpret it as a "garden," but the primary meaning of the word is the same.) "Dr. Robinson mentions a press much longer and more shallow. In such an one Gideon thrashed his wheat in some obscure corner of the vineyard, where he would cover it over with boughs or leaves and conceal it from the Midianites. How well this simple wine vat in the stone illustrates the expression, 'treading the wine-press alone'! Hard by one of these we found a large deep cistern hewn in the rock, and little converging channels about 4 inches wide cut above it to drain the water from the upper part of the vineyard. The cistern had been wrought with a natural roof, and a square opening in the centre. A few yards below this was a circular opening in the ground, about a yard in diameter, like the mouth of a well, but really the mouth of an ancient granary, or 'silo,' for keeping and concealing corn. It swelled into a round chamber below, about 8 feet deep and more than 9 feet in diameter, carefully plastered wherever it was not hewn out of the native rock, and having very much the shape of a large flask or demi-john. Such 'silos' are still universally used by the nomad Bedouin for storing their grain, and exist in great numbers in and around favourite camping-grounds. More than once I have had a fall, through my horse, when galloping over a plain, setting his foot on the treacherous roof of one of these empty granaries. It was to such hidden stores as these that the ten men referred, who appealed to the treacherous Ishmael, 'Slay us not, for we have treasures in the field of wheat, and of barley, and of oil, and of honey' (Jer. xli. 8)."

The importance of the land assigned to Manasseh consisted in its including not only fertile parts of the land, but such important cities as Shechem (Josh. xvii. 2), one of the most beautiful spots in all the land, well watered and to this day the site of one of its chief towns. Samaria also was in Manasseh's lot, and Tirzah the beautiful, now Teiâzîr (Song vi. 4), which was the capital of the northern kingdom before Samaria (1 Kings xiv. 17, xv. 33, xvi. 23, 24). Other positions which should be noted are Ferâta, representing "Ophrah of the Abiezrites," 6 miles south-west of Shechem; and Taanach, on the edge of the plain of Esdraelon, so often the scene of battle. The very extensive area, reckoned at some 1300 square miles (Conder), was, however, but partially possessed by the tribe of Manasseh. Occupying the hill-country which afforded access to the mountain-land of Ephraim, it is no wonder if the whole north-western part of the country "is full of the old fortified villages of Manasseh, every one of them a natural stronghold, and full of deep gorges, a perfect network twisting down towards the plain of Esdraelon." Across that portion cutting off the northern extremity of Carmel, ran the great road by which from the days of Thothmes III. of Egypt, as doubtless long before, armies crossed from the plain of Sharon over into that of Jezreel—the pathway of caravans, as in Joseph's time.

Shechem was the central *city of refuge* for Western Palestine.

ISSACHAR.

JOSH. xix. 17–23.

76. The greater part of the plain of Jezreel, or **Esdraelon, fell to the lot of Issachar**. To the west it was enclosed by Zebulun, whose boundary ran from Jokneam, where the river (Kishon) descends from the northern steeps of Carmel, known as Jokneam of Carmel (Josh. xii. 22), and identified with Tell Keimûn. Thence it went to Sarid, the position of which is uncertain. As the *r* and *d* are easily confused in Hebrew, we may conjecturally read Sadid, which would suit Tell Shadûd. Chesulloth, or Chisloth, is no doubt to be placed at Iksâl, and the next frontier town Daberath at *Dabûrieh*, a mile north-west of Mount Tabor. From Jokneam to this the border ran almost in a straight line from east to west for a distance of 16 miles. From this point eastwards Issachar marched with Naphtali, the boundary line going down the Wâdy Bîreh on the north side of the Little Hermon, or Jebel Duhy range, to the Jordan. This range is also identified with the hill of Moreh named in Judg. vii. 1. It may be traced on the Physical Map, running parallel with the valley of Jezreel farther north.

The possession of Issachar was a desirable one (Gen. xlix. 14, 15); and many of its towns are named in Bible story. **Jezreel** lay on the westmost point of the range of Gilboa, where it runs off into the plain; and Engannin just 7 miles due south of it. Six miles north-west of Engannin lay **Taanach**, with Rummâneh (Hadad-Rimmon?) close beside it, 4 miles beyond which again lay Legio, generally identified, on the testimony of Jerome, with Megiddo, though other place it at Tell el Mutasellein, 1 mile farther north.

Captain Conder proposes Tell Mujedd'a, lying as a sister-fortress opposite to Bethshean on the south, holding the eastern entrance to the great plain. The name seems the same, and there are several respects in which such a site would suit better than Legio (Lejjûn).

G

The ruins indicate that Mujedd'a marks the site of a large and ancient town well supplied with water from fine springs (see note, § 98). On the other hand, if Rummâneh be, as suggested, Hadad Rimmon, the "valley of Megiddon" must be the pass in the mouth of which Legio lies (Zech. xii. 11). Meanwhile this point must be regarded as unsettled.

Along the northern boundary lay towns so well known as *Shunem* and *Nain* and *Endor*, on the slopes of Jebel Duhy close to the plain. Upon its fertile plain the "locusts" of the east came up to reap the corn which the Israelites had sown and tended. One of its mountains was possibly known as the Har Megiddo—the Armageddon of prophetic symbol (Rev. xvi. 16). Though now little cared for, the remains of wine-presses at *Zerin*, or Jezreel, and other indications, tell how much more fertile this land once was than the traveller passing through it would suppose.

As already pointed out, the district of Zartanah beneath Jezreel "stretched from Bethshean southward to Abel-Meholah" (for references see Index). The territory of the tribe of Issachar was one of the 12 divisions of Solomon (1 Kings iv. 12).

There is no doubt about the site of the great fortress of **Bethshean**, which was given out of the territory of Issachar to Manasseh. Standing on the hill of Jezreel looking eastward down the Wâdy Jâlûd, an arm seems stretched out to bar the way, at the extremity of which the great mound of Beisan, the ancient Bethshean, is clearly seen guarding the entrance to the valley. From the interesting notice in the *Memoirs* issued by the Palestine Exploration Society, vol. ii., pp. 101–113, we gather the following particulars of this great fortress. It stands on the south bank of the Jâlûd, which there passes close to the hills on the north side of the plain. These hills run eastwards to within a mile of the Jordan. To the south of it there is a small plain beyond the mountains of Gilboa, which do not reach so far eastward as the northern hills. From this plain a marsh, caused by neglected irrigation, sends other three brooks through Bethshean, which is very abundantly supplied with water. The hill is a very commanding one, set just where the great Jezreel plain breaks rapidly down some 300 feet to the "Ghôr" of the Jordan. The form of the hill and the basaltic character of the rock led Robinson to the conclusion that it is the cone of a crater. In the centre is the Tell el Hosn, or "the fortress." Many columns fallen and yet erect tell the grandeur of the town in Roman times. The theatre is the best preserved Roman work in Western Palestine. The walls include an area of over $\frac{1}{3}$ of a mile; but the ruins and ancient sepulchres spread far around.

One remarkable feature of this plain is the river Kishon. It rises on the northern slope of Tabor at El Mugheiyû, and gathering its waters about the roots of Tabor east by Endor and westwards at the base of the Nazareth range, it flows westward as the Nahr el Mukutta. Often the springs that feed it are suddenly swollen by heavy rains, and the plain becomes all at once an impassable morass, just as in the olden time when Sisera and Barak fought there. The Nähr el Mukutta has been identified with the "waters of Megiddo." There is greater resemblance in the name as it appears in the Egyptian records, where, according to Brugsch, Megiddo is called "Makitha." The determination of this, as of many other matters of interest, must wait till the land is delivered from the hands of its present possessors and wasters, and when thorough and free search of its many *Tells* will be possible.

The territory of Issachar was in superficial area very much the same as those of Benjamin and Dan.

ZEBULUN.

JOSH. xix. 10-16.

77. We have traced the boundary of Zebulun as far as it marched with Issachar, describing a straight line due west from Jokneam to Tabor. North-westwards from Jokneam the boundary ran by the base of Carmel to the sea. At the other, the eastern extremity of the straight line described, it went up to Japhia or Yâfa, a mile to the south of Nazareth, and passing Nazareth (which is never named in the Old Testament), the boundary went north to Gath-hepher or Gittah-hepher, where (2 Kings xiv. 25) Jonah was born. His tomb is now shown at El Meshed, not far from Seffûrieh, or Sephoris. Ittah Kazin, the next landmark (Josh. xix. 13), is unknown; it must have lain near Khurbet Kenna on the line from Gath-hepher (or Gittah-hepher) to Rimmon, now Rummâneh, 3 miles northward. From

Rimmon it was drawn to Neah, which is unknown. The northmost point of this boundary was Hannathon, now Deir Hanna, 6 miles north of Rimmon. At this town, which is on the north of the plain of Buttauf, the northern boundary of Zebulun descended by the valley of Jiphthah-el, the name of which lingers in Jephat, 6 miles down its course on the north side. It is the Jotapata of Josephus (*Wars*, iii. 6 and 7), who also mentions a town Japha that lay near it. Scarce 5 miles west by north of Jefat is Cabul of 1 Kings ix. 13, now Kabûl, 2 miles north of which lies Y'anim. This Conder proposes for Neiel (Han-N'aial), which lay on the border between Zebulun and Asher (Josh. xix. 27). From the same place we learn that the boundary went thence to Bethdagon, now Khurbet Dâûk, within 3 miles of the sea-coast, ending at the mouth of Shihor Libnath, identified with the Belus. The worship of Dagon extended, as thus appears, from Philistia to Phœnicia in the north, one of many indications of their close relations. Of the towns of Zebulun not thus indicated, the more important are Nazareth, between 3 and 4 miles west of which we find Mahlûl, representing the rabbinical name of Nahallah; 2 miles farther west Semûnieh, or Shimron (§ 74), some 3 miles north of which is Beit Lahm, the Bethlehem of Zebulun. Kattath (Josh. xix. 15) is identified by Dr. Tristram with Kana el Jelil, the Syriac form of whose name is Katna. Van de Velde, taking Zebulun, Josh. xix. 27, for a town, proposed to identify it with 'Abilin, 3 miles south of Cabul. Ajalon of Judg. xii. 12 may be 'Ailût, 2 miles north-west of Nazareth, to which Elon belonged, who judged Israel after Ibzan of Bethlehem. The territory of Zebulun was among the smallest, ranking with the area of Ephraim, as did also Asher, next to be described.

ASHER.

Josh. xix. 24–31.

78. We are unfortunately not so well able to define Asher as the other tribe territories; partly, no doubt, because to the north no other tribe boundary helps us, but chiefly because the district in which Asher settled was remote from the rest of the land, and lay up among the mountains, the maritime plain included in his lot never having been taken from the Phœnicians (Judg. i. 31). The tribe was

not a small one (Num. i. 41; 1 Chron. xii. 36), and it is possible it spread much farther north than the Litâny, seeing Joab went as far as Riblah in taking the census of Israel. From some expressions, it would seem as if the territory of Asher as at first assigned went south of Carmel; but if so, some of the land in the first instance given to Asher must have been ceded to Zebulun, which certainly reached to the Bay of Acre and possessed the north slopes of Carmel. Josh. xix. 24-31 contains the list of Asher's towns. Some of these doubtless were of little account (1 Kings ix. 11-13). The principal were certainly held by the Phœnicians or Canaanites, as Tyre and the Great Zidon and Accho (or Acre). For note on Tyre, see § 115.

The following of the towns of Asher may be reckoned as pretty well identified; they are but a few of the number given in Joshua. Achsaph is El Yâsîf (Conder). Hebron or Abron should rather be Abdon, which is 'Abdeh, at the north of the plain of Acre, 4 miles inland from Achzib, now Ez Zib on the coast. Hammon is probably Umm el 'Amud, 7 miles north of Ez Zib on the coast: this place (a Laodicea of Greek times) was sacred to Baal-Hammon; an interesting notice of its remains and of two altars found there is given in *Heth and Moab*, p. 87. Kânah lies 10 miles north-east of Hammon, and Hozah is placed by Conder at 'Ezziyah, half-way between them. Ramah is placed by Tristram close to Tyre.

Of Sidon, which lay 20 miles north of Tyre, there is no occasion to speak, nor of Sarephath or Sarepta, 8 miles north of the mouth of the Litâny.

It may be interesting to read the following regarding Aphek of Judg. i. 31, as throwing light on the worship of the Sidonians and Bible allusions to it:—

"The Nahr Ibrahim is the ancient sacred river of Adonis, which we found sinking rapidly, a reddish turbid stream with a broad margin of reeds and rushes. From the theatre of rocks at Afka, high up on Lebanon, with its groves and cascades, the sacred river plunges down its deep gorge and hastens to the sea. Jibeil, Afka, and Baalbeck are almost in one line in the direction of the summer sunset and the winter sunrise; and not far east of Jibeil the old temple of Adonis was excavated by Renan, while Phœnician antiquities abound on every side. Here, then, we find ourselves at the very centre of the Phœnician worship, the holy Byblos, the city of Adonis and Osiris. The great coffin by the shore might to the imagination be the one which, covered with sea-weeds, was washed by the waves from Egypt, and stranded at Byblos. It held, says the myth, the mutilated body of Osiris, and it was made a pillar of the king's house till the faithful Isis, having vainly flitted over the Serbonian swamp, followed her lord to Phœnicia, and restored to life the limbs mangled by the dark northern Typhon. It was here that Philo, the sacerdotal recorder of Phœnician legends, was born. . . . Here also, at midsummer, the women went out to the river to bewail Adonis (their lord), or Tammuz (the son of life), and feigning to find his head in the sea, or his infant form in a cradle of papyrus on the waters, rejoiced to celebrate his new birth. The cradle was fabled to come, like the coffin of Osiris, from Egypt, where the Alexandrian women had, with tears, committed it to the waves. Not only does Lucian tell us this, but a Phœnician Scarabæus represents the ceremony, and in Isa. xviii. 2 we find the Egyptian land thus denounced: 'Woe to the land, says the prophet, that sendeth ambassadors by the sea in vessels of bulrushes upon the waters;' and Procopius already perceives the true meaning of the passage.

"At Afka, the ancient Aphek, named from the 'springs' (such being still the Syriac meaning of the word), stood till Constantine's time the shrine of the mourning Venus, with booths (Succoth) for the temple-consecrated women, who resembled exactly the votaries at Indian shrines, or in the fane of Ann among the Accadians. The image had her hand wrapped in her robe, and into the sacred spring by her temple fell every year the star or heavenly fire called Urania. Her votaries cut off their long tresses in grief for Tammuz, who, born from 'the bitter tree' (Amos viii. 10) which was torn open by the boar, was again slain at midsummer by the same boar, so that his blood dyed red the sacred river of Adonis, and the crimson anemone by its banks" (*Heth and Moab*, pp. 76, 78).

These forms of the worship of the sun spread from Phœnicia over all Palestine, and were practised even in the house of the Lord at Jerusalem (Ezek. viii. 13-16), thus reverting to the Chaldean idolatries from which Abraham went forth to come into Canaan.

From the north-western bounds of Israel this vile idolatry came. There also, at Nazareth, grew up and thence came forth to Israel "the Sun of Righteousness with healing in His wings."

NAPHTALI.

JOSH. xix. 32-39.

79. The territory of **Naphtali** lay immediately to the west of the sea of Galilee and the waters of Merom, the tribe of Asher just described possessing the plain and lower hills to the west of it. The

boundary to the north is indefinite. Joshua's description of the land of Naphtali gives first its length from Heleph in the north-west, to the south-west, where it touched the Jordan at Adami, 5 miles south of the Sea of Galilee (Josh. xix. 33). Allon there named is probably to be rendered oak, "oak at Zaanaim," or Bit-Zaanaim (Judg. iv. 11). This is contracted now into Bessûm (the Kadesh of that passage must be the town of that name overhanging the Sea of Galilee 5 miles eastward). Close by in the valley, east of Tabor, lie Adami (Dâmieh), Jabneel (Yemma), and possibly Nekeb, called by the Talmudists Tzidetha, which is no doubt the present ruin Seiyâdeh. But Tristram notes the recovery of Nakib in the Ard el Hamma between Tabor and the Sea of Galilee (which, however, is not given in the Survey Map). Lakum is not known, but is conjectured by him to be *Kefr Kamma*, within 2 miles of Bessûm. From this district the line ran westward to Tabor, or Aznoth-Tabor, which cannot be more certainly fixed, and up to Hukkok (Yakûk), which is but 4 miles west of Gennesareth, at which point therefore the territory of Naphtali must have been very narrow. At Hannathon, the boundary between Zebulun and Naphtali turned westwards till Naphtali met Asher (Josh. xix. 34) in the west.

The cities of Naphtali named in Joshua are *fenced* cities. They have nearly all been identified. Ziddim is placed at Hattin, which was Caphar Hittai, the "village of the Hittites" where Madon lay (§ 74). Hammath is the well-known Hammam or Emmaus on the shore of the Sea of Galilee, not 2 miles south of Tiberias. Rakkath is the old name of Tiberias, and long clung to it. Chinneroth may have stood on the site afterwards occupied by one of the towns in the plain of Gennesareth. Adamah may be recognised in Damieh, 5 miles south-west of Tiberias. Ramah lies 15 miles west of the north end of the Sea of Galilee, and Hazor has been identified with Hadîreh by the Jebel Hadîreh, 12 miles north-east of Rameh, and within 3 or 4 of Kedesh next named. Kedesh, famous as a stronghold, lay west of the Lake Huleh (§ 74). Edrei (Y'ater) is close to Hepher (Beit Lif) on the north-east, and 5 miles north of it is Mujeidil, once Migdal-el. The other cities will be found in a central line north and south—En or 'Ain Hazor, 5 miles west of Yakûk, at

Hazzûr, where is a spring; Bethshemesh, probably Khurbet Shema, 6 miles to the north of Hazzûr; Iron (Y'arûn), 7 miles yet farther north; Beth Anath, 4 miles to the north of Iron, now 'Ainîtha; and Horem, at Khûrbet Hârah, 3 miles beyond.

To the north of the Lake Huleh lay Abel, also called Abel-Beth-Maachah; Dan or Luz; and far north, at the uttermost boundary of the tribe, Ijon, now Merj Ajûn, by which the westmost branch of the Jordan flows. Janoah mentioned with them (2 Kings xv. 29) is now Yanûh. Giscala, famous for its resistance to the Romans, now El Jish, lies 5 miles north-west of Safed, which is still an important Jewish town. The New Testament sites around the Sea of Galilee will be best considered in connection with the history of our Lord's journeys. The territory of Naphtali was among the largest, having an area of 800 square miles, or twice as much as Issachar's. To it belonged *Kedesh*, the northmost *city of refuge* in Western Palestine.

CHAPTER VII.

PALESTINE IN THE TIME OF THE JUDGES AND OF DAVID.

THE details of the tribe boundaries being disposed of, and a key thus furnished to the Book of Joshua, we may take up the narratives of the following books of Scripture so as to illustrate the gain from a more exact localization of their scenes.

THE BOOK OF JUDGES.

80. So far as not already described, the following notes on the topography of this book will be sufficient to enable the reader to follow its narratives. The history of the successive Judges is given in Scripture very briefly. It begins with a notice of the opening campaigns of the several tribes in their allotted inheritances, and preserves for the most part only a record of failure.

Judah and Simeon, whose lot was really henceforth in all respects a common one, made common cause against their foes. In the northwest they defeated Adoni Bezek, the ruins of whose town yet remain below the plain of Ajalon, 6 miles to the south-east of Lydda. It lay afterwards within the tribe of Dan. Then they turned their arms southward to the district of Hebron, and south of the Salt Sea at Zephath or Hormah; Gaza, Ashkelon, and Ekron in the land of the Philistines, being taken but not permanently held. Jerusalem had been among the places first taken, and was apparently made the headquarters of the united armies, Judg. i. 7, 8; but from verse 21 we learn that the Benjamites did not drive out the Jebusites from Jerusalem, an indication that there was, as Jewish tradition says, and as the line of boundary seems to require, a division of Jerusa'em between Judah and Benjamin. The cities named in the remainder of the first chapter can be traced, so far as known, from the Index. Bochim, the scene of Judg. ii. 1–5, is quite unknown; it must have been near where the ark was—either, therefore, Shiloh (xviii. 31), or more probably Bethel (xx. 26–28); possibly there is an allusion to Allon Bachuth (Gen. xxxv. 8, marg.).

81. Of the Judges or "Saviours" whom God raised up to deliver Israel, the first was **Othniel**, nephew of Caleb, who prevailed against *Cushan-rishathaim*, when he came like Kederlagomer of old from Babylonia to subdue this nation, the renown of whose conquest of Canaan was spread far and wide. Not improbably he was invited by those whom Israel had subdued. For eight years he oppressed Israel.

Next Eglon of Moab crossed the Jordan and took Jericho, "the city of palm-trees," and dwelt there till **Ehud** the Benjamite, a near neighbour of, and probably special sufferer from the oppressor, killed him. The Gilgal named (Judg. iii. 19) is the camp of Israel, whose "quarries" or "stones" were possibly those erected by Joshua, if not a sacred circle of heathen worship which had before given a name to the spot. Seirath (ver. 26) was most probably near Ehud's home in Benjamin, and may have been the Mount *Seir* of Josh. xv. 10, on the border of Benjamin west of Jerusalem (now Saghir). The position suits the narrative.

The next oppression was suffered from the hand of the Philistines whom **Shamgar** defeated, but no locality is indicated in the brief mention of his deliverance of Israel.

The great victory gained by **Deborah and Barak** is detailed with minute and most helpful exactness. Deborah's home was between Ramah and Bethel, beneath a palm-tree, which is spoken of as if not a common tree; yet there are several about Jerusalem now, which has the same climate. Er Râm lies just half-way between Bethel and Jerusalem. It was in the territory of Benjamin; but the whole of what was afterwards given to Benjamin was in the first instance assigned to Ephraim. This may explain the frequent use of the name "Mount Ephraim," as for example in the preceding story of Ehud. Deborah sent to the north for Barak of Kadesh, in Naphtali, where Jabin the oppressor lived. The men of Naphtali, if they would be delivered, must strike for their liberty. The Kadesh at which Barak rallied his forces was by Tabor and Zaanaim (§ 88)— not the great Kedesh which lies 25 miles farther north. It lay on the edge of the hills looking down upon Kerak at the southwest corner of the Sea of Galilee. As he crossed the plain with his forces eastward to Mount Tabor, he passed the black tents of Heber the Kenite. Sisera, captain of Jabin's forces, dwelt in *Harosheth*, still known as El Harathiyeh, which lies under the shadow of the highest part of Carmel, about a mile north of the river Kishon. His forces must have advanced eastwards, and gone beyond Tabor with the purpose of gaining the low ridge on the north-east of Tabor, by which alone it is connected with the hill country about it, so as to surround and exterminate the unarmed mob with Barak and Deborah. At the command of Deborah, Barak descended towards Endor (Ps. lxxxiii. 10), 3 miles due southward from Tabor. The storm of Jehovah overwhelmed the Canaanites and turned their own chariots, wherein they trusted, against them. For as the springs about Tabor poured down their sudden floods, their "wheels drave heavily," and in the overthrow Sisera, who himself had led the attack to the east of Tabor, lighted off his chariot, and fled on foot to Zaanaim, 6 or 7 miles north-westwards—far enough, after the march and battle he had come through. There he slept his last sleep in the tent of Jael. The name of Meroz stands in the Song of Deborah in close and marked contrast to the honoured name of Jael (Judg. v. 23, 24). The contrast is yet more significant when we recognise that the inhabitants of Meroz were Jael's neighbours. It is identified with Murussas, 12 miles south-east of Zaanaim, and at just the same distance from Kadesh, the home of Barak, who without doubt had specially summoned them to "the help of the Lord against the mighty."

82. The brilliant exploits of **Gideon** take us to districts already pretty fully described. His native town was Ophrah of the Abiezrites. Captain Conder's suggestion of Feráta is quite acceptable. It lies on the ridge of the hill running west from Gerizim, and is about 7 miles from Shechem, with which his family was so closely connected (Judg. ix. 1). It was a high place of Baal (1715 feet).

Gideon in all probability led his forces through Shechem and by the road past Thebez (Judg. ix. 50, now Tubâs), 10 miles north-east of it; through Thirsah (Teiâsîr), 2 miles beyond, and passing close by Bezek (1 Sam. xi. 8), now Ibsik, which lay on his left 2 miles north of Thirsah, descended into the plain of Bethshean. The Roman road between Shechem and Bethshean (Scythopolis) followed the course just traced. Gideon must then have turned westwards by the base of the mountains of Gilboa, reaching the Ain el Jem'aîn, "the well of the two companies," which Conder proposes to identify with the well of Harod of Judg. vii. 1. It is just possible he took the direct north road by Engannin and on to Jezreel, and that the well Harod was the great fountain by Jezreel (1 Sam. xxix. 1).

The rendering of Josh. vii. 3 is doubtful; it may mean, "Whosoever is fearful and afraid, let him return and go round by Mount Gilead;" that is, by the way just come round the eastern end of Mount Jâlûd—evidently the more ancient name of part if not of the entire Gilboa range. The Midianites were encamped by the hill Moreh on the north.

The pursuit of the defeated Amalekites and Midianites was by Bethshitta (Bethshûtta), 3 miles north of 'Ain el Jem'aîn, about half-way between Jezreel and Bethshean on the north side of the Wâdy Jâlûd. Thence they fled to Zererath or Zartanah, and to Abelmeholah. Tabbath last named (Judg. vii. 22) is unknown. Gideon had sent messengers southward through all Mount Ephraim to take the fords of Jordan, and prevent the Midianites from crossing, and this was done from Bethbarah (probably opposite Jericho), so that many were taken. The site of Zuweil edh Dhiab, 17 miles south of Bethshean, "the den of the wolf," has been connected with the name of Zeeb, " the wolf;" and Ash el Ghorab, "the raven's peak," 2 miles south of it, with that of Oreb. The suggestion that these preserve the names of the two princes of Midian slain on the west of Jordan is interesting, and is possibly correct. The pursuit of the Midianites went by Succoth to Peniel, and eastwards of Jogbehah, for which see § 61.

The after history of Gideon's house, more specially of Abimelech, who was crowned in Shechem as king, does not range far from that city. He went to Arumah (Judg. ix. 41), most probably El 'Ormeh,

7 miles south-east of Shechem. At Mount Zalmon, which lay on the direct line between El 'Ormeh and Ferâta, 4 or 5 miles south of Shechem,—the Salmon of Ps. lxviii. 14,—he and his men cut down branches wherewith to burn the tower of Shechem. Having destroyed it, he went to Thebez, the position of which is given above.

The scene of **Jephthah's** fight with, and pursuit of Ammon, has been fully described already, § 59–60, as well as the Bethlehem of **Ibzan** and the Ajalon of **Elon**, § 77. Pirathon, the home of **Abdon**, has been placed by Conder at Feron, on the edge of the hills, 15 miles west by north of Shechem. The identification is good, as it is an important and ancient site.

83. The valley of Sorek was the scene of the exploits of the great hero of the tribe of Dan—**Samson**. Already several of the towns in that valley have been noticed. Of these, Zorah, at first assigned to Judah, but afterwards allotted to Dan, was one of the chief. Its position is described, § 72, and that also of Eshtaol. In the little plain on the western edge of which they lay, "the camp of Dan" had been formed when a detachment of the tribe prepared to seek a home in the far north by the sources of the Jordan. Zorah and Eshtaol were within 2 miles of each other; Bethshemesh was 2 miles due south of Zorah, and to the east suddenly rose the mountain on which stood Baalah, or Kirjath Jearim, so that "the camp" was close to it, on the west (Josh. xviii. 12).

Here, in Mahaneh Dan, "the camp of Dan," the Spirit first began to move the son of Manoah of Zorah (Judg. xiii. 25, marg.). Timnath, where he sought a wife, and among whose vineyards he rent a lion, is but 4 miles down the valley from Zorah in a south-westerly direction. When he went to Ashkelon to provide the garments due to those who had found out his riddle, he made a journey of 25 miles south-westwards. Etam, where he hid, is probably Beit 'Atab, 5 or 6 miles up the valley from Zorah. "It is pre-eminently a 'rock'—a knoll of hard limestone, without a handful of arable soil, standing above deep ravines, by three small springs. The place is also one which has long been a hiding-place, and the requirements of the Bible story are met in a remarkable way; for the word rendered 'top' of the rock Etam, is in reality 'cleft' or 'chasm;' and such a chasm exists here

—a long narrow cavern, such as Samson might well have 'gone down' into, and which bears the suggestive name Hasûta, meaning 'refuge' in Hebrew, but having in modern Arabic no signification at all. This remarkable 'cave of refuge' is 250 feet long, 18 feet wide, and 5 to 8 feet high. At its north-eastern extremity there is a rock shaft 10 feet deep leading down from the surface of the hill" (*Tent Work in Palestine*, and *Memoirs*, iii. 137).

Lehi, Ramath Lehi, and **En Hakkore**, "the well of the crier" (Judg. xv.), must be about the same region; the latter may be 'Akûr on the opposite side of the valley from Etam, and a play upon the name 'Ain 'Akûr such as we often meet with. This would confirm the identification of Samson's "rock Etam." At 'Akûr there is a "good spring."

Other traditions cling to this valley, on which much weight cannot be put, though they are of some interest. The valley between Beit Atab and Akûr bears the name of Wâdy Ismaîn, *i.e.* "the valley of Ishmael," which may be a reminiscence of Samson's prayer as was "En Hakkore"—*Ishmael* meaning "heard of God" (Gen. xvi. 11). Beit Atab was at one time the possession of a native family which bore the name Beit Lehhâm. Can this be connected with the Lehi of Samson's exploit? Commenting on the tenacity of the old names, Clermont Ganneau says: "It is worthy of remark that the ethnic name—that is, the name by which the *inhabitants* are known, and which is derived from the locality—is very often more archaic in form than the name of the *place* itself. There are many examples of this interesting fact which may prove very useful in testing the accuracy of proposed identifications" (*Spec. Papers*, p. 325). It is most probable that originally the name Lehi was given to the jaw-like gorge itself, from its serrated, tooth-like cliffs. The name "Shen" or Ha-shen, *i.e.* the tooth, occurs also farther up this same valley (§ 86), and is similarly used in 1 Sam. xiv. 4 of Bozez and Seneh. If we read, as it is most likely we ought, "to Lehi" instead of "into troops" (2 Sam. xxiii. 11), then this valley would also be the scene of the heroic feat of Shammah, the third of David's mighty men, which so closely resembled the achievement of Samson. Ramath Lehi, "the jawbone height," might be one of the prominent hills on either side of the ravine, such as Khurbet Sammûnieh. See description of the Wâdy Ismaîn and the road by it between Bethshemesh and Bethlehem (p. 118).

Gaza, whose gates Samson carried off by night, and where he died, is yet an important town in the very south of Philistia, on the edge of the desert.

84. The places named in the remaining chapters of Judges are for the most part easily found. In tracing the journey of the Levite of Mount Ephraim from Bethlehem, it will be noticed that as early as this time Jerusalem is called a "city of a stranger," and if, as is very probable, there were really two towns here, the traveller from Bethlehem passed close to "Jebus," and thence to Gibeah. This Gibeah—the name means a hill, and occurs very frequently—has usually been placed at Tell el Ful, 4 miles or so north of Jerusalem. It is very doubtful if this is Gibeah of Saul. From 1 Sam xiv. 2, it would seem as if the name applied to the eastern district of Benjamin, as well as to more than one town situated there. The "pomegranate-tree," or "Rimmon," in the text just quoted is doubtless the Rimmon of Judg. xx. 45—the Migron or "precipice" of which may be the "rock" of this place where the Benjamites sought shelter.

The Gidom of Judg. xx. 45 cannot be identified.

TOPOGRAPHY OF FIRST SAMUEL.

85. The first verse of this book contains the name of **Ramathaim-Zophim**. Where were the two Ramahs or heights of the watchmen? Some would identify Ramah, which was Samuel's birth-place, with Er Ram, 5 miles north of Jerusalem, but this hardly suits. Ramathem, mentioned in 1 Macc. xi. 34 along with Lydda and Ephraim, so as to suggest that it lay between them, as having been taken from Samaria and added to Judah, seems to have been the same. The most probable position for this Ramathem would be about Ram Allah, an important site, now a Christian village 3 miles southwards from Bethel. It stands just to the west of the watershed close to Beeroth. One mile and a half west of it is *El Muntar*, "the watch-tower," which may preserve the memory of the Zophim or watchers of 1 Sam. i. 1, and be the twin Ramah which the name Ramathaim requires. One mile south of El Muntar is Kh. Bir Shâfa, in which the ancient name Zuph may still be recognised. Fortunately **Shiloh**, where **Samuel** spent his youth at the tabernacle, is known as Seilûn. Its position has been pointed out 10 miles to the north of Bethel. He was still young when the ark of God was taken and carried into the land of the Philistines from Ebenezer (afterwards so called)

to Ashdod and Ekron, whence it was returned to Bethshemesh, lying 12 miles up the valley from Ekron ('Akir). Ashdod or Azotus, now Esdûd, lies on the coast 12 miles south of Ekron. Kirjath Jearim is 4 miles "up" from Bethshemesh. After being twenty years neglected, the ark was sought for in a time of religious revival (chap. vii.), and a place, doubtless, prepared for it "on the hill." Just such a levelled platform as remains at Shiloh has been found at Khurbet 'Erma. (See Appendix I.)

Captain Conder visited it to see what evidence of the identification could be traced on the spot, and gives the following account of it :— "A bold spur running northwards from the southern ridge was characterized by a small natural turret or platform of rock, rising from a knoll which stood covered with fallen masonry above a group of olives, beneath which again the thickets clothed the mountain. This knoll represented the ruins of 'Erma, which on closer inspection proved to be a site undoubtedly ancient and presenting the aspect of an old ruined town. . . . On the east is a fine rock-cut wine-press; on the south, a great cistern covered by a huge hollowed stone, which forms the well-mouth, and which, from its size and its weather-beaten appearance, must evidently be very ancient. Rude caves also occur, and the ground is strewn with fragments of ancient pottery. But the most curious feature of the site is the platform of rock, which has all the appearance of an ancient high-place or central shrine. The area is about 50 feet north and south, by 30 feet east and west; the surface, which appears to be artificially levelled, being some 10 feet above the ground outside. The scarping of the sides seems mainly natural, but a foundation has been sunk on three sides, in which rudely-squared blocks of stone have been fitted at the base of the wall. On the east this wall consisted of rock to a height of $3\frac{1}{2}$ feet, with a thickness of 7 feet. There is an outer platform, about 10 feet wide, traceable on the south and south-east; and a flight of steps 3 feet wide, each step being 1 foot high and 1 foot broad, leads up to this lower level at the south-east angles. There is a small cave under the platform, and the ruined houses extend along the spur principally north and south of this remarkable rocky tower" (*Palestine Quarterly Statement*, Oct. 1881, p. 265).

The presence of a cave under the rock, as well as the prominence of the site, confirms the belief that this is Baalah—a high-place of Baal, which became afterwards more memorable as the abode of the ark till David took it up to Jerusalem.

86. For at least part of the time during which the ark abode at Kirjath Jearim, the tabernacle was at Nob (1 Sam. xxi.), which lay near Jerusalem on the north. It was to the ark of the covenant, no

doubt, Israel sought at the end of the 20 years it had remained neglected at Kirjath Jearim; for the period mentioned 1 Sam. vii. 2 can only refer to such a neglect, the ark remaining there very much longer than 20 years in all—from three months after its capture, till David removed it—a period of at least 60 to 70 years.

Mizpeh—the watch-tower—was the rallying-place of Israel during this time. It is probably the Maspha over against Jerusalem, where the Israelites used to pray (1 Macc. iii. 46). Unfortunately its site is one of the much-disputed points of Palestine topography. The difficulty is much increased by the frequent recurrence of the name. (1) There is the hill now known as Neby Samwil, which rises from the plain, 5 miles north by west of Jerusalem, and beyond which lies Gibeon, whither the tabernacle was taken after the slaughter of the priests at Nob. There is great probability that this site, suggested by Dr. Robinson, is the true one. (2) Sôba, 6 miles west of Jerusalem, has been also suggested, but it could hardly be said to be over against Jerusalem, being on the far side of the Wâdy Beit Haunina, though its name is suggestive of Mizpeh, being from the same root. (3) The Mount of Olives has been also proposed, but it could not be the Mizpeh of Jer. xli. 10–12—an objection equally fatal apparently to Scopus, or Shafat, or any point on Olivet; though of all positions suggested, Olivet is the one most accurately described as "over against Jerusalem" (compare Mark xiii. 3). Possibly Olivet was the "Mashpa" of Josephus, though not of Samuel. Placing it at Neby Samwil, most of the incidents of 1 Samuel are easily understood. The first battle in which Israel successfully rebelled against the Philistine oppression—against which Samson did little more than protest—was fought here (1 Sam. vii.), and the routed enemy was pursued to Bethcar, now known as 'Ain Karim, just as Bethshemesh down the same valley has become 'Ain Shems. Close to it is Deir Yesin, which preserves the name of Shen (ver. 12), which should rather be Ha-shen, and is by the LXX. given as Yasan. Between this and Mizpeh, Samuel set up the memorial-stone of Ebenezer. It has been proposed to place this at Deir Aban, much farther down the valley, within a mile or two of Bethshemesh, but this seems too near the Philistine country, and the memorial would rather be erected on the battle-field. Deir Aban is far more likely the stone of 1 Sam. vi. 18.

The places which Samuel went to on circuit were Bethel, the Gilgal near Jericho, and Mizpah. His home was in Ramah, which is distinguished from Mizpah, though its locality is not known. It can scarcely be Er Eram, which is so near where Gibeah of Saul must have been that it would be difficult to understand how, in that case, Samuel and Saul were ignorant of one another (1 Sam. ix. 17-19) when they met—most probably at Kirjath Jearim (*Palestine Quarterly Statement*, 1882, p. 63). Josephus states that Samuel and Saul met at Ramah, but this is a confusing conjecture based on the mention of the seer's house. Samuel, who went from place to place officially, would have several houses. The Bible gives no ground for the assertion. It would almost appear also that Ramah was distinguished from Ramathaim Zophim ; but there were, and are, many places of the name, which means "a height." Possibly Khurbet of Sammûnieh may be the Gibeah or hill that was by Kirjath Jearim. It is a striking conical hill, about a mile east of Khurbet 'Erma, and south of Khurbet Sûffa, rising conspicuously from the deep Wâdy Ismain on its northern side. (See Note, p. 118.)

87. **Gibeah of Saul,** though its precise position is doubtful, lay most likely in the north-western part of Benjamin, where Jeba and Sahel Jeba or "plain of Geba," now are, on the edge of the Wâdy Suweinit, some 6 miles east of Nebi Samwil. Some place it farther south, near Tell el Ful, whereabout a Gibeon must have been (Judg. xix. 11, 12). Josephus, *Wars*, v. 2, 1, says Gabaoth-Saul was 30 furlongs from Jerusalem, near the "valley of Thorns," or Wâdy Suweinit, which would indicate Geba. Saul left his father's house to seek the strayed asses (1 Sam. ix. 4) through the land of Shalisha and Shalim, and through the land of Benjamin (or of the south ?), and came to the land of Zuph. The line he took is unknown ; but one might conjecture he went along the north boundary of Benjamin and round by Shilta and Selbit, which is Shaalbim (Judg. i. 35; § 72), to Sûffa (§ 72); and that after his anointing he returned by Rachel's sepulchre and Jerusalem (the plain of Tabor is unknown), and homewards to

Gibeah, passing on his way "Gibeah of God," which may be Neby Samwil.

Bezek, where he gathered the men of Israel to relieve Jabesh Gilead, lies on the edge of the hills just over against Jabesh. Its position is defined, § 82.

Michmash, where next he rallies his forces against the Philistines, lies on the north side of the Wâdy Suweinit, "eastward" from Bethaven, § 63 and 95. From this he retired on their approach down to Gilgal, from whence the more timorous fled across the Jordan. The Philistines sent out companies to make raids northward by Ophrah, eastwards by Zeboim, and westwards by Ajalon, while Saul lay helplessly on the south of their camp. Then it was that Jonathan climbed over from Seneh to Bozez (§ 63), and the Philistines were driven from Michmash by Bethaven and Ajalon down to their own land. The *Carmel* mentioned (xv. 12) is now Kurmul, 7 miles south of Hebron; its position is described in the next section.

88. The anointing of **David** at Bethlehem (chap. xvi.) causes the interest of the after story to centre in him.

The scene of his memorable victory over the giant was in the Wâdy Elah, between Shocoh and Azekah. The former is now Shuweikeh, situated at the point where the Wâdy Sûnt, or Elah, descends from the hills; the latter, now Deir el 'Ashek, lies in the open below the Wâdy Surâr. Close to this in the place required is Beit Fased, in which we can trace the Ephes Dammim of the narrative.

"In further illustration of this episode, I found that much discussion had occurred as to words used in the narrative, one meaning a broad, flat valley; . . . the other a ravine or narrow channel. It was supposed that a gorge must exist somewhere, and this point explorers were required to clear up. On visiting the valley, I could find no such gorge; but the true meaning at once became apparent on the spot. The *Emek* or broad valley has in the middle of it the *Gai*, or narrow channel. The water of the turbid winter torrents has dug a deep channel in the middle of the valley. The course is strewn with smooth white pebbles, and the steep banks are built up of them. This therefore, it seems to me, is the channel which separated the two hosts" (Captain Conder, "Manchester Address," *Palestine Quarterly*, 1876, p. 40).

The site of Gath, whence Goliath, David's foe, came (as also his after-friend Ittai), and where David sought shelter with Achish, is with greatest probability placed by Dr. Porter at Tell es Sâfi, which commands the lower part of the valley of Elah, "an isolated, conical hill in the plain, like a sentinel of a watch-tower, or fortress, and on that account there was so much struggling for its possession" (Herr Conrad Shick). "The magnificent natural site of Tell el Sâfich, standing above the broad valley, which seems undoubtedly the valley of Elah, and presenting on the north and west a white precipice of many hundred feet, must have made this place one of importance in all ages. . . . Gath, so placed, guards the entrance of the valley, and is about 6 miles from the scene of conflict" (*Memoirs*, ii. 415, 416).

Map III. of Southern Palestine, p. 76, will help the reader to follow the wanderings of David as he fled from Saul. Gibeah, Ramah, Naioth, Nob, and Sechu are not fixed with certainty. (See Index.)

The cave of Adullam has been found by M. Ganneau, the recoverer of Gazer, at 'Aîd el-Mâ. Here was the royal city of the Canaanites (§ 54). A row of small caves exists there—large caves would be too cold to be habitable—the position was a very well chosen one, and for one like David, hovering between the lands of Israel and Philistia, exceptionally convenient. It is about 2 miles up the valley from and south of Shocoh. Three miles farther south, still ascending the valley, is Keilah. Driven from Keilah (Khurbet Kila), David retired up to the hill Hareth or *Kharas*, situated 3 miles to the east, upon the road from Hebron to Adullam, by which his ancestor Judah doubtless travelled. Thence he fled through Hebron to Ziph, 4 miles to the south of it. The "wood" of Ziph should be *Choresh* of Ziph, which Conder recovered in Khoreisa, scarce 2 miles south of Ziph. This place, Khoreisa, should be noted, for here took place the interview between Jonathan and David (xxiii. 16–18). Carmel—*Kurmul*—lies 2 miles to the south of it, and Maon, *Main*, a mile and a half beyond Carmel.

" One is at once struck with the fitness which the plateau presents for the adventures of the fugitive bandit chief who was destined to become the King of Israel. The inhabitants, like Nabal of Carmel, are rich in sheep and oxen. The villagers of Yuttah owned 1700 sheep, of which 250 belonged to the sheikh. All along the borders of the Jeshimon and Beersheba deserts there is fine pasturage, to which the peasants descend in spring-time, having made some sort of agreement with the neighbouring Bedawin to protect them from other tribes. Thus we find perpetuated the old system under which David's band protected the cattle of Nabal" (*Tent Work*, ii. 88).

Still hard pressed by Saul, David turned eastward to the cliff or "Sela" in the Wâdy Malâki. This is the "Sela Hammahlekoth" (xxiii. 28), where he was so nearly captured when Saul was called off the prey just within his grasp, by the tidings of a Philistine invasion—as Peden on our Scotch hills was hid, in answer to his prayer, in the mantling mist, and found when it cleared off that the dragoons in pursuit of him had been suddenly summoned to other work.

David then went down to the shelter of Engedi, by the Salt Sea; probably ascending in the spring-time to the cooler heights as the summer heat made Engedi unbearable. It was in one of the caves about Engedi that David cut off the skirt of Saul's garment (xxiv. 1-22). On Saul's departure, David returned to the more genial pastoral land about Maon and Carmel (xxv. 1); but had to leave it when, instigated by those men of the place who were of Nabal's spirit or family, or were afraid of one whom they thought the cause of the great man's death, Saul once more came in pursuit of David. For the last time Saul and David exchanged words by the Hill of Hachilah, the ridge El Kôlah, 6 miles to the east of Ziph. On the north side of El Kôlah are "the caves of the dreamers," in which it can scarcely be doubted lingers a dreamy memory of the sleeping king of Israel and his slumbering guards (xxvi. 3-16).

Ziklag, where he had a dwelling among the Philistines, has been placed by Major Kitchener at Zuheilikah, 11 miles east by south of Gaza. There the crown of Saul was laid at David's feet by the Amalekite, who brought the tidings of the death of Saul and Jonathan upon the mountains of Gilboa.

Hebron was David's first capital. Here he was close by the places among which he wandered in Saul's time, and the people whom he had conciliated by gifts and favours (1 Sam. xxx.), the people of his own tribe of Judah. Here Abner came to make terms with David. The well of Sirah, whence Joab recalled him, still remains close by the high road, little over a mile to the north, as does also the pool in Hebron where David hanged the murderers of Ishbosheth.

Note.—The following is a description of the Wâdy Ismaîn, which, though seldom now visited by travellers, must have been of old the scene of many conflicts between the Israelites and Philistines from the days of Samson to those of David. By the rough road here described the ark was taken from Kirjath Jearim, "the city of the woods," by Ephratah, to Jerusalem (Ps. cxxxii. 6) :—

"Riding down the great gorge, which under various names runs down from near Gibeon to Bethshemesh, we gradually ascended the southern slopes. Before us was the notable peaked knoll of Khurbet Sammûnich, a conspicuous feature of the view up the valley from Surah ; and leaving this on the right we followed an ancient road along the slope of the mountain. Here and there remains of sidewalls are visible, and there can be little doubt that this is a branch of the Roman road from the vicinity of Bethlehem leading to Bethshemesh. In front of us, far beneath, we saw the white bed of the torrent twisting in bold bends between the steep slopes which rise fully 1000 feet to the hill-tops. Both slopes were rocky and rugged ; both—but especially that to the south—were clothed with a dense brushwood of lentisk, arbutus, oak, hawthorn, kharub, and other shrubs ; while in the open glades the thyme, sage, etc. carpeted the ledges with a thick fragrant undergrowth" (*Palestine Quarterly Statement*, as quoted, p. 112).

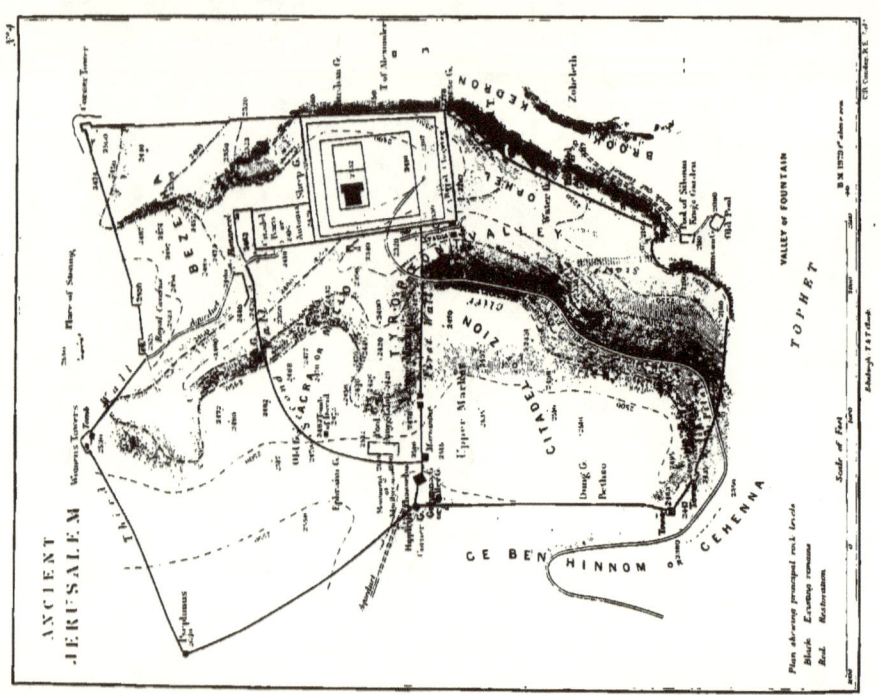

CHAPTER VIII.

THE DAYS OF THE KINGDOM.

(*See* MAP IV.)

89. WITH the capture of **Jerusalem** by David, a new era began in Israel's history, and new interests grew up about it as the capital of the kingdom and home of the temple. The topography of Jerusalem is a tangled and thorny subject, and few points can be regarded as settled.

The first thing to be done in such controversies is to clear the ground. This has happily been done to a large extent by the engineers who have worked for the "Palestine Exploration Fund." At nearly 300 points has the original rock-level been ascertained. The score of sieges, and many burnings, which the limestone buildings of Jerusalem have passed through, have accumulated a vast amount of formless debris, which, slipping down into the hollows, has changed completely the original contour of the site. Map IV. embodies the results of these observations. On all sides, save at the north and north-west, the city was surrounded by deep valleys. On the north a plain extends "into the country" for a mile and a half; while on the north-west the ground rises rapidly to about 100 feet above the highest point of the site of the city. From the north and north-west alone, therefore, were all assaults directed against Jerusalem by its besiegers.

90. On the east the **Valley of the Kidron** separates it from the **Mount of Olives**, which is in fact a spur from the watershed running out north of Jerusalem, and bending round in a southerly direction. Its height is just about that of the general watershed (2682 feet), and but 150 feet above the highest point of the city. It is from the Mount of

Olives the best view of the city may be had. For though not much higher, the lie of the city slopes down eastwards, so that one looks on it as on a book inclined towards the reader. The valley of the Kidron is quite narrow, and the rock of Jerusalem rises steep on the west. The bed of the stream was originally 40 feet deeper than it now is; and it has been thrust 70 feet eastward by the rubbish poured down from the city walls above. As it goes southward a little beyond the line of the temple, the Mount of Olives droops, rising again into the "**Mount of Offence**" so called, past which, to the south, the Kidron valley becomes a rugged gorge. The Mount of Offence is in a line due east of the southern point of "the Citadel of Zion." On its western slope is perched **the village of Siloam**, where is the rock or "stone of Zoheleth" (1 Kings i. 9), now called "Ez Zehwele" by the villagers—a rocky plateau projecting into and slightly overhanging the Kidron valley. By rude steps cut in the face of it, the women of Siloam daily descend for water to the "Virgin's Fountain," or Enrogel, which is right across the valley, and but 70 yards from the rock.

Another steep valley or **ravine**, descending from the west of Jerusalem and sweeping round by the south, meets the Kidron valley at the Bir Eyub, over 700 yards south of the stone of Zoheleth, at the point on the right-hand corner of Map IV. marked "1979 feet above sea." This it will be observed is 556 feet below the highest point of "Zion." This valley, now called Wâdy Rabâbeh, is usually identified with the valley of the Son of Hinnom—the *Gai* Ben-Hinnom, sometimes contracted into Gehenna. The south side of this valley is steep, though not so steep as the precipice of Zion. Opposite the mouth of the valley which divides the city was Tophet, and on the hillside immediately south is the traditional site of Aceldama (Acts i. 19). The summit on the south side of the valley over against Zion is known as the "Hill of Evil Counsel."

91. It should be kept in remembrance that the "mountains round about Jerusalem" are not much higher than the hills on which the city is built; and that its strength consists in the deep valleys which surround it save on the north and north-west.

The city may be said to stand on two spurs of the central watershed of Palestine already described. Of these the westmost is much the larger and higher. As it leaves the watershed it goes first in a south-easterly direction, and then contracts into a very narrow neck, beyond which it expands again and reaches due south, terminating in a sudden and inaccessible precipice. The eastern spur is very much, indeed almost exactly, of the same form on a lesser scale. Its true form has been entirely concealed, and its apparent size enlarged, by the filling up of the hollows at its neck, and by the construction of the great artificial temple-platform on its southern half. Though the depression of the **Tyropœon valley** is clearly visible from Olivet, no one had any idea of the extent to which it had been filled up by debris, until exploration discovered the true rock-levels as shown on the Map.

Note. — The portfolio of Jerusalem drawings published by the Palestine Exploration Fund, reveals the true face of the ground. The bearing of this on the disputed sites in Jerusalem is manifest. The highest point marked is 2532, just south of David's Tower (so called). The highest contour-line traced round Zion is 2529. Following the contour-line 100 feet lower (2429), it will be found on the west of Zion just where Pilate's aqueduct from Etam first touches it, and at the north-east corner, well up the western branch of the Tyropœon valley, a little east of the Pool Amygdalon. The contour-line, yet another 100 feet lower, is found in the valley south of Zion just where the "G" of the name Gehenna is on the accompanying Map, and on the west just where the line of the "first wall" joins the temple wall. All lying east of a line along the hillside between these two points is lower by 200 feet than Zion.

The proper names of these different hills on which the city is built have been much disputed. **Each of the two spurs, or ridges, being divided, there are four hills to identify.** A careful study of Scripture usage indicates a very considerable latitude in the interchange of the names Jerusalem and Zion, and they are unquestionably often used as synonymous. A more difficult question is as to the interchange of the names "Zion" and "city of David." The most important passages as to this are, (1) 2 Sam. v. 6-9, and 1 Chron. xi. 4-7, from which it appears that David took first the stronghold or castle, and that thereafter Joab gained entrance into the upper and stronger position committed to the lame and blind as adequate to hold it ; (2) 2 Chron.

iii. 1, v. 2, which show clearly that Zion or "the city of David" was not Moriah.

We have also descriptions of the city by Josephus, which help us to understand how, in his time, the various names were appropriated. He never uses the name Zion at all, which confirms the impression that it had by his time become a general name for the whole city; otherwise it is not easy to see why he never employs it in his descriptions of the different parts of the city, and his minute accounts of their successive capture. The following passages of Josephus may be consulted: *Ant.* vii. 3; *Wars*, v. 4. From them it appears that he regarded the south-west hill as "the citadel," the north-west as "Acra," the north-east as Bezetha, and the south-east as Moriah, of which the extremity was known as "Ophel." Undoubtedly the south-western hill must always have been the strongest position, as it was always the last to be stormed. Protected everywhere, save at the narrow neck on the north-west, it was a natural fastness. Acra was a knoll standing out between the two branches of the Tyropœon, and was originally about 30 feet higher; but was cut down in the time of the Maccabees because it dominated the temple. Though still higher than the temple site, it was so reduced that the high walls of the temple and its tower of Baris (afterwards Antonia) sufficiently covered it.

It is important to note the depth of the Tyropœon valley between the hills marked "citadel of Zion" and "Acra," as now ascertained, corresponding with Josephus' description of the separation of the "upper market-place" from "the lower city."

Note.—In the description given of the hills on which Jerusalem stood, the generally-accepted identifications have been followed. There are points on which certainty can probably never be attained; but on the whole there seems no clear evidence warranting the adoption of any other of the many proposals. One of the most recent of these is the transference of the whole of the Jerusalem of David to the eastern spur, on which the temple stood. But reducing the size of the temple courts to the uttermost, the area which would remain for David's city is far too small. It is inconceivable that the much lower position of Ophel would be occupied, and "the height of Zion" left unoccupied. It would perhaps solve some difficulties to take the eastern hill as the site of the city of David, "the lower city" which he took first, and where he dwelt, and to set the fastness of the Jebusite on the southern part of the higher western hill; assigning the eastern spur to Benjamin, and the western to Judah. In that case the Tyropœon, or "cheese-maker's," valley would be identified with the valley of Hinnom. The fact that there is no notice of that valley by that or any like name in Scripture, and no mention of the "valley of Hinnom" by Josephus, has suggested to many the identity of the two. A most ingenious note will be found in Dr. Bonar's *Land of Promise*, p. 486, proposing to find the Hebrew Geben-hinnom in the Greek Tyropœon. He supposes that Josephus, took the first two syllables of the name Geben-hinnom for "*Geben*," the Hebrew for "cheese," and translated it by the Greek equivalent; and he points to an exactly similar mistake by the LXX. in Ps. lxviii. 16. The suggestion is worthy of more notice than it has received (see *Memoirs*, Jerusalem vol., p. 291). Captain Conder suggests valley of "money-changers," pointing out that as late as 1500 A.D. the part of the city immediately over this valley was called Khân es Serf, "change" or "silver" in Arabic, which would correspond to a Hebrew root "to smelt." The money-changers still have their shops in David Street, which runs down from the Jaffa gate in the line of the Tyropœon. Other derivations have been proposed, but the whole is matter of conjecture and uncertainty. If the valley now found to descend from the west between "the citadel of Zion" and "Acra," turning southwards, and dividing "Zion" and Ophel, be identified with "the valley of Hinnom," it would be necessary to include in it the whole "ravine" where Tophet lies on the south to its junction with the Kidron valley at the Bir Eyub.

92. The **water-supply of Jerusalem** belongs also to the natural features of the site. It has always been chiefly dependent on reservoirs or cisterns in which the surface water collected. Of these there are very many, the whole temple-area being honeycombed beneath. Much water was always needed in connection with the temple services. The chief spring is Enrogel, the position of which has been described (Map IV.). At this spring a large tank or reservoir has been formed to which a long flight of 30 steps leads down. The modern Arabic name, 'Ain Umm ed Deraj, "the spring of the Mother of Steps," is given it from these steps. From this fountain, which flows out of the base of the temple hill, a **tunnel** was cut through Ophel to feed the **pool of Siloam** (see Map). Forty years ago, Dr. Robinson made his way, with great difficulty, from the fountain to the pool. The actual length of the tunnel, including its numerous windings, is 1706 feet. Recently an inscription was discovered upon

the side of the tunnel at the point where the workmen from each end had met in the centre. It is thus rendered by Professor Sayce, line by line, as it is cut in the rock. The blanks mark words obliterated.

(1) (Behold) the excavation. Now this (is) the history of the tunnel : while the excavators were still lifting up
(2) the pick towards each other, and while there were yet 3 cubits (to be broken through) . . . the voice of the one called
(3) to his neighbour, for there was an (?) *excess* in the rock on the right. They rose up . . . they struck on the west of the
(4) excavation ; the excavators struck, each to meet the other, pick to pick. And there flowed
(5) the waters from their outlet to the pool for a thousand two hundred cubits ; and (?)
(6) of a cubit, was the height of the rock over the head of the excavators.
—*Survey of Western Palestine,* Jerusalem vol., p. 347.

At about 50 feet from the spring, a passage branches off westwards 17 feet deeper into the hill, and ends in a hollowed basin 3 feet deep for retaining the water. Over this basin is a shaft 40 feet in height, from the top of which (where an iron ring was found for the rope of the water-bucket) a passage leads to a stair which ascends to another passage with vaulted roof opening upon the top of the hill. By this means water could be drawn from the fountain without going outside the walls, or descending from the top. This may have been the work of Hezekiah (2 Chron. xxxii. 4).

The spring of Enrogel rises in a cave, measuring 20 feet to the back and 7 feet across ; the steps and vaulted chamber leading to it are modern. A serpentine tunnel, 67 feet long, probably an earlier outflow, runs towards the left, off which the Siloam tunnel branches.

A notable peculiarity of the spring is that it is intermittent. It is so directly dependent on rainfall, that while in winter it gushes forth three to five times a day, in summer it does so twice, and in autumn but once a day. The natives ascribe this to a dragon, which swallows the water when awake ; while he is asleep it gathers and flows freely away. "It is interesting to note that a similar dragon which 'keeps back the waters' is the enemy of the Indian rain god, Indra, whose contest with this dragon and delivery of the waters is constantly noticed in the Vedas. The modern Jews believe the waters of this pool to be a sure cure for rheumatic complaints. They often go in numbers, men and women together, and stand in their clothes in the pool waiting for the water to rise."—*Survey of Western Palestine*, Jerusalem vol., p. 366.

The **Pool of Siloam**, as now visible, at the south end of Ophel, is but a small portion of a large rock-pool. From it a channel goes to supply a lower pool, probably also older, and which may be the one called by Josephus Solomon's Pool (*Wars*, v. 4, 2). There is no doubt as to the identification of the Pool of Siloam, and the waters of Shiloh were those which flowed through the tunnel.

Another spring in Jerusalem is once mentioned, En-Hat-tannin, "the dragon's spring" (Neh. ii. 13). As we have seen, the peculiar feature of the Virgin's Fountain has associated a dragon with it also. The site of this well is unknown. Just outside the temple area, some 120 feet on the west, is the *Hummâm esh Shefa*, "the bath of healing." This may possibly be the pool of John v. 2. The 'Ain es Shefa supplies it. The observations made do not quite certainly warrant the conclusion that it was "a spring;" but it is marked as such on Jerusalem plans, Plate VI., and it has evidently been long used, its sides having from time to time been raised in different styles of building, as debris accumulated about it to a depth of 80 feet. "The portion cut in the rock seems to be of great antiquity." This may be "the fountain" of Josephus (*Wars*, v. 6, 1).

There are also **two pools** outside the north-western angle of the temple walls, which are kept constantly supplied by an aqueduct from the north, and, some think, by a subterranean spring also. It may be assumed that the two branches of the Tyropœon were natural water-courses, gathering the rain or spring water from the north and west. One large pool, "Amygdalon," or "Hezekiah's" Pool, was constructed in the neck of the western ridge; another, now often called Bethesda (not improbably " Bezetha" originally), was similarly placed in the neck of the eastern ridge. This latter may have also been designed as a moat to defend the north temple wall.

Besides these local means of supply, **Jerusalem was fed from the hills beyond Bethlehem.** At Etam, at the head of the Wâdy Urtâs, are fountains which fill "the pools of Solomon," together with the stream fetched by a tunnel from as far as the Wâdy Arrûb, 6 miles south of Etam. By Bethlehem and Rachel's tomb, along the plain of Rephaim, the water was conducted to Jerusalem. In most ancient times, before the pools of Solomon were made, it kept a high level, passing into Jerusalem probably at the western head of the Tyropœon, and flowing down it towards Siloam. The traces of this oldest and highest aqueduct are lost on the plain of Rephaim; possibly it was destroyed, or hidden, to keep it from besieging armies. After the three pools were made at Urtâs, the water, flowing then at a lower level, was taken down the valley on the west of Jerusalem, crossing over it to the side of Zion, round which it wound its course up the Tyropœon to the temple, which it supplied. A few years ago, after a partial repair, the water actually flowed again by this course for a short time into the temple cisterns. An older channel for this supply has been traced on part of Zion, so that the existing aqueduct may be the work of Pontius Pilate, of which Josephus speaks (*Ant.* xviii. 3, 2).

The water-supply, though important, was not, however, a chief point in determining the site of a fortress. Many villages in Palestine are planted for safety on hill-tops at considerable distance from water. Nothing can be inferred from this, therefore, as regards the original site of "Zion." A notable illustration will be found in the case of Rabbath Ammon (§ 94). "The city," says Ewald, "is known to have been called Jebus by the Canaanites; and since this name may signify a *dry* mountain, so that, changing the name but preserving the signification, it might be called Zion, we may draw the conclusion, confirmed by all the circumstances, that the erection of the whole city began from the broad dry mountain to the south, which easily formed a strong citadel, whence the rest of the city gradually spread farther and farther to the north and east." Other scholars, it must be remembered, would translate Zion as the "sunny."

93. The course of **the walls of Jerusalem** may be traced on the Map. The **first wall** ran round the south-western hill. Starting from where the Tower of David, so called, now stands, it ran due east along the southern edge of the Tyropœon, a strong well-fortified wall, on which much labour and skill were expended to render it impregnable. It went round the western and southern border of the same hill, a rock-

scarp 50 feet high, with bases of towers every 400 feet, still marking its course. There are also parts of the deep fosse or gutter which ran without the wall yet remaining. A second wall surrounded Acra, or Millo.

Regarding the course of **the second wall**, there has been much discussion, stimulated by the interest attaching to the traditional site of the Holy Sepulchre. A glance at the plan of the ground will show the impossibility of supposing a wall so built on Acra as to exclude the Church of the Holy Sepulchre. Indeed, it is more likely that the second wall included more than is represented on Map IV., extending farther north, and returning by the western edge of the northern branch of the Tyropœon. How far the eastern ridge, where the temple was built, was then occupied with dwellings and fortified does not appear; but the presence of a threshing-floor on its highest point, and the "much building on Ophel" as late as the times of Uzziah, Jotham, and Manasseh (2 Chron. xxvi. 9, xxvii. 3, xxxiii. 14), indicate that it was neither so built upon, nor fortified, as was the natural citadel of Zion, on which the defence of the city depended. The Pool of Siloam seems never to have been enclosed within the walls (Josephus' Speech to Jews, *Wars*, v. 9, 4), and the king's gardens spread below Siloam. At the north end of this ridge, Bezetha, the "new city" of Josephus, stood, on which, in the time of the Maccabees, tents were pitched (1 Macc. vii. 19). Houses and markets nestled in the valley between the hills. Here Joab's buildings may have been (1 Chron. xi. 8). While on the south-western edge of the citadel of Zion, David planted his barracks and armoury.

The position of **Acra** was certainly occupied very soon, as necessary for the defence of the city, and here most likely stood the "outpost" David first captured, and the fortress palace in which he dwelt. The three years' labour of the Maccabees in lowering this rock by at least 30 feet, and filling up the valley on the east, have destroyed, as was their design, its commanding importance. But it is quite possible David had a dwelling upon Ophel also, for Eastern monarchs have many palaces for themselves and their wives and families. The great palace of Solomon stood on the eastern hill adjoining the temple on the south, possibly supplanting a humbler royal residence; for the king's sons had each houses of their own in David's time (2 Sam. xiii. 8, xiv. 24, etc.).

The description of the temple site may be best given, once for all, in the account of Herod's buildings (§ 101–104). It is not possible, and is not necessary, to attempt in this handbook to describe the probable positions of the many gates of Jerusalem of which we read in Nehemiah.

The whole area of the city was at no time very great. Altogether, including the temple area, it did not amount to 250 acres. "Great Babylon" had probably 72,160 acres. But the island-site of Tyre, which affords a much fairer case for comparison, did not exceed 200 acres. Solomon and Hiram appear in this history as allies on equal terms; and one can hardly suppose Solomon's capital to have been less than Hiram's. The population cannot have been as great as is often represented; it possibly never exceeded 30,000 permanent residents. Of course at feast times it was crowded. The figures of Tacitus and Josephus seem great exaggerations. The number of inhabitants has an obvious bearing on the dispute as to the area of the city; and in considering it, we can hardly suppose the houses to have been of any great height, like the many-storied tenements of modern times, though doubtless they were "compactly built together."

The following remarks and *note* of Ewald's on the obscure words Millo and Silla may help to their better understanding:—

"The fortification of the city at the time of David was limited, as far as we can recognise, to the broad mountain of Zion on the south, which became the nucleus of the whole city. In the walls of this 'city of David,' however, a weak point must have been observed, which Solomon improved at considerable expense. This was probably to the north-east, westwards therefore of the temple, not far south of the spot—perhaps even upon the very spot—where the later fortress of the city lay. The only passage besides that just adduced from which we may gather a little more definitely the situation of Millo, is that in 2 Kings xii. 21 (20): 'Beth-Millo, which goeth down to the steps,' for Silla or Salla is probably abbreviated from *soolah'm*, 'steps' (or '*ladder*,' Gen. xxviii. 12), so that it results that from this structure a flight of steps led down into a deep valley. Now such a flight certainly led down from Zion on the west, and another on the south, into the vale of Hinnom (Neh. iii. 15, 19). The mention of Millo so early as in 2 Sam. v. 9 is plainly only a brief description in the language of a later day of the part of the city intended. That Millo is much the same as Akra is proved also by the version of the LXX. 1 Kings xi. 27, and elsewhere. Zion, as well as the mountain north of it, appears to have sloped down rather low into the valley of the Tyropœon, so that Solomon had an earthwork thrown up there, and within the lines erected a fort, which might serve as a powerful defence alike for Zion and the temple. This fortification, which derived from the earthwork the name of Millo, or more fully Beth-Millo, was evidently of considerable extent, and took some years to complete; moreover, it is still spoken of in the following centuries. Later still, Solomon appears to have carried the wall round the mountain on the north and east; since the eastern hill with the temple and palace, and the northern, on which the population of the capital was rapidly increasing, formed one whole with Zion, and required defence. Of course, besides this, the temple, as such, had its own walls. The most northern portion of the city, however, which was so closely connected with Zion, bore from that time the name of Mishneh, *i.e.* second city, which we might translate by New-town" (Ewald's *Hist. of Israel*, iii. 258).

94. The incidents of **David's** later years occurred for the most part on familiar ground.

One of his first acts was to fetch up the ark of God from Kirjath Jearim (2 Sam. vi.). To this Ps. cxxxii. undoubtedly refers. The poet there describes inquirers for the neglected ark as hearing of it at Ephratah or Bethlehem, and finding it in Kirjath Jearim, "the city of the woods." This indicates the road by which the ark was brought up (p. 118). The scene of Uzzah's solemn death is unknown, but the name Peraz (Uzzah) was already connected with the valley-plain of Rephaim (2 Sam. v. 18-20).

In after times, when his kingdom was established (2 Sam. viii.), as well as greatly extended, he was drawn into war with the Ammonites (2 Sam. x.). Their capital, or chief city, Rabbath-Ammon, was an exceedingly strong city, and in many points resembled his own rock-fortress of Zion, as may be seen from the following account:—

"For picturesqueness of situation, I know of no ruins to compare with Ammon. The most striking feature is the citadel, which formerly contained not merely the garrison, but an upper town, and covered an extensive area. The lofty plateau on which it was situated is triangular in shape: two sides are formed by the valleys which diverge from the apex, where they are divided by a low neck, and thence separating fall into the valley of the Jabbok, which forms the base of the triangle, and contained the lower town.

"Climbing up the citadel, we can trace the remains of the moat, and crossing it find ourselves in a maze of ruins. The massive walls

—the lower parts of which still remain, and which, rising from the precipitous sides of the cliff, rendered any attempt at scaling impossible—were evidently Ammonite. As I leant over them and looked sheer down about 300 feet into one wâdy, and 400 feet into the other, I did not wonder at its having occurred to King David that the leader of a forlorn-hope against these ramparts would meet with certain death, and consequently assigning the position to Uriah. The only possible point from which that officer could have advanced was at the apex where the low neck connects the citadel with the high plateau beyond, but even here he would have had to charge up an almost hopeless escarpment. This is confirmed by the account of Joab's messenger to David describing the incident. Portions of the colossal gateway and the massive wall flanking it, at the point where the low neck joins the apex of the triangle, still remain to attest the truth of this narrative, and to identify the spot where Uriah met his fate. Joab afterwards took the lower city, which he called 'the city of waters,' indicating very probably that the Jabbok was dammed into a lake near the lower city, to which the conformation of the valley would lend itself; but the citadel still remained, and was upon the point of being taken, doubtless because its water supply was cut off, and the provisions, after a siege which must have lasted nearly two years, had become exhausted. So David arrives to take part in the final capture of the citadel" (*Land of Gilead*, p. 259 ff.).

The flight of David over Olivet, the hiding of Jonathan and Ahimaaz by Enrogel close under, and so hid by, the city walls, the journey over the plain of Jordan to Mahanaim, and the fight in the wood of Ephraim, where Absalom was slain by his friend and counsellor Joab, can be easily followed from the description of those parts already given. In Conder's *Handbook to the Bible*, p. 341–342, will be found an ingenious suggestion as to David's tomb. It seems to have been well known till the overthrow of Jerusalem (Acts ii. 29), but the determination of its actual position is inextricably mixed up with the discussion of the precise position of the part of Jerusalem called "the city of David" (Appendix III.).

THE DIVIDED KINGDOM.

95. When the land was divided between Rehoboam and Jeroboam, the territory remaining to David's house was very small. It is fully represented in size by the county of Perth. Much of it is of little value, being but desert. It was, moreover, shut in on every side,

The rival kingdom was on the north, the Philistines on the west, and the Arabians on the south. One of the first necessities, therefore, for Rehoboam was to erect fortresses for the defence of his land (2 Chron. xi. 5–12). In the fifth year of his reign his capital was spoiled by Shishak of Egypt. Besides the brief notice of this calamity given from the Jewish side in the Bible (1 Kings xiv. 25, 26, and 2 Chron. xii.), there remains the Egyptian record at Karnak, from which it appears that Shishak, or Sheshank, had come to the help of Jeroboam, who had before sought refuge in, and now help from, Egypt; that he not only conquered and gave to Jeroboam such frontier positions as Ajalon, Bethhoron, Gibeon, and Ephraim, to strengthen him against Judah, but that he subdued for him Taanach, Bethshean, Megiddo, and other Canaanite fortresses, as also the Levitical cities within his territory, which held out for Rehoboam (2 Chron. xi. 13, 14). **The boundary between Judah and Israel** was the valley of Ajalon on the west, and eastward the Wâdy Suweinit, or "valley of thorns," on the edge of which stood Gibeah of Saul. The proverbial "Dan to Beersheba" became "Geba to Beersheba" (2 Kings xxiii. 8). Bethel seems to have belonged sometimes to the one and sometimes to the other, but usually was held by Israel (§ 71). Rehoboam's son Abijah took it and kept it in his time (2 Chron. xiii.). Baasha of Israel recovered it, and proceeded to build Ramah (*Er-Ram*) to protect it; but on being diverted by the attack of the Syrians, he removed the material he had collected, and strengthened his frontier at Geba and Mizpah (2 Chron. xvi. 6).

This borderland, which henceforth was so often the scene of war, is about the most rugged part of the whole land. A narrow watershed winds about the head of the valleys, which cut deep into the hills on the east and the west (§ 63). Ephraim, whence Abijah addressed Israel, is doubtless Ephraim, the Ophrah of Benjamin, which lay 5 miles north-east of Bethel, and is identified with the site of the modern village of Taiyibeh, just beyond Ai. This Ephraim is most likely the Apherema of 1 Macc. xi. 34. Jeshanah, which Abijah took, is now 'Ain Sinia, 5 miles due west of Ephraim, forming with it and Bethel a "trilateral" for the defence of Jerusalem upon the north. In Isaiah, chap. x. 28–31, is a vivid description of the approach of the Assyrian king by this route against Jerusalem. He comes to Ai, 10 miles north of Jerusalem, having left his baggage at Michmash, and crossed **the deep gorge to** Migron (the precipice) at Geba, where his camp is pitched for the night ; Ramah, or Ha-Râmah, now Er-Ram (but 2 miles east), trembles, Gibeah of Saul (possibly at Sahel Jeba, "the plains of Gibea," not 1 mile off) fleeth ; Laish and Gallim (unknown, Beit Jala, near Bethlehem, is much too far off), Anathoth (now 'Anâta, is 3 miles north-east from Jerusalem over the Mount of Olives), Madmenah, Gebim (both unknown), are all in alarm and outcry, and preparing for flight ; but the Assyrian shall advance no farther than Nob (possibly Mizpeh, see Appendix I.). His march is stayed at the northern end of the Olivet range, from which, at Scopus, the last destroyer of Jerusalem viewed the city (Josephus, *Wars*, v. 2, 3).

KINGDOM OF ISRAEL.

96. The territory which revolted from David's house and formed the northern **kingdom of Israel**, was much greater, but it wanted the unity and seclusion which were the strength of Judah. The actual outbreak of revolt occurred at Shechem (1 Kings xii.), and there in the first instance was Jeroboam's capital. On the east of Jordan he fortified Penuel, to maintain his hold on the dwellers in "the wood of Ephraim" and the other trans-Jordanic territory, and to cover his eastern frontier. At Bethel in the south, and Dan in the north, he set up the calf-worship so often alluded to by the prophets. Bethel had certainly, and Dan almost as certainly, been sacred places of worship from before Israel's time. Close to the site of Dan is a dolmen-centre (§ 39), and not far to the west is a great mound, still known as Tell el 'Ajjul, that is, "the hill of the calves." The adoption of these sites and their familiar heathen rites was as thorough a rejection of Jehovah's worship at Jerusalem as Jeroboam could have devised. The beauty of Tirzah attracted Jeroboam (§ 82), and it became the capital of the northern kingdom till Omri purchased the hill of Shemer and built **Samaria** (1 Kings xvi.). The position was well chosen, for the hill stands out as a great "mamelon" entirely clear on every side. On this conical mountain Omri perched his city; and so unassailable was it by the engines of war in ancient times, that it seems only to have been reduced, often as it was besieged, by starving it out. Ahab, Omri's son, built Jezreel on the westmost spur of the mountains of Gilboa. The site is a choice one, though now occupied by a miserable village. Nothing but the rock-cut wine-presses remain of its once enviable vineyards. From its site

a fine view is had eastward towards Bethshean and the mountains of Bashan beyond Jordan, by the Wâdy Jâlûd, up which Jehu drove his chariot (2 Kings ix. 17-20); and westward, along the plain of Esdraelon (or Jezreel), shut in by the hills of Nazareth on the right and the Carmel range on the left. Three or four miles due north lies the Shunem of Elisha. Away over the Jordan lay Ramoth Gilead, on whose plain Ahab was mortally wounded when at war with Syria, aided by Jehoshaphat.

97. Jezreel is closely linked with the history of **Elijah**, as it was during that prophet's ministry that Ahab was building his palace and city there. From Ahab's and Jezebel's rage he went and hid by the brook Cherith. The expression "before Jordan" seems, as usually, to mean *east* of Jordan and the Jarmûk (§ 69), or one of its tributaries may have been the hiding-place of "the inhabitant of Gilead." With his meeting there with the priests of Baal, **Carmel** is indissolubly associated. The scene was not the highest point of Carmel; though it, no doubt, was a place of sacrifice, and the stones still there may mark the spot where Vespasian, according to Tacitus, offered sacrifice in honour of an ancient custom. It commands a magnificent view. Eastward the eye ranges for 20 miles over the plain towards the mountains of Gilboa and Jezreel at their base 18 miles off. The site of Nazareth is marked by a tower on the hill to the north of it, for lying 12 miles away in a basin of the hills right across the plain it is not itself visible. The name Mahrakah, or burning, attaches to the summit, but the scene of the sacrifices to Baal and Jehovah has been placed on a plateau just below it. "There is a cliff at the north side of El Mahrakah some 50 or 60 feet high, and beneath is a little plateau, with a well cut in the rock, and shaded by a large tree. The well (Bîr el Mansûrah) contained water in the autumn of 1872" (*Memoirs*, i. p. 265). "It is a glade overlooking the plain, somewhat in the shape of an amphitheatre, and completely shut in on the north by the well-wooded cliffs. No place could be conceived more adapted by nature to be that wondrous battle-field of truth. In front of the principal actors in the scene, with the king and his courtiers by their side, the thousands of Israel might have been gathered on the slopes, witnesses of the whole struggle and its

stupendous results" (Tristram). Dr. Thomson (*Land and Book*, p. 484) thinks this well would not hold out in a drought, and supposes Elijah to have had water fetched from the springs of Kishon. But Tristram mentions his finding molluscs attached to the stones within its cistern, "which, unlike most of the other families of fresh-water molluscs in Palestine, never bury themselves in mud, and are very sensitive to removal from water, existing only in permanent streams and pools. They are found in all the perennial rivers of the country, and in such fountains as those of Engedi and Jericho, but never in the streams or wells which are occasionally dry. We examined all the fountains of the neighbourhood, but in this one, and this alone, did we find this little *Neritina*, plainly showing that this spring continues to flow when all the others are dry." As the Mahrakah is at the south-eastern or landward end of Carmel, 12 miles from the sea, it could not have been thence the water was fetched if this was the spot. Mr. L. Oliphant has suggested another site 1 mile north of Mahrakah, within 10 minutes of the top of the hill, and at the same distance from tanks, from which he says "water in any quantity, even at that time of drought, could have been supplied, and within a hundred yards of which the path leads down to the Tell el Kussis (the hill of the priests), the traditional site of the massacre" (*Palestine Quarterly Statement*, 1884, p. 44). He mentions also what, with the many rock-cut wine-presses and the olive-presses still found, illustrates the excellency of Carmel in the days of its cultivation, that within a radius of $2\frac{1}{2}$ miles of the spot where he would locate Elijah's sacrifice, he counted the ruins of no fewer than twelve ancient towns and villages on the various hill-tops and mountain spurs which surround it. Thus has Carmel, famed for its beauty and fertility and population, become a wilderness (Isa. xxxiii. 9; Amos i. 2). Elijah's flight from Jezreel to Beersheba was a journey of 100 miles; and from thence to "*the* cave in Horeb" was 250 miles more. The last scene in Elijah's life takes us back to familiar ground. With Elisha he went to Gilgal, now Jiljiliah. Thence they went to Bethel, 7 miles south by east. From Bethel they went down past Ai to Jericho. From Jericho they crossed the plain to the Jordan by the other Gilgal, where so long the camp of Israel had stood, and where the covenant rite of circumcision had been renewed. Over Jordan they went dry-shod, as Israel had come, and went on beyond it, till they were beneath the shadow of Pisgah, whence Moses had looked upon their track, and there in manner as in place the departure of Elijah was as that of Moses.

Tiphsah, the scene of King Menahem's cruel outrage (2 Kings xv. 16), now bears the name of Tafsah. It is 8 miles south-west of Shechem.

KINGDOM OF JUDAH.

98. Turning again to the Kingdom of Judah, we may mark some of the more memorable places in its later history. First. Against Asa, Rehoboam's grandson, came Zerah the Ethiopian some thirty years after the invasion of Shishak, and encamped at Mareshah (2 Chron. xiv.). Asa confronted him there, in the valley of Zephathah, and smote him and pursued him to Gerar. Mareshah is no doubt Mer'ash, 1 mile south-east of Beit Jibrin, and Asa may have been encamped at Sâfieh on the other side of that city. Zerah, who very probably was an Ethiopian conqueror of Egypt (Brugsch) seeking to possess the Philistine country and advance his conquests thence, was thus overthrown.

Second. In the days of Asa's son Jehoshaphat, the Moabites, Ammonites, and others came up by Engedi "by the ascent of Ziz," 2 Chron. xx., the name of which appears in the earliest name Hazezon Tamar, and also survives in the modern name Wâdy Husâsah of a valley running north-westwards from Engedi. These Moabites and their allies, ascending to the level of the Jeshimon, and crossing it in a north-westerly line, would strike the road between Hebron and Jerusalem near where the ruins of Breikût now stand. Conder recognises in this the name Berachah. "The valley of blessing" would be in that case the broad, flat, fertile Wâdy 'Arrûb, where the invaders, emerging from the gorge leading up from the wilderness, and spreading their tents, may well be supposed to have quarrelled over their spoil, or their future route, and so, as they fell on one another, to have been inextricably entrapped by the surrounding ambushments.

Third. In the days of Uzziah (2 Chron. xxvi.), the Edomites were subdued and Elah rebuilt at the head of the Red Sea ; the Philistines also were so entirely defeated that the walls of their chief cities were cast down ; the Arabians, too, were conquered who dwelt in Gur-Baal, as also the Mehunim, or Maonites. Maon lies 8 miles due south of Hebron ; from thence a ridge runs out southward trending to the west, which, 18 miles from Maon, ends in the prominent hill *El Ghŭrrah*, "a square-topped hill, some 1800 feet above the sea." To the west of this ridge is the Wâdy Ghŭrrah, draining towards Beersheba. In the hill El Ghŭrrah we may recognise the eastern limit of the Arabians whom Uzziah subdued along his whole southern boundary "to the entering in of Egypt."

Fourth. The site of **Megiddo**, where Josiah fell, is yet undetermined.

Robinson placed it at Lejjûn, at the edge of the plain of Esdraelon, 9 miles west of Jezreel. Thomson prefers "the bold artificial 'Tell el Mutzellim,'" about a mile to the north of Lejjûn, undoubtedly the site of an ancient city, and a strong position naturally. Conder suggests Mujedd'a, an important site with ruins of a strong city, 3 miles south of Bethshean, as a twin fortress with it, closing the eastern end of the plain of Jezreel. Megiddo was an important fortress even before the time of Israel's coming into the land, and is mentioned in the Egyptian records in the narrative of the campaign of Thothmes III. against its inhabitants, and those of the neighbouring Kadesh. (See *Records of the Past*, vol. i.) "Geuta," 'Ai, 'Anzu, Tuti, Raba, and the waters of Kaina, are named in his lists at Karnak. These have been identified by Conder, with great likelihood, as Jett, Kefr, R'ai, 'Anza, Umm el Tût, Raba, Ka'ûn, which will be found lying from west to east on a line 8 miles north of Samaria, the last-named being 4 miles south of Mujedd'a. His enemies "were standing at the main roads of Aaruna" (no doubt Arâneh, 5 miles north of Umm el Tût) to resist his descent into the plain of Jezreel by Engannin. He may have crossed the hills down into the Jordan valley to outflank them, and seize Megiddo undefended. There is a curious passage in the travels of an Egyptian officer in the time of the Judges, journeying south, whose words are thus translated by Brugsch (ii., p. 106, Eng. ed.) :—"Describe Bethsheal (*i.e.* Bethshean), Thargaal, the Ford of Jirduna how it is crossed. Teach me to know the passage, in order to enter into the city of Makitha (Megiddo) which lies in front of it." Others translate "Jelden" for "Jirduna," which *might* be Jalûd, though both forms suggest Jordan.

As regards the scene of Josiah's defeat and death, it is connected also in a special way with Hadad-rimmon. If this be Rummânch, as most think, it takes us rather towards Lejjûn than Mujedd'a.

A difficult passage occurs in 2 Kings xxvii. (see also 2 Chron. xxii. 9) in describing the flight of the king of Judah from Jehu, when he went out with his cousin the king of Israel to meet Jehu coming up the plain of Jezreel from beyond Jordan. Captain Conder suggests that he turned and fled to the north. "The garden house" he retains as "Beth-haggan," placing it at Beit-Jenn; the ascent of Gur he would put at Kâra; and Ibleam he identifies, as Dr. Thomson before had done, with "Yebla," supposing him to have taken the road away from Jezreel, bending round, after he was wounded, by the chariot road which led past Bethshean to Mujedd'a. If he fled south, and Ibleam be regarded as the same as Bileam, and placed at Belameh south of Engannin, he must have turned west thereafter, if Megiddo were at Lejjûn; if it was at Mujedd'a, he would cross the hills like Thothmes, eastward. At Engannin he was equidistant from both sites; but to turn from Engannin to Lejjûn was nearly to face right about; to turn towards Mujedd'a was to go off at a right angle to his left.

If Josiah came up the Jordan valley to resist Pharaoh coming eastward by the plain of Esdraelon, he might very well take his stand at Mujedd'a, but the difficulty as to Hadad-rimmon already mentioned, remains.

Fifth. Riblah, where Josiah's son was put in chains by the triumphant Pharaohnecho, lies 35 miles north-east of Baalbeck on the Orontes (see § 37, 78).

WARS OF THE MACCABEES.

99. Before passing to the New Testament history, it may be well to give a brief account of the places which became notable during the wars of the Maccabees. The home of Matthias, the father of those heroes, was at Modin, 16 miles north-west from Jerusalem, on the way to Lydda, by the valley of Ajalon. He was the great-grandson of Hasmon of the line of Eleazar, and hence the name of Hasmoneans. The first encounter which Judas, son of Matthias, had with the Greek soldiers was at the top of the pass of Bethhoron, down which, as in ancient times, the routed foes of Israel were driven. His second battle was fought, and won, at the foot of the valley of Ajalon at Emmaus, also called Nicopolis (not the Emmaus of Luke, § 118), where he surprised the enemy. A third assault was attempted by the valley of Elah, and met and repelled at Bethsur, where the road up that valley attains the watershed 15 miles south of Jerusalem. Having made good his possession of the capital, Judas made successive raids,

southwards by Acrabbim against the Idumeans, and eastward against the Ammonites, whom he overthrew at Jazer, on the ravine which formed the old boundary of Gad (§ 56). When revenge for this defeat was attempted against the Jews in Bashan, he hastened to their relief, first at Bozrah, then at Dametha, now Dâmeh, in the Argob, following his smitten foe to Ashteroth Karnaim, which is 150 miles from Jerusalem. The next attack of the Greeks under Lysias was delivered from the south, and was met by Judas at Râs Sherifeh, close by the springs of Solomon's pools beyond Bethlehem, where his forces were overawed by the elephants used by the Greeks and routed utterly. This is known as the battle of Beth Zacharias. After a skirmish at the village of Salama, *Selâmeh*, below Modin, in which he was victorious, Judas lay in ambush for his foe Nicanor at Adasa, 1 mile north of Neby Samwîl, and falling unexpectedly upon him, slew him and scattered his forces in precipitous flight down the valley of Ajalon. His last battle was on the old border of Judah and Israel, near Bezetho, *Bir es Zeit*, 10 miles north-east of Eleasa, *Il'asa*, near Modin, whence he started. Here he was defeated and slain. The position of other cities mentioned in Maccabean story are known and already described, save perhaps Jamnia (Map V.), the ancient Jabneel, now *Jebnah*, which commanded the plain at the foot of the valley of Sorek, near which was also Cedron, now *Katrah*. As the whole effort of the Maccabees centred in the defence of Jerusalem and its holy place, the area of their conflicts, save in the raids of Judas, was very limited, and their battle-fields lay about the city, or the approaches to it from the east and south and north.

Of the other apocryphal books as Judith, so far as needful, brief descriptions of the towns named will be found in the Index.

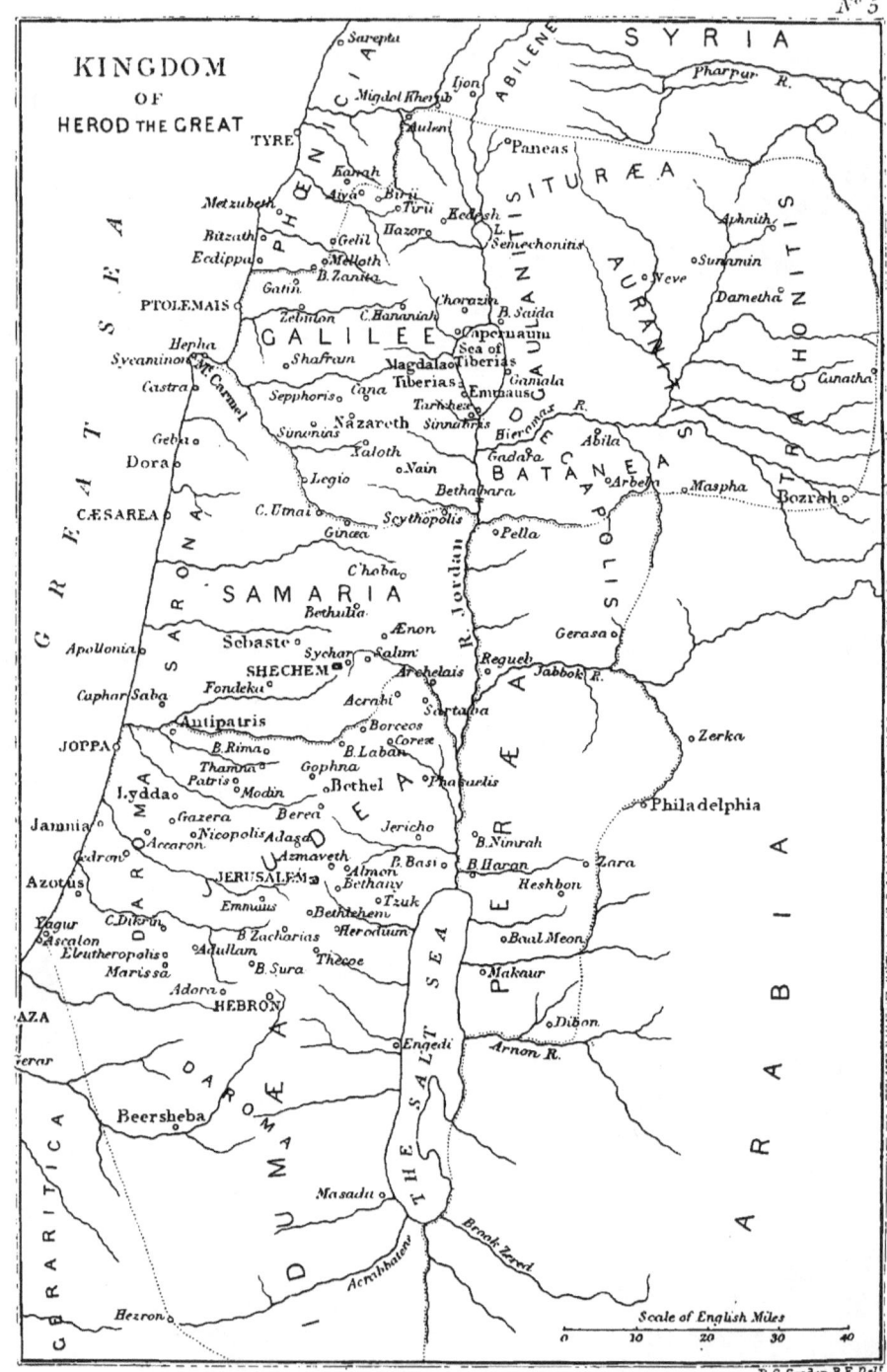

CHAPTER IX

PALESTINE OF THE NEW TESTAMENT.

(*See* MAP V.)

TERRITORIAL DIVISIONS.

100. A COMPARISON of Maps II. and V. will show the changes in the territorial divisions of the land which followed the captivity of Israel and Judah. In accordance with the custom of the Assyrian conquerors to transfer the nations they subdued from their own lands to break up their associations and national unity and fuse them with other tribes, Israel was carried far off to the east, and eastern peoples were planted in Israel (2 Kings xvii.). These formed a new centre of religious and national life in **Samaria**, which was regarded by the Jews with fierce antipathy. We see this already in the days of Ezra and Nehemiah. In the days of the Maccabees the enmity was intensified. According to the rabbis, Samaria was no part of the Holy Land, it was the land of the Cuthim. The exact bounds of this "heathen" or "alien" district are not easily fixed. Considerable difficulty is caused by the habit of the Romans to give "towns" to favoured governors for the sake of their revenues chiefly, while the surrounding country was left under the local ruler of the district. For example, Josephus (*Ant.* xv. 4) recounts how the insatiable Cleopatra acquired the cities along the sea-shore of Palestine as well as Jericho on the east, and rented them to Herod. The scruples of the Jewish rabbis led them to deny a place within the Holy Land to Cæsarea and Ascalon where there were heathen temples. But the general line of demarcation of Samaria may be easily stated. On the south it very much corresponded, as might be expected, with the boundary between Benjamin and Ephraim (§ 71). That boundary was however not so fixed,

especially about Bethel on the watershed, as is commonly supposed. It shifted with the relative strength of the northern and southern kingdom, even before the captivity, and during the time of the Maccabees also. At one time Lydda, Ramathem, and Apherema (1 Macc. xi. 34) were taken from Samaria and added to Judea. The first and last are known as Lydda and Ophrah, and the central Ramathem must have been about Ramallah, in the mountains of Ephraim. At a later time the territory of Judea went as far north as Shiloh and Lebonah, within 10 miles of Shechem. To the east of this the boundary must have descended to the Jordan by the Wâdy Far'ah, and on the west to the north of Tibneh and Antipatris, which were in Judea, reaching to the Mediterranean, and cutting off the upper part of the plain of Sharon, where Cæsarea stood, which was not in Judea (Acts xii. 19).

On the north, the south border of the great plain of Esdraelon —the boundary of Manasseh—was the limit of Samaria.

Galilee was divided into "upper" and "lower." Lower Galilee included all Issachar and Zebulun and what of Naphtali lay west of the Sea of Galilee. Upper Galilee contained the rest of Naphtali's inheritance, Asher's portion having become Phœnician.

The various districts included in the ancient lot of Manasseh to the east of Jordan are laid down on the Map (and see § 23); these constituted the territory of **Philip the tetrarch** (Luke iii. 1). Gad and Reuben were embraced in "**Perea**."

Judea was divided into eleven toparchies, and besides these included Gebalene, which was the Edomite "Mount Seir;" the Negeb, or Daroma; the whole sea-shore of Philistia, from about Gerar in the south, by Ekron and Lydda to the Samaritan border; with the Shephelah, or lower hill district, which lay between Philistia and Judah. The Samaritan district alone was held to be "without" the land of Israel, and so defiled that what passed through it was rendered impure.

The number of "Herods" mentioned in Scripture, and the frequent changes in the districts they ruled, is confusing.

The following table may help the reader of the Gospels and Acts to understand the territories which were, at different times, under the rule of the several members of that family:—

1. Herod the Great. His kingdom is shown on Map V.
2. On his death his kingdom was divided among his sons thus:—
    (1) Archelaus had Judea, with Samaria and Idumea, till 7 A.D. (Matt. ii. 22).
    (2) Antipas had Galilee and Perea (Luke ix. 7–9, xiii. 31, xxiii. 5–12).
    (3) Philip had Batanea, Trachonitis, Auronitis, Gaulonitis, and Iturea (not to be confounded with Philip of Mark vi. 17, who had no dominion).
3. Herod Agrippa I., grandson of Herod the Great, succeeded bit by bit to all his kingdom. *First*, in A.D. 37 he received (3); *second*, A.D. 39 he received (2); and *finally*, A.D. 41, the much-coveted territory (1) was given him. He died A.D. 44 (Acts xii.).
4. Herod Agrippa II., son of preceding, in A.D. 52 received (3), and A.D. 54 some towns, including Tiberias, in Galilee and Perea. He is Agrippa of Acts xxv., and sided with the Romans against the Jews when Jerusalem was destroyed A.D. 70.

THE TEMPLE OF HEROD.

101. **The temple at Jerusalem** is the link between the Old and New Testament. As originally built by Solomon, it stood on the hill of **Moriah**. Its size was not great. Immediately adjoining it on the south stood the great palace of Solomon. The hill thus consecrated is surrounded on every side by valleys, save at the north-west, where it is joined by a narrow neck (§ 91) to the higher hill of Bezetha. Afterwards, to separate it entirely, a moat was cut, which excavations have shown to be 150 feet wide, and 60 feet deep, on the side next the temple. The temple did not stand close to this cutting, for here the ridge was too narrow, being contracted by a valley discovered to have run where now the north-east corner of the Haram is. The fortress "**Baris**" of the Maccabees, and Antonia of later times—"the castle" of Acts xxi. 34—stood over this moat on the south and protected the temple. The area now vacant, about the Mosque of Omar, which occupies the site of the temple, is thus far greater than the temple area of even Herod's time; and that was, as Josephus avers, double that of Solomon's.

Right opposite on the slope of Olivet one has the best view of the great vacant space which now stretches for one-third of a mile north and south (see *East Wall*, Map IV.). It reaches from the south-east corner, where the rock-level 2278 is marked to the end of the *black* line, just beyond the mark 2320. The whole space between the east wall and the citadel, where the valley is shown, is now levelled up by an enormous accumulation of rubbish which entirely obliterates all traces of the valley above ground. Looked at from Olivet, the wall seems about 40 to 50 feet high outside; within it is little more than half of that, owing to the accumulation of debris. The wall from top to bottom, where it crosses the bed of the valley, is, however, actually 170 feet. The lower courses of masonry are hewn at the joints and round the margin, securing thus a good joint, but the faces are exceedingly rough, the undressed centres projecting from 12 to 20 inches in some cases. Mason marks have been found 100 feet under ground, which have been pronounced Phœnician. From the trickling of paint on their upper side it is clear the mark was put on before the stone was laid in its present position, and suggests that the stones here used belonged to an earlier building, and have been built in upside down. It is quite likely that stones cast down from Solomon's walls would be used by Herod's workmen in an underbuilding which would not be seen, just as they have been found.

The way in which this deep valley came to be filled up is thus described (Josephus, *Wars*, i. 7, 3):—

"But Pompey himself filled up the ditch that was on the north side of the temple, and the entire valley also, the army itself being obliged to carry the materials for that purpose. And indeed it was a hard thing to fill up that valley, by reason of its immense depth, especially as the Jews used all the means possible to repel them from their superior station; nor had the Romans succeeded in their endeavours, had not Pompey taken notice of the seventh days, on which the Jews abstain from all sorts of work on a religious account, and raised his bank, but restrained his soldiers from fighting on those days; for the Jews only acted defensively on Sabbath days. But as soon as Pompey had filled up the valley, he erected high towers upon the bank, and brought those engines which they had fetched from Tyre near to the wall, and tried to batter it down; and the slingers of stones beat off those that stood above them, and drove them away; but the towers on this side of the city made very great resistance, and were indeed extraordinary both for largeness and magnificence."

Southward of this valley of Bezetha the rock rises rapidly till at the Golden Gate (which occupies the position of an old gate which some identify with the "Beautiful Gate") the accumulated debris is but 30 feet deep. For 400 feet or so, the rock runs about level; thereafter it slopes downward rapidly till at the south-east corner it is some 80 feet below the present surface. At that corner the wall, as it stands, is 156 feet high. The masonry here is about the best in all the walls, and some of the stones are very great (Mark xiii. 1). One, at the angle, a good way above the present surface, is 26 feet long, and over 6 feet high by 7 feet broad. It must weigh over 100 tons. It is said to be the heaviest though not the longest in the walls. It is known that a bridge spanned the Kidron. Sir C. Warren would place it opposite the Golden Gate, where a span of 600 feet would need to be crossed; others therefore propose to put it about 100 feet from the south end of the wall where the distance to a corresponding height on the side of Olivet would be but 300 feet, and where two great archstones project from the wall. The position of this bridge, known as **the red heifer bridge,** cannot now be fixed.

The appearance which the wall suddenly presented to one coming over Olivet from the east, must have been most impressive. Terraces once existed, formed by great retaining walls, parts of which have been found, but which, with the soil and the roadways they upheld, have been hurled into the Kidron. The drawings of Sir C. Warren show a vast accumulation of about 70 feet of rubbish plastered, so to say, upon the western side of the Kidron valley, with the effect, as already stated, of pushing the course of the stream 70 feet eastward, and lifting it up the eastern side 40 feet above its original level. But though some considerable portion of this is, without doubt, the debris of Solomon's city and temple, and may have hid the base of Herod's great wall, that wall must have been, on the average, 80 to 100 feet high, as seen along its whole course in the time of our Lord.

102. The other **walls enclosing and retaining the great** levelled **platform** on which the temple stood, were not seen to the same advantage. From the south-east corner **the south wall** runs westward for about 920 feet. This is 100 feet beyond the whole breadth of the eastern ridge at this point: and by so much does the wall cross beyond the valley bed between Moriah and Zion, and rest upon the eastern slope of the latter hill. As **the western wall,** which is 1600 feet long, is built

over and across ancient aqueducts, it seems more than probable that the original enclosure of the temple was much narrower, and rested wholly on Moriah, to which exclusively sanctity was ascribed. Close to the southern end of the west wall are the projecting stones which formed the spring of **Robinson's Arch**, and more than a third of its length to the north those of **Wilson's Arch**. These arches are so called from their discoverers. The bridge to which the former belonged led across the Tyropœon to a point on Zion at the same level, 350 feet westward. The spring-stone indicates an arch spanning 40 feet, at which distance the first pier of the bridge was accordingly found. It stood above an older pavement between the two hills. Beneath it 20 feet of rubbish were found lying on the top of an old rock-cut passage, which was 12 feet high, and a cistern, out of which a conduit was traced north and south for a considerable distance. No doubt this is the bridge more than once mentioned by Josephus (*Wars*, i. 7, 2). The key-stone, with its neighbours, was found where it fell upon the old pavement just mentioned.

Between the two arches named (Robinson's and Wilson's) is that part of the wall familiar as "**the Jews' Wailing Place.**" At this point, though there is still a steep descent to it, the rock was found to be 80 feet below the present surface. Close by a colossal lintel stone, 24 feet long, may be seen only 10 feet above the level of the ground. For other 20 feet the side pillars go down into the rubbish; through it (known as Barclay's gate) a passage led up by an ascent to the level of the temple courts within. Four such entrances led from the west into the courts. On the south are yet the remains of two of the subterranean passages which led up an ascending tunnel into the temple area.

The present north wall includes the site of **Antonia**, which stood on a rock 20 feet higher than the level of the temple courts; the ground, elsewhere so greatly levelled up, being at this north-west corner levelled down.

The age of these walls it is quite impossible to determine. Some parts may be as old as Solomon's day, though this seems improbable. It is much more likely that we see in the great substructures of the present walls the work of Herod—at some places building on the older foundations and using what of the old material was available. The mixed style and quality of work in the undoubtedly oldest parts would be thus accounted for.

103. The **Citadel** on the north was an exceedingly strong fortress. There of old stood in all probability the Tower of Hananeel—afterwards the famous Baris or Antonia. It had four great towers, with an inner court. It was an almost impregnable place. During the Roman possession, it was a convenient watch-tower over the temple courts which it overlooked, the soldiers being always at hand to quell the oft-recurring riots there (Acts xxi.). It was in reality a "fortress palace;" for it was also the **Prætorium** of Pilate. When this part is cut off from the present Haram area, it will be seen that the remainder, as indicated by the red lines on the Map, is approximately a square such as the temple court is stated to have been.

Along the south side of the temple court ran the famous **Royal cloister** of Herod, which was 105 feet broad, being divided into three arcades; the centre one being 45 feet broad and 100 feet high, and the two side ones each 30 feet broad and 50 feet high. This cloister was thus alone greater than York Minster or Westminster Abbey. The bridge which crossed the Tyropœon at Robinson's arch ran straight with the central colonnade. At the south-east corner the roof of the cloister was 326 feet above the bed of the Kidron. The height of the **pinnacle**, which is said to have risen at that corner, is unknown; whatever it was, it must be added to that giddy height of 326 feet. Round the other sides the cloisters were only double, not treble as at the south. That on the east was, according to Josephus, *Ant.* xx. 9, 7, **the porch which was called Solomon's** (Acts iii. 11, v. 12; John x. 23). He says it was in a deep valley. Possibly a great wall found during the excavations, 46 feet out from the Golden Gate, may have been connected with its substructure, as Josephus assigns it just this width (*Wars*, v. 5, 2). In the same place Josephus adds: "When you go through these (first) cloisters unto the second (court of the) temple, there was a partition made of stone all round, whose height was three cubits; its construction was very elegant; upon it stood pillars, at equal distances from one another, declaring the law of purity, some in Greek, and some in

Roman letters, that 'no foreigner should go within that sanctuary;' for that second court of the temple was called 'the Sanctuary,' and was ascended to by 14 steps from the first court. This court was foursquare" (see also *Ant.* xv. 11, 5, and *Wars*, vi. 2, 4). In 1871, Mons. C. Ganneau entering a cemetery at the north-west of the Haram area, noticed a stone with Greek letters which proved to be one of the inscribed stones thus mentioned by Josephus. On it is written : " No stranger to enter within the railing and enclosure about the holy place, and whoever is taken will himself be to blame for his death following" (*Memoirs*, Jerusalem vol., p. 423). The words of the inscription explain Acts xxi. 28, 29, xxiv. 11, and xxvi. 21 ; as also Eph. ii. 12-22. From the fact that Trophimus, whose "supposed" bringing within the "holy place" provoked the riot which ended in Paul's imprisonment, was an Ephesian, we may be sure the peculiar significance of the apostle's words was perfectly understood, and the personal reference appreciated.

104. Within this "partition wall" called "Soreg," was an area said to be 500 cubits square ; here, not quite in the middle, but to the west of the northern half, stood **the temple** proper. It included, first, **the court of the women**, 8 feet higher than the outer court. Ten feet above that again was the **court of Israel**; then **the court of the priests** on a level 3 feet higher ; and lastly, **the temple floor**, 8 feet above this, and therefore 29 feet above the level of the outer court of the Gentiles. It is most interesting to know that these levels correspond exactly with the ascertained rock-levels round about the Sakhrah or "holy stone," now covered by the Mosque of Omar. That stone undoubtedly was of old time the resting-place of the ark of the covenant. "The house" on the mountain was 70 cubits wide by 100 cubits long. The façade was 100 cubits in breadth and height, and was gilded, and over its great entrance "was spread out a golden vine, with its branches hanging down from a great height, the largeness and fine workmanship of which was a surprising sight" (*Ant.* xv. 11, 3). The Sakhrah projects from the floor of the mosque, a bare and undressed rock, at a level of 2446 feet above the sea. In front of it stood the great altar of burnt-offerings. A line from the temple entrance through the centre of the altar reached to the highest point

of Olivet, due east. The summit of Olivet was but 90 feet above the top of the temple façade. Beneath the rock have been found vast reservoirs for water, one of which, called the Great Sea, could alone contain 3,000,000 gallons. It is not possible to trace all the elaborate system of water storage and draining till free access is obtained for examination of the whole area. Such arrangements were absolutely essential in connection with all the sacrifices and ablutions of the temple services.

The building was undertaken by Herod to conciliate the Jews; and similarly the great enlargement of its "court of the Gentiles" was designed to please the Gentiles. It was begun B.C. 20, that is, 16 years previous to our Lord's birth, the vulgar era being in error by 4 years. A year and a half completed the temple itself; but 8 years were occupied on the surrounding buildings, and from that time onward the work of adornment went on, so that when our Lord was "about 30 years of age" (Luke iii. 23), it had been 46 years on hand (John ii. 20).

OTHER BUILDINGS BY HEROD THE GREAT.

105. Herod's buildings were not confined to Jerusalem. Of his other more important buildings may be mentioned Cæsarea, which became a most important garrison city, covering an area little less than Jerusalem itself. It lies on the Mediterranean some 32 miles north of Joppa (Acts x.) and 25 south from Carmel (Josephus, *Ant.* xv. 9, 6, and *Wars*, i. 23). Twelve years were spent on the work; the construction of the artificial harbour being a great undertaking. Here Herod built a temple in honour of Cæsar, after whom the city was named (see *Memoirs*, ii. 13-29, for full plans of the ruins, etc.). To show if possible yet more entirely his disregard for all religions, he built also a temple for the Samaritan worship upon **Gerizim**. This was originally set up by Sanballat, and was soon transformed into the scene of all the more wonderful incidents of traditional importance. The sacred rock, which has a cave, lies on the eastmost point of the summit of the mountain. Ruins, chiefly of Christian buildings, are scattered about. To the west, on a spur of the moun-

tain by which travellers usually ascend, is the Samaritan place of Passover observance—a dry-stone enclosure, within which is a small trough where the lamb is still roasted yearly. The claim that here was the scene of Gen. xxii. has been already mentioned. To this mountain the woman of Sychar undoubtedly referred (John iv. 20). The interest of Samaritan tradition is, however, rather a matter of archæology than of geography.

Samaria, which had been taken after a year's siege by John Hyrcanus, B.C. 109, and then devastated, Herod also rebuilt, when on the death of Antony and Cleopatra, Augustus bestowed it on him. Remains of his buildings vindicate the accounts of Josephus (*Ant.* xv. 8, 5; *Wars*, i. 20, 3, and 21, 2). According to his usual custom, Herod named it after the Roman emperor, calling it Sebaste, the equivalent in Greek for Augustus. It is referred to in Acts viii. 5 as the scene of Philip's preaching and working of miracles. And apparently it was here he first met with and baptized Simon Magus. Though in the R. V. it is translated "the city of Samaria," many regard the correct rendering to be "*a* city of Samaria;" but of those who do so, several understand the city "Sebaste" to be intended though not named.

Two other places where Herod's great activity was displayed were Machærus in the gorge of the Callirhoe (§ 26 and § 111) and Jericho. The latter grew under him into wealth and fame. About it he built forts, a new town, named Phasælus from his brother, a great palace, and a splendid theatre. There he died, and in his theatre his death was announced to a relieved people. Destroyed in a tumult soon after his death, his palace was rebuilt with yet greater magnificence by Archelaus, who founded yet another new town, and called it after his own name, and watered it by an aqueduct from Neæra or Naarath. It was one of the most beautiful and wealthy places of the land in our Lord's time, and many priests and Levites dwelt in it (Luke x. 31, 32). The way down from Jerusalem to Jericho is a steep and wild pass, often to this day the haunt of robbers. The distance is about 18 miles, and the road goes "down" from Jerusalem, which is 2500 feet above sea-level, to Jericho, which is over 800 feet below it. (See also Betharam in Index.)

SCENES OF OUR LORD'S LIFE.

106. At **Bethlehem**, *Beit Lahm*, 5 miles south of Jerusalem, Jesus Christ was born. A long accumulating story invested the town already with peculiar interest. It stands on a narrow ridge which runs out eastward from the watershed. The ridge is made up of two swelling heights, the greater being on the west. "On both north and south are valleys rapidly deepening eastwards, on the terraced sides of which grow vines, olives, and fig-trees. The position is naturally strong, and the fields which roll away eastward attractive to husbandmen like Boaz and sheep-masters like Jesse. Bethlehem has no natural water-supply. To the north-west of the town are 3 ancient and extensive cisterns on a flat rock-terrace, which are called Bîr Dâûd, traditionally the well by the gate of Bethlehem, 2 Sam. xxiii. 14–16" (*Memoirs*, iii. 28). Dr. Wilson pointed out the accuracy of the narrative which calls it always a "well," not a "spring," though the incident might have suggested the latter (*Lands of the Bible*). The site of Bethlehem is beyond dispute; it is mentioned as early as the time of Jacob, and as late as that of Nehemiah. It is to-day a town with a population of 5000 inhabitants, who are industrious and wealthy; they have numerous flocks and herds, and the wine of its extensive vineyards is reckoned among the best which the Land yields. The traditional spot where the manger stood is at the eastern end, where stands the oldest Christian church now existing, undoubtedly the work of the Emperor Constantine. As for the value of the tradition which locates our Saviour's cradle here, that is another matter. The traveller, who finds it guarded by the glittering bayonet of a Turkish soldier set to keep Roman and Greek Churchmen from fighting, feels there is a mistake somewhere. It is a comfort to know that there is no necessity to believe that the true spot is thus desecrated. It has been suggested that the "inn" of Luke ii. 7 is the "inn" of Chimham, Jer. xli. 17, which possibly preserved the name of Barzillai's son, rewarded by Solomon at David's direction (2 Sam. xix. 38–40; 1 Kings ii. 7) with an inheritance at Bethlehem.

107. "**Nazareth**, where He was brought up," lies far away in the hills of Galilee. Its position has been already described. The range

of hills in the upper hollows of which it nestles, rises precipitously 950 feet from the western half of the plain of Esdraelon on the north. The town is not visible even from Carmel, as it lies 1½ mile back from, and 140 feet lower than the front of the range. When in the town, nothing is visible beyond the smooth hill-tops which shut it in. As a Christian town, it is clean and pleasant-looking in comparison with other towns and villages; but it has no special features of beauty. It was an unwalled, retired village, courting obscurity in its upland hollow, and in consequence unnamed in the Old Testament or by Josephus. Apparently the town lay to the west of the site it now occupies. A cliff running down into it, showing several precipices over which a fall would certainly be fatal, is "the brow of the hill" on which it then stood.

The view from the hill above the town on the north is extensive. Standing there one sees, over and beyond the south edge of the enclosing hills, the whole length of Esdraelon east and west, and the hills of Manasseh and Ephraim to the south. Carmel, but a dozen miles away, appears, as seen through a pure atmosphere, almost within touch, and its shadow running as far again north-westward into the sheen on the Mediterranean, is a striking object. Tabor raises its rounded top just over the eastern edge of the basin. Behind it is the Little Hermon range, round the foot of which from north to south lie Endor, Nain, Shunem. Beyond to the right are the mountains of Gilboa and the ruins of Jezreel at their westmost point. In the distance eastward and northward are the Bashan mountains, rugged with long-stretching ridges running from what seem extinct volcanoes. Over the rough plateau of the Galilean hills, the great three-peaked Hermon, scarred and snow-topped, fills in the picture. Northward the eye must in our Lord's time have rested on an attractive prospect. Sepphoris, *Seffûrich*, made by Herod Antipas the most important city of Galilee, taking precedence of Tiberias even, was scarce 4 miles off; and many of the 240 towns numbered, but unhappily not named, by the historian, must with their houses and vineyards and oliveyards and gardens have enlivened and enriched the scene. The only water-supply, beside cisterns, is from the "Virgin's Well;" and in this, as has often been observed, we have the only remains of what existed when our Lord grew up there. " The threshing-floors are on the south below the town." The present population is said to be over 5000, that of Seffûrieh to the north being probably about the half. When twelve years of age, our Lord went up, according to custom, to the Passover with Joseph and Mary. Tradition fixes Beeroth, *Bîreh*, 9 miles north of Jerusalem, as the place from which they turned back to seek Him. As the usual resting-place on the first night of the return journey, it is probably correctly determined, *if* they journeyed through Samaria.

Fifteen gently-rounded hills " seem as if they had met to form an enclosure" for this peaceful basin ; they rise round it like the edge of a shell to guard it from intrusion. It is "a rich and beautiful field" in the midst of these green hills—abounding in gay flowers; in fig-trees, small gardens, hedges of the prickly pear; and the dense rich grass affords an abundant pasture. The expression of the old topographer, Quaresimus, was as happy as it is poetical: " Nazareth is a rose, and, like a rose, has the same rounded form, enclosed by mountains as the flower by its leaves" (*Sinai and Palestine*, p. 365).

"The scenery in the Nazareth hills differs very much in different parts ; round the city itself it consists of rolling, rounded mountains of bare white limestone, but on the west these are hidden beneath a growth of forest trees ; but for the greater part of its extent it is very dense, especially near Harosheth (El Harithîyeh, § 81), a place thence named, where underwood more or less thick is found. Through this forest runs the beautiful valley called Wâdy el Malak, generally rendered 'King's Valley,' but perhaps better 'Valley of Pasture.' Such a valley, with its cool brook and clear springs, its broad corn-fields and patches of turf, its flocks and herds, we may suppose David to have in remembrance in the twenty-third Psalm. On either side the slopes are covered by the oak forest, and innumerable wild doves find shelter for their nests among the branches. For quiet beauty we saw nothing in Palestine equal to this valley" (*Tent Work*, p. 157).

108. **Cana of Galilee** was near Nazareth. There are three candidates for the honour of being the home of Nathanael and the yet greater honour of being the scene of our Lord's first miracle. These are (1) Kefr Kenna, about 5 miles from Nazareth on the road to Tiberias; (2) Khurbet Kâna, 8 or 9 miles north of Nazareth on the farther side of the plain of Buttauf, which at its upper end is a marsh, lying at the base of Jebel Kâna, not 2 miles east of Jotapatah (Josephus, *Wars*, iii.

6 and 7). Dr. Robinson reported this place as having the name Kâna el Jelil, and Sir C. Wilson also says he got it so from a herdsman on the spot; but the evidence seems conclusive that this name is not known among the Moslems, the native Arab peasantry, but only among the Franks. Certainly it cannot be the Cana of Josephus (*Life*, § 16 and 17), where his camp was fixed to command Sepphoris and Tiberias, and from which he made a sudden night-march on the latter. The site of Khurbet Kâna is unsuitable in itself for a camp, needless so close to Jotapatah, and quite remote from the required position. There is no evidence of ruins or water-supply indicating an ancient site. (3) At Reimeh, but 1½ mile from Nazareth, Captain Conder found 'Ain Kânah, to which he draws attention, but there is nothing to indicate that here was a town of that name. The tradition in favour of (1) seems correct. The objection that the town was called Cana, not Kefr Cana (which means "village" of Cana, as in the name Capernaum) repeated by Trench *On the Miracles*, is of little force, and is entirely removed by the discovery of ruins close to the beautiful spring on the west of the town called simply Kenna. Josephus describes his camp as at "a village of Galilee which is named Cana." John may have used the designation Cana of Galilee to distinguish it from the too well-known Cana in Judea, near Antipatris, where Antiochus had fallen in battle with the Arabians (see Josephus, *Ant.* xiii. 15, 1, and Lightfoot, vol. ii. p. 580).

Dr. Zeller, whose residence at Nazareth gave him special facilities for inquiry, is explicit in declaring that the northern Khurbet Kâna is *not* known as Kâna el Jelil among the natives, and that its site has nothing in its favour. The following is his description of Kefr Kenna :—

"*Kefr Kenna* lies 5 miles north-east of Nazareth on the direct road to the Sea of Galilee. It is bordered toward the west and north by the plain of Buttauf. Its situation is particularly suitable, pretty, and healthy, for the village lies on a hill gradually sloping down towards the west, so that the houses, built in terraces up the slope, receive the cool west wind, which has through the plain of Buttauf a free and strong current over the village. On the south the village is separated by a valley from the higher mountains, separating it from Mount

Tabor and the plain of Jezreel. At the south of the village is a copious fountain of excellent water. ... The village covers only the middle and southern slope of the hill, whilst there are sufficient traces that in former times the village was *at least thrice as large*, and the excellent situation, with the copious supply of water, certainly afforded space for a large place. The gardens at the foot of the hill are luxuriant, and the pomegranates produced there the best in Palestine."
... He also notices the existence of cisterns and foundations of great antiquity at the conical hill, or Tell, Kenna already mentioned (*Memoirs*, i. pp. 257 and 391–394). The distance from Kefr Kenna to Tiberias is fully 12 miles (as the crow flies), to *Khan Minyeh* nearly 15, and to *Tell Hum* 17. The road over the highlands is easy, but the descent from there to the Sea of Galilee is steep and tedious, adding a good deal to the length of the journey. To whichever claimant be finally awarded the title to be the scene of the incidents in our Lord's life recorded in John's Gospel, we are in no doubt as to the neighbourhood in which his early years were spent among acquaintance and kinsfolk in and about Nazareth.

Nain, which our Lord must have often seen, if not often visited, lay 8 miles south of Cana, and in a direct line, scarcely so far from Nazareth. It lies on a bare hill at the end of the Little Hermon range, looking out to the west over the plain of Esdraelon. The old rock-cut tombs are the only interest of the now miserable hovels of fanatical Moslems which occupy the site. They are to be seen, both east and west of the town, but the chief places of ancient burial were on the east. They are, appropriately, the only remains of the little town which would have been nameless in Bible story but for our Lord's restoration to its weeping widow of her dead son (Luke vii. 11). It is an easy day's journey from Capernaum (see margin, R. V.).

109. The record of **the Baptist's ministry** is short, and the localities named are few. He was born in the hill country of Judea—tradition says at 'Ain Karim, 4 miles west of Jerusalem; but as to this Scripture is silent. The first place at which we meet him, which we can with tolerable confidence determine, is also the most interesting—the scene of our Lord's baptism, of which we read John i. as at **Bethabara**, or, in Revised Version, Bethany beyond Jordan. Tradition had located

this at the ford over against Jericho; and one reading *Betharabah* (R. V. margin), "the house of the plain," is so far in favour of this. Only Betharabah was a town of Benjamin (Josh. xviii. 22), and therefore *not* beyond Jordan. Possibly the explanation of the doubtful reading of this place is that it refers to Bethabara which led over into *Bethania*, that is, Bashan (§ 23). It was the great ford—and still bears the name of "the ford"—from the eastern end of Esdraelon to Batanea. From thence our Lord could easily reach Cana of Galilee by the third day, whichever of the three rival sites be accepted. "The house of the ford" might be on the east of the river—"in Bethania beyond Jordan."

John also baptized in "Ænon near to Salim, because there were many waters there" (R. V. margin). Ænon simply means "springs," the plural of the often-recurring 'Ain or "En." The Salim of this place is no doubt the Shalem of Gen. xxxiii. 18, and some 7 miles north is 'Ainûn, at the head of the Wâdy Fâr'ah, which is the great highway up from the Damieh ford for those coming from the east by the way of Peniel and Succoth. The situation was a central one, approachable also from the northward (§ 82) and from all Samaria, and by the central main road from the south. The assumption that the place where John baptized must have been in Judea, at least not in Samaria, is without show of proof. It should be recollected, moreover, that John's ministry was nearing its completion, and the Christ having come and entered on His ministry in Jerusalem and Judea, John might withdraw into the half-alien Samaria to prepare His way there also. So it came to pass naturally enough, that when our Lord at the close of His first ministry in Judea had to leave it, He passed northward by Jacob's well at Salim near to the scene of John's labours. Very possibly when he proceeded northwards from Sychar he visited his forerunner at Ænon.

110. **Sychar** is often confused with Shechem, from which it is a mile and half distant. But it is now correctly placed at 'Askar, called in the Samaritan chronicle Ischar, and which, it has been already suggested, is the ancient Asher in the border of Ephraim (§ 73). The woman of Sychar probably drew near the well with her pitcher during the heat of the midday when the field labour, in which possibly she

was engaged, was necessarily suspended. **The well of Jacob**, where she found her Saviour waiting alone for her, is off the main road which leads round the base of Gerizim into the vale of Shechem. If our Lord passed north by Ænon, He would not go by Shechem, but by the route described in § 82—by Tirzah and Bezek, into the plain of Bethshean, then called Scythopolis, ascending by the great Damascus road, which passes Mount Tabor on the east, and striking off westwards when beyond Tabor, to Cana. Over the well of Jacob a church was built, one of the ruined vaults of which covers the mouth of the well. Close by, on the north, is the traditional place of Joseph's sepulchre, and right overhead towers the steep precipice of Gerizim, " this mountain " to which the woman pointed. There is no dispute as to the correctness of the identification of this well with that of Jacob (§ 41), and it is the only spot in Palestine of which we can say with certainty that just here Jesus Christ sat and rested when weary with His journey. It is not to be supposed that He had travelled that morning from Jerusalem, which is over 30 miles away ; or even from Bîreh (§ 107), the distance from which was over 20 miles. There is nothing in the narrative to indicate from what part of Judea our Lord and His disciples started on their northward journey to Cana of Galilee.

111. Apparently the Baptist was not unfamiliar with **Tiberias**, which Herod Antipas built and named from the Emperor Tiberius. The site was that of the ancient Rakkath, a town of Naphtali, whose lot lay on the west of the Sea of Galilee. The town preserves its old site and name, *Tŭbarîya*, and has yet some 2000 inhabitants, about half of whom are Jews. There is no mention of our Lord visiting it. It became a most influential centre of Jewish life and faith, from about the middle of the second century, when the Sanhedrim settled there. There the Mishna was compiled by the close of that century. To this period also must be ascribed the synagogues, the remains of which are yet found in this district. A very full report on these is embodied in a most valuable and conclusive discussion of the matter by Major Kitchener in the "Special Papers" of the *Survey*, pp. 294-305. He fixes their date between 150 A.D. and 300 A.D.

The stronghold of **Machærus**, where John was sent prisoner and afterwards beheaded, was far beyond Jordan in the gorge of the Callirhoe (§ 26).

"The citadel was placed on the summit of the cone, which is the apex of a long flat ridge, running for more than a mile from east to west. The whole of this ridge appears to have been one extensive fortress, the key of which was the keep on the top of the cone, an isolated and almost impregnable work, but very small, being circular, and exactly 100 yards in diameter. The wall of circumvallation can be clearly traced, its foundations all standing out for a yard or two above the surface, but the interior remains are few; one well of great depth, a very large and deep oblong cemented cistern, with the vaulting of the roof still remaining; and—most interesting of all—two dungeons, one of them deep, and its sides scarcely broken in, were the only remains clearly to be defined. That these were dungeons and not cisterns, is evident from there being no traces of cement, which never perishes from the remains of ancient reservoirs, and from the small holes still visible in the masonry, where staples of wood and iron had once been fixed. One of these must surely have been the prison-house of John the Baptist" (Tristram, *Land of Moab*, p. 259).

112. On hearing of the Baptist's death, our Lord, with His disciples, "withdrew apart to a city called **Bethsaida**" (Luke ix. 10, Revised Version). In the other Evangelists this is described as a "desert place" (Matt. xiv. 13; Mark vi. 31), and on "the other side of the Sea of Galilee" (John vi. 1). There the crowds flocked to Him on foot, crossing the Jordan by the ford, 2 miles above the lake. **The scene of the miraculous feeding of the multitude** which followed is, with general consent, placed at Butaiha, at the north-east corner of the Sea of Galilee. Here stood Bethsaida, advanced by Philip from the rank of "a village" to that of "a city," and named by him Julias; and which, as within his territory in Gaulonitis, was not at all likely to be designated as "Bethsaida of Galilee" (John xii. 21). Josephus calls it simply Julias (*Life*, § 72). Though some have thought the site is preserved in the name Mesadiyeh, there are no decipherable remains there; and the probability is that great changes have taken place along this coast, such as are plainly seen at Tiberias, by volcanic action or subsidence which forbids any great hope of the recovery of lost sites.

The following narrative of Canon Tristram's experience is a most exact illustration of the Gospel history, and of great importance in helping to determine the topography. He sailed across from Mejdel on the springing up of a fresh breeze *from the western shore.* After visiting the scene of the feeding of the 5000, and touching at two or three points on the eastern shore, he says :—"But now the wind continued to increase, and the farther we were from a lee-shore the better. The boat would not beat, and, with its lateen sail close to the wind, made very little way. We were nearly in the centre of the lake, so far as we could judge by the distant lights on shore, for it was now pitch dark, and, finding we made only lee-way, had to take in the sail and ply the oars. My boatmen, two young Jews and a Moslem, wished now to run to the south, and wait at anchor for the morning, rather than pull any longer. I insisted, however, on their trying to make the western shore. Vividly now came home to my mind, as I squatted down under the shelter of the little poop, with the waves beating over our bows, the story of the disciples all night toiling in rowing, for the wind was contrary (Mark vi. 48). It was eleven o'clock before we reached Tiberias"[1] (*Land of Israel,* p. 418).

113. Was there a second Bethsaida?—a **Bethsaida of Galilee** on the west? Although eminent names are ranked against this supposition, it seems to be required by the statements of Mark vi. 45, 53, altogether apart from any question as to the site of Capernaum; for if the disciples left Bethsaida on the eastern side for Bethsaida "on the other side," it is hardly possible to refuse to admit the conclusion that there were two, without impugning the accuracy of the Gospel historians. Bethsaida of Galilee was in **the land of Gennesareth,** which is identified with the marshy plain *El Ghuweir,* which stretches for 3 miles along the shore of the lake in its north-west corner.

The southern boundary of the plain is where the Wâdy el Hamâm descends from Hattin, a precipitous gorge leading from the plateau above, and there Mejdel represents the ancient Magdala, best known as the home of Mary, who ministered to the Lord of her substance, and to whom first, after His resurrection, He showed Himself. The waters of the Wâdy el Hamâm, swelled by the strong spring of the 'Ain es Surâr, form a broad perennial stream, used to irrigate the plain. There are other springs and streams which water the whole

---

[1] Another interesting account of a precisely similar experience is graphically told in Mrs. Mentor Mott's *Stones of Palestine,* p. 13. From the frequency with which travellers have met with such storms, we may almost certainly conclude that the two occasions recorded in the Gospels were not the only ones on which our Lord and His apostles were in jeopardy on the Sea of Galilee by night. See § 17.

plain abundantly. At the north end of it is Khân Minia (or Minyêh). Here there must have been in former times a dense population. The great Damascus road passed this way, "running from Beisan up past Mount Tabor on the east ... on through Lûbieh, and thence down the steep decline of the first step of the plateau, to the village of Hattin. From thence it crosses the plain to the mouth of the Wâdy el Hamâm, down which it plunges. Emerging on the plain of Gennesareth, it follows along the coast as far as Khân Minia. It then strikes north (leaving the sea-shore).... This road is still the caravan route to Damascus" (*Memoirs*, i. 379). Hereabout by the sea, and the great high road, Capernaum must surely have stood (Mark iv. 13, 15). For at Capernaum there was a military garrison, and also a custom-house, where probably duties were levied on merchandise passing from or to the east. This became distinctly Christ's "own city" when He left Nazareth, and here most of His mighty works were done.

There is no reason to suppose it a large place—Josephus speaks of it as "a village" (*Life*, § 72), into which he was carried after a fall from his horse, and from which he was the same night removed to Tarichææ at the south end of the lake. The account of this which he gives is of little use to determine the position, as he was at the time of his fall drawing his enemy away from his defences by pretended flight. There are three positions in which Capernaum has been located—(1) at the 'Ain Mudauwerah at the south of the plain ; (2) at Khân Minia, at the north of the plain ; and (3) at Tell Hum, 3 miles farther north along the shore. At the latter are many remains, including that of a synagogue ; but there is every likelihood that the synagogue dates from the great Jewish revival in the second century of our era (§ 111) ; and however much we should desire to identify these remains with that synagogue in which our Lord so often taught, there does not seem any evidence to warrant the confidence of Sir C. Wilson in placing Capernaum here.

Whether at one end of the plain of Gennesareth or the other, it was undoubtedly in that plain, and on the great high road, where alone a custom-house and military station would be planted. The rock-cut aqueduct which winds round the promontory at the north end of the plain is a clear proof that there was once here a city of no inconsiderable size, for the supply of which it was laboriously made. Sir C. Wilson and others place Bethsaida here; but more probably this aqueduct at Khân Minia marks the fountain of Capernaum which, according to Josephus, watered the plain (*Wars*, iii. 10, 8). A comparison of Mark vi. 45 and John vi. 17 proves that these two cities were very close together; while Matt. xiv. 34 and Mark vi. 53 fix the position of both in the land of Gennesareth.

The absence of extensive ruins is not of great account on a marshy plain, in a volcanic country, in view of subsidence so remarkable as that at Tiberias, and of the practice of quarrying from old ruins. The early tradition as to the sites of those cities is of very little value, and is contradictory.

Of the three places named (Matt. xi. 21-23) **Chorazin** alone is fixed by general consent. At Kerazeh, two miles and a half up the Wâdy Kerazeh from Tell Hum its ruins have been found. Here many houses are still comparatively well preserved, and among them the remains of a fine synagogue. The date of these buildings is not known; though in all probability, like others of the same design and workmanship, their date must be put between 150 A.D. and 300 A.D. Possibly further exploration may yet recover the lost sites of Capernaum and Bethsaida.

114. Tarichéæ or Kerak was situated at the south end of the Sea of Galilee, and defended the road passing up from the Jordan valley. It was a place of great strength; a bridge connected it with the other side of Jordan, and another bridge still passable crosses the river a mile lower down. By these the east and west of Jordan were brought together. Of the towns of the district known as **Decapolis**, the capital Bethshean, or Scythopolis, was on the west; the other towns were on the east, reaching out as far as Canatha, 60 miles over the Hauran on the east of Trachonitis, and scattered over Perea and Gaulonitis from Rabbath Ammon (Philadelphia), on the south to the north as far as Damascus, which was sometimes reckoned among "the ten cities," on which special privileges were conferred by the Romans. The only two of interest to the student of Scripture are (1) **Pella**, south-east from Bethshean, where the Christians, before the destruction of Jerusalem,

fled in obedience to the Lord's injunction, Matt. xxiv. 16. Extensive ruins covering much ground on a low terrace thrust forward into the Jordan plain, from the tableland above, and bearing the name *Fahil*, now mark the site. (2) North of Pella on the south bank of the Jarmûk was **Gadara**, now Um Keis. The Roman remains here are wonderful; on the old road "ruts of the chariot-wheels are deeply marked, and numerous sarcophagi lie strewn thickly; there are said to be 200, many of them in an excellent state of preservation."... "There are many tombs whose stone doors still swing on their hinges in the massive basalt framework." "The *fellahin* often use these tombs for dwellings, as well as granaries" (Oliphant). While Gadara gave its name to the district of the Gadarenes, it was not the scene of the miraculous cure of the demoniac and destruction of the herd of swine. Beyond doubt Dr. Thomson has rightly placed that at **Gerza**, or Kerza, at the foot of the hills where the Wâdy Semakh opens upon the little plain which edges the sea, right opposite Magdala. As more than one traveller has testified, since Dr. Thomson recovered the true site, the whole requirements of the narrative are perfectly satisfied. Gerza is about 8 miles from Gadara.

To Dr. Thomson we are indebted also for a notice of the ruin of Ed Delemîyeh, 1 mile north of Jarmûk, where he suggests the **Dalmanutha** of Mark viii. 10 may have been. The corresponding statement of Matt. xv. 39 substitutes Magadan (R. V., not Magdala), which Ewald suggests is Megidon. There is nothing, therefore, unlikely in the identification, as our Lord may have passed into the plain of Beisan, and the Abelmolah of Elisha, having purposely withdrawn from Capernaum and its neighbourhood.

115. From the shores of the Sea of Galilee our Lord, in the last year of His ministry, took a journey to **Tyre and Sidon**. Leaving Capernaum with His disciples, He took apparently a quiet track over the hills of Galilee to Tyre, 35 miles across the Map, but necessarily a much longer road to travel. "He arose and went away into the borders of Tyre (and Sidon). . . And again He went out from the borders of Tyre and came through Sidon" (Mark vii. 24, 31, R. V.).

The position of Tyre has been already more than once pointed out. When our Lord visited it, it was still in its glory as a busy seaport.

On the north was the Sidonian harbour, and on the south the Egyptian, each being about 12 acres in area. There are still remains which tell of its old busy days, though the doom prophesied has at last overtaken it (Ezek. xxvi.-xxviii. 19). In excavating, great heaps of shells have been turned over, from which the famous dye had been obtained, and broken lumps of glass that mark the site of its not less famous glassworks. It was a busy and heathen city when He passed by the sands of its sea-coast. "The beach" (Acts xxi. 5) over which the sea rolls unbroken, as distinguished from the rocks of Tyre, stretches north and south. Along it, doubtless, the Saviour went by Sarepta to Sidon. Surafend, which bears its name, has moved 2 miles up the hill from the ancient site of Sarepta, most probably to gain a position of greater security. On the old site not a house remains, though the foundations of the old dwellings may be traced close to the sea at two places, extending over a mile. From its fallen stones, and those quarried from the site of Tyre, it is said, both Acre and Beyrût have been largely built. Sidon seems to have been an older and once a greater city than Tyre (see references in Index to Genesis and Joshua). Its name marks its first beginning as a fishing village,— the name is familiar as the latter part of the name Beth-Saida; but in Homer's day it was famed for its silversmiths, and in that of Xerxes for its shipbuilders. It was, about 350 B.C., burnt by its inhabitants, who perished in its flames to the number of 40,000, rather than fall into the hands of the Persians. It rose again round its fine natural harbour, which encloses 20 acres, nearly equalling both harbours of Tyre combined, and in our Lord's time was a thriving commercial city and a home of learning (§ 78).

Another journey He made with them to **Cæsarea Philippi**, or *Banias*, at the foot of Hermon, which was in all probability the scene of the transfiguration.

The last months of our Lord's life were spent on the east of Jordan (John x. 40). After a brief visit to Jerusalem, He retired to **Ephraim**, Ophrah of Benjamin, afterwards *Apherema* (§ 95, 100), a village perched on a conspicuous eminence and with an extensive view, 13 miles north of Jerusalem, now called Taiyibeh. A Roman road ran down the Wâdy Taiyibeh by which, doubtless, He reached the Jordan valley, and gaining the Roman road which ran northward, crossed by one of the bridges over Jordan, into Perea again.

By **Jericho** He passed once more to Jerusalem for His last Passover.

116. The Mount of Olives lies, as already described, close to Jerusalem on the east, separated only by the narrow valley in which the Kidron flows. Coming out of the city, the road descends the

western side of the valley, and immediately ascends after crossing a very small bridge. The valley is often called "the valley of Jehoshaphat," which is most probably from an early Christian tradition, localizing the prophetic vision of Joel iii. 2; though the word which the prophet uses is inapplicable to the Kidron. At the head of the valley to the north of Jerusalem is "Shafat," which not improbably is the Sapha (Josephus' *Ant.* xi. 8, 5) at which the Jews, headed by their high priest, met and saluted Alexander the Great, and thence the priests ran by his side till he came into the city. From the eastern side of the Kidron several roads branch off. One, north-eastwards over to Anâta, $2\frac{1}{2}$ miles distant, the **Anathoth** of Jeremiah, crosses the hill, passing on the south of *Râs el Meshârif,* "hill-top of the high places," the northmost summit of the range of Olivet. Another road ascends straight up the mountain to its highest point, a branch going off to the right, which, crossing the southern shoulder, winds down upon the eastern side towards Bethany. Yet a third line of road, avoiding the height, bends round the south side of Olivet in the hollow between it and the Mount of Offence, and reaches Bethany within 2 miles of the city by an easier road. Most probably David took the northmost in leaving the city, and it is on the whole most likely that our Lord took the central road when He entered it in triumphal procession. Stanley (*Sinai and Palestine*) describes the approach by the southmost road.

Bethany, now named El-'Azirîyeh, from Lazarus, nestles in a sheltered nook at the point where the road over the summit descends into the southern one. There is no question as to its identity. On the other hand, the site of **Bethphage** is unknown. The recent discovery of a carved and painted rock shows where the traditional site was, well up the face of the hill, on a ridge joining the central and southern spurs which run eastward from the summit and the south shoulder, and over which the road, by the summit, from Bethany to Jerusalem passes. But the suggestion of Ganneau, that the Kefr et Tûr, the village on the summit, is Bethphage is more probably correct; for, as Lightfoot shows, Bethphage was, according to the Talmud, within the bounds "of Jerusalem," *i.e.* within the 2000 cubits' distance from the city walls to which it gave its name, and "the district" that lay between the walls and the top of Olivet was called Bethphage, as Bethany was the name of the adjoining district on the east (*Opera*, ii. 44, 198, 409); for so, as the name of the district, must we take Bethany in Luke xxiv. 50. When the remains of the traditional Bethphage were being excavated, the inhabitants of Bethany claimed "the find" as theirs!

At the foot probably of the Mount of Olives was "**The Garden of Gethsemane.**" Its position is not known. Neither of the two traditional sites have any evidence to favour their claim, and it is not at all likely that privacy such as was sought in Gethsemane could have been found at the very junction of the roads leading over the mountains to the city. It was by the Kidron (John xviii. 1); but whether farther up the valley than where the Bethany road crosses the Kidron, or among the gardens down below Siloam, we cannot tell.

117. **Calvary** was nigh to the city. The form of the mountains on which Jerusalem sits require us to locate Calvary somewhere to the north or north-west. It is most likely that the crucifixion of our Lord and the two malefactors took place at the ordinary place of execution; and that when they dragged Stephen out of the city the multitude would instinctively make for the usual spot "without the gate" where offenders were stoned (see Lightfoot, *Op.* ii. 718). The Talmud places it without the three camps: (1) that of the Shechinah, or the Temple; (2) that of the Levites, or the Temple courts; and (3) that of Israel, or the city of Jerusalem. The narratives of the evangelists require a position outside but nigh to the city,—near enough for easy communication, as when Pilate sent, when the even was come, to inquire of the centurion if Jesus were already dead, while Joseph waited for the answer to his petition for His body. It must have been near enough to a highway for passers-by to address the crucified,—an highway that led "into the country." It was also visible from "afar off" (Matt. xxvii. 32; Mark xv. 21, 29, 40, 44; Luke xxiii. 26, 49; John xix. 20, 41, 42). The Hebrew *Gool-gŏh-leth* merely means a head, and was so used (Num. i. 2; 1 Chron. xxiii. 3, 24); but it was also used (2 Kings ix. 35) for a bare skull, such as "Calvary" denotes. There is no need to press the popular description

which the name preserves, beyond requiring a rounded "head," so situated as to fulfil the conditions of the narratives of the evangelists. There is indeed such a spot on the north of the city just without the gate, now called the Damascus gate, but earlier known as St. Stephen's gate.

The hill "Bezetha" is all hollowed beneath by the "royal quarries," as they are called, out of which a large part of the city and possibly the Temple was built. But besides this subterranean quarry there is another which cuts Bezetha in two. The north wall of the city east of the Damascus gate is built upon the southern edge of it. The northern side, facing towards the city, presents a rocky precipice of about 50 feet high at a distance of 500 feet from the city wall. The top of the knoll behind it is rounded and dome-like, and is 110 feet higher than the sacred rock of the Temple, of whose enclosure it commands a view. "A sort of amphitheatre is formed by the gentle slopes on the west; and the whole population of the city might easily witness from the vicinity anything taking place on the top of the cliff. The knoll is just beside the main north road. It is occupied by a cemetery of Moslem tombs, which existed as early as the fifteenth century at least. . . . The hill is quite bare, with scanty grass covering the rocky soil, and a few irises and wild-flowers growing among the graves. Not a tree or shrub exists on it, though fine olive groves stretch northward from its vicinity. . . . The hillock is rounded on all sides but the south, where the yellow cliff is pierced by two small caves high up in the sides. . . . In 1881 it was found that a Jewish tomb existed on a smaller knoll west of the north road, about 200 yards from the top of the first-mentioned knoll" (*Survey of Western Palestine*, Jerusalem volume, p. 432).

There is no exaggeration in this description, nor in the statement that when the setting sun lights up the limestone brow and casts the two caves here spoken of into deep shadow, one looking from the western city wall can scarce fail to see what would suggest the name of Golgotha.[1] But we do not know what changes have taken place

[1] See *British and Foreign Evangelical Review*, January 1879, p. 112. The effect there described was noted and sketched before the discovery that it was the traditional place of stoning had been published, and was entirely unsuggested by it.

on the rock face during these eighteen centuries. It is, however, interesting to find that one Jewish tradition points to this hill as the "Beth-has-sekîlah," or "house of stoning," and even indicates one of the caves in the face of it as the spot whence the condemned were thrown down; while Christian tradition, as old as the fifth century, fixes this as the locality of Stephen's stoning. The discovery of what seems to be a tomb of the Herodian age proves the place to have been both without the gates, and nigh to rock-hewn sepulchres. The tomb referred to had been built over; and from the manner in which the rock in which it is hewn had been scarped, as for the foundation of a fortification, some think it was the site of "the women's towers" of Josephus (see Map IV.). Being thus built over before the destruction of the city, its existence was unsuspected. The rock of the Beth-has-sekîlah is now known as "El-Heidemîyeh," which means "cut off" or "destroyed." The Moslems say this is a corruption of Heirimîyeh, or Jeremiah, whence the "grotto" is named, but it is most likely that it refers to the quarrying of the rock; unless it be that the old use of the place still lingers in the name, as a memory of those who were there destroyed or cut off (Hos. iv. 6, x. 7, 15). With the Christian tradition of Stephen's martyrdom and the Jewish tradition of the place of execution pointing us to it, and from its answering better than any other place now existing the requirements of the Gospel history, it is scarce possible to resist the impression that if not here, yet hereabout, the crucifixion of our Lord was accomplished. Still the evidence, though most suggestive, is so incomplete, that we must add, "but no man knoweth of His sepulchre unto this day."

118. A similar veil seems drawn over the site of the **Emmaus** of Luke xxiv. Of several suggested identifications only two require attention here. From Luke's narrative we learn that it was 60 stadia from Jerusalem, or about 7½ miles. Josephus also mentions that when the Jewish cause had been finally overthrown, Vespasian gave orders that all Judea should be sold, a place being reserved for 800 disbanded Roman soldiers; and this military colony was planted at Emmaus, 60 stadia from Jerusalem. There can be no doubt that Luke and Josephus write of the same Emmaus, as to the exact

distance of which from Jerusalem they thus agree. Another well-known Emmaus (afterwards called Nicopolis, now *Amwas*) was situated 160 stadia from the capital, and in one ancient MS. this reading is found in Luke xxiv., embodying the belief of Eusebius and Jerome. But there is no reason to doubt the accuracy of our received text; and Josephus speaks of both places in language which shows he did not regard them as the same. The two sites where it has been proposed, with any show of reason, to place Emmaus are :—(1) El-Kubeibeh, just 60 stadia to the north-west of Jerusalem. The name it now bears means "little dome" in Arabic, and is derived from the Crusaders' church, the remains of which are yet to be seen there. The Crusaders said they found the name at this spot, which may be the more readily believed, because, as a well-known Emmaus already existed, with high ecclesiastical authority in its favour—a place they had possession of—they had no motive to invent an Emmaus, and thereby discredit received tradition. The name also lingers in the Wâdy el Hummâm and Khurbet Hummâm, within 2 to 3 miles off. But yet more strongly in its favour is the existence of Kolônia (which means *colony* and must mark a *Roman* colony) between it and Jerusalem. In a land conquered and depopulated, 800 Roman soldiers would not, of course, be content with a small village; and in this case, as in others (§ 116), the name of the village would apply to the whole district round it which belonged to its inhabitants. The position was eminently suitable for a military colony. Roman roads crossed it, and joined it with other garrisons, as Antipatris and Cæsarea. It is, as the history of the land from Joshua to Judas Maccabeus clearly proves, the military key of the land. Other suggestions in its favour, from the identification of Mozah (Josh. xviii. 26) at Beit Mizzeh, near Kolônia, cannot be discussed here. The upland retired hollow where El-Kubeibeh nestles, and from which nothing can be seen, save at one point where the surrounding hills, slightly dipping as they meet so as to leave a notch in the basin-rim, afford a glimpse of the Mediterranean, is impressively appropriate as the possible scene of that secret self-manifesting of the Lord to His two disciples. If here or hereabout to the north-west Emmaus lay, the road "into the country" would be the same which led "out of the country" past the scene of Calvary and in by the northern gate (Mark xv. 21, xvi. 12).

(2) The other claimant put forward by Captain Conder, who discovered it, has undoubtedly in its favour,'the strong support of the name Khurbet Khamasa, *i.e.* " the ruins of Khamasa," which may well be " the ruins of Emmaus." The site is about 8 miles from Jerusalem to the southwest. There are ruins, of a Crusaders' church apparently, beside a beautiful spring, and a Roman road leads past it down to the plain of Philistia. No tradition remains to explain the planting of the church, and the name was recovered by the officers of the Survey, without, in the first instance, any perception even of its original meaning. An attractive account of it is given in the *Survey Memoirs*, iii. p. 36 (see *Quarterly Statement*, April 1879 and October 1884). Beyond this summary of the evidence for these two identifications it is scarce warrantable to go here, and it is of all things most unwarrantable to attempt the creation of " holy places " in Palestine.

ACTS OF THE APOSTLES.

119. The history of the first years of the Church in Palestine do not introduce us to many new localities. Appropriately we are drawn westward to the shores of the Mediterranean. In the way down to Gaza, Philip, directed by the Holy Ghost, joined himself to the eunuch of Ethiopia reading in his chariot Isaiah's prophecy of Messiah's death. Gaza, *Guzzeh*, is a very ancient town (Gen. x. 19), and is an important place still, though no vestige of the ancient city remains. From its position on the edge of the desert it has always been a market town and the residence of a military governor. It stands on an isolated mound 180 feet above the sea, from which it is about 2 miles distant, and is surrounded by gardens; it is said to have still a population of 18,000. On the sea-coast 12 miles to the north is the Philistine town of Askelon, famous of old for the worship of Venus Derceto, or Atergatis, the Syrian Venus. It is named for the first time in the cuneiform inscriptions by Sennacherib (Rawlinson, *Herod.* i. p. 247). An excellent account of it is given in the *Land and Book*, p. 345 ff.

After parting from the Ethiopian treasurer somewhere on the way to Gaza, Philip came to **Azotus**, or Ashdod of the Philistines, now Esdûd, 3 miles from the sea. It is familiar as a Philistine city in early times, and an interesting mention of its capture by the Assyrians is alluded to, Isa. xx. 1 (see Sayce's *Fresh Light from the Ancient Monuments*, pp. 128–143). It is now a poor Moslem hamlet, surrounded with beautiful gardens. One sarcophagus remains as a token of the ancient grandeur of what Herodotus calls "a great town in Syria" (Bk. ii. 157). Twelve miles to the south-east is the cliff on which of old Gath of the Philistines stood (§ 88), and 9 miles north is Yebnah, a large village standing conspicuously on a hill, the Jamnia of Maccabean and the Jabneel of earlier times. Four or five miles east of it is Akir, the ancient Ekron of the Philistines. The position of **Joppa** is well known; it stands on a hill or hummock, covered with white, flat-roofed houses, visible at sea long before the low sandy shore-line can be seen. **Lydda** lies inland 11 miles to the south-east on the road to Jerusalem, across the plain of Sharon. Here was the scene of Peter's labours (Acts ix. 32–43) among the saints already gathered into a Christian community. Joppa is a miserable port, yet it served in Solomon's time; and from it, in probably a very small vessel, Jonah took his passage. The harbour is small and difficult of entrance. To the north of Lydda and 11 miles from Joppa is Râs el 'Ain, identified as the site of **Antipatris**, built by Herod and named after his father. Through it ran the Roman road northward from Lydda to Cæsarea, which lies 32 miles from Joppa by the coast-road which Peter would take, and 28 from Antipatris by which Paul was taken (Acts x. 23, 24, xxiii. 31, 33). A Roman road has been traced going by the maritime plain north to Tyre.

120. From Cæsarea Paul sailed as a fugitive after his first visit to Jerusalem subsequently to his conversion, and there he lay from the summer of 58 A.D. till the autumn of 60 A.D. Cæsarea was built by Herod as a new capital, but its glory was of short duration (§ 114). It is still famous as the home of Eusebius, who was also probably born there about 260 A.D. He published, beside other works bearing on the subject of this Handbook, the celebrated *Onomasticon*, giving alphabetically the designations of the cities and villages mentioned

in Holy Scripture in their native tongue, with a description of their locality and their modern names.

From Cæsarea the Apostle of the Gentiles sailed for the last time from the land of his fathers, touching the next day at "the great Sidon," named, in the same verse with Gaza (Gen. x. 19), as the utmost border of the Canaanite, — named ofttimes in Israel's history, though never possessed by Israel,—named when our Lord once passed through it (Mark viii. 31, R.V.), and looked across that western sea into which He now sent forth Paul to witness of Him at Rome (Acts xxiii. 11). As His apostle sails from Sidon, the last volume in the Land's great history is closed; for no more than the brilliant exploits of the Maccabees before He came, can the fierce heroism of the Jews, the untiring devotion of pilgrims, or the romantic chivalry of the Crusaders, one or all of them, command the serious interest of mankind in a country which bears on it the footmarks of Jesus Christ.

APPENDIX.

I. (p. 112).

THE various *sites* of the *tabernacle* were Shiloh, Gibeon, Nob, and apparently Mizpeh (1 Sam. vii. and x.). The two first only are known. Nob, "the high place," lay just north of Jerusalem, and was a place of some military importance (Isa. x. 32). The tabernacle was there in Samuel's time. Precisely the same is true of Mizpeh. It is remarkable that they are not both named in any one passage (such as Josh. xix. 26, and Neh. xi. 32), in which lists of the towns are given in the locality where they must both have been. Mizpeh is associated with Gibeon, "the great high place," in several places; and Nob is similarly conjoined with it in the Talmud (*Pal. Quar.* 1875, p. 37). Robinson's identification of Neby Samwîl with Mizpeh is most probably correct; it is 1¼ mile from Gibeon. Conder's suggestion that it is also Nob seems not improbable. It is remarkable that on Neby Samwîl, a similar levelled platform to that at Shiloh has been traced. "There is a scarp of rock some 5 or 6 feet high running north and south, a narrow trench is cut between this and a sort of platform of rock, which is occupied by buildings. North of the church there is a sort of sunk court about 250 feet north and south, by 500 feet east and west, to which the narrow passage leads. On the north-east of this is a flat platform of rock reached by steps with a cave below. . . . East of the platforms are two large shallow reservoirs communicating with one another . . . and there are two curious shallow recesses in the scarp" (*Memoirs*, iii. p. 151). There seems more than accidental agreement between this and the description of Shiloh by Sir C. Wilson: "The Tell slopes down to a broad shoulder, across which a sort of level court 77 feet wide and 412 feet feet long has been cut. The rock is in places scarped to a height of 5 feet, and along the sides are several excavations and a few small cisterns" (*Pal. Q. S.* 1873, p. 37). With these may also be compared the platform found at Kirjath Jearim, where doubtless a place was made for the ark, similar to the tabernacle in which it should have been. Admittedly the site of Mizpeh and Nob is uncertain. There may have been more than one Mizpeh in the neighbourhood of Jerusalem. But the facts above given indicate a solution which is perhaps less beset by difficulties than any other yet suggested.

II.—MOABITE STONE (p. 73).

In 1869, Dr. Klein found at Dhibân an engraved stone of black basalt. Unfortunately the cupidity or superstition of the natives led to its being broken to pieces before it could be removed; but the pieces were nearly all recovered. The subjoined translation is that given by Professor Sayce. Mesha who set it up is the Moabite king mentioned in 2 Kings iii. 4–27. The monument is extremely valuable, because it is the only specimen beside the Siloam stone, of the form of the Hebrew letters used in ancient times, and because of the light it casts on the use of the name "*Yahveh*," the proper form of our "*Jehovah*," and other matters of interest affecting the history and religion of Israel. The stone is about 4 feet high, and 2 broad, rounded at the top; it is now in the Louvre at Paris.

"I, Mesha, am the son of Chemosh-Gad, king of Moab, the Dibonite. My father reigned over Moab thirty years, and I reigned after my father. And I erected this stone to Chemosh at Kirkha, a (stone of) salvation, for he saved me from all despoilers, and made me see my desire upon all my enemies, even upon Omri, king of Israel. Now they afflicted Moab many days, for Chemosh was angry with his land. His son succeeded him; and he also said, I will afflict Moab. In my days (Chemosh) said, (Let us go) and I will see my desire on him and his house, and I will destroy Israel with an everlasting destruction. Now Omri took the land of Medeba, and (the enemy) occupied it in (his days and in) the days of his son, forty years. And Chemosh (had mercy) on it in my days; and I fortified Baal-Meon, and made therein the tank, and I fortified Kiriathaim. For the men of Gad dwelt in the land of (Atar)oth from of old, and the king (of) Israel fortified for himself Ataroth, and I assaulted the wall and captured it, and killed all the warriors of the wall for the well-pleasing of Chemosh and Moab; and I removed from it all the spoil, and (offered) it before Chemosh in Kirjath; and I placed therein the men of Siran and the men of Mochrath. And Chemosh said to me, Go take Nebo against Israel. (And I) went in the night, and I fought against it from the break of dawn till noon, and I took it, and slew in all seven thousand (men, but I did not kill) the women (and) maidens, for (I) devoted them to Ashtar-Chemosh; and I took from it the vessels of Yahveh, and offered them before Chemosh. And the king of Israel fortified Jahaz and occupied it, when he made war against me; and Chemosh drove him out before (me, and) I took from Moab two hundred men, all its poor, and placed them in Jahaz, and took it to annex it to Dibon. I built Kirkha, the wall of the forest, and the wall of the city, and I built the gates thereof, and I built the towers thereof, and I built the palace, and I made the prisons for the criminals within the walls. And there was no cistern in the wall at Kirkha, and I said to all the people, Make for yourselves, every man, a cistern in his house. And I dug the ditch for Kirkha by means of the (captive) men of Israel. I built Aroer, and I made the road across the Arnon. I built Beth-Bamoth, for it was destroyed; I built Bezer, for it was cut (down) by the armed men of Dibon, for all Dibon was now loyal; and I reigned from Bikran, which I added to my land, and I built (Beth-Gamul) and Beth-Diblathaim and Beth-Baal-Meon, and I placed there the poor (people) of the land. And as to Horonaim, (the men of Edom) dwelt therein (from of old). And Chemosh said to me, Go down, make war against Horonaim and take (it. And I assaulted it, and I took it, and) Chemosh (restored it) in my days. Wherefore I made . . . year . . . and I . . ."

III. (p. 130).

Much stress has been laid (*Encyc. Brit.*, art. Jerusalem) on the allusion in Ezek. xliii. 7-9 to the "carcases" of Jewish kings in or near the temple precincts, as proving that the eastern hill must be the "city of David" in which David and other kings were buried. But (1) the prophet's language is vague, and it is known that at least more than one place of royal sepulture existed at Jerusalem. (2) Any carcases of the kings buried in the palace close by the ancient temple-court must have been removed when Herod enlarged it. David's was not displaced (Acts ii. 29), therefore the allusion is not to his sepulchre. (3) "The sepulchres of David" (Neh. iii. 16), near Siloam, cannot be those referred to by Ezekiel. The expression there is equivalent to "royal sepulchres." The garden of Uzzah, where several kings were laid, was apparently near Siloam, and is most probably the place referred to; but certainly neither was that David's sepulchre. We may conclude that there were therefore at least three places of Royal sepulture, which renders any inference from their position very uncertain. The more so that each of the four hills on which the city stands has eminent authority in support of its claim to be the site of David's sepulchre. The steps leading down from the city of David may very well have been made for direct descent to Siloam from the western hill, to avoid a detour by the bed of the Tyropœon.

IV. (p. 92).

Tappuah is generally translated "apple." Tristram maintains it is the apricot that is meant (*Land of Israel*, p. 598). "Everywhere the apricot is common; perhaps it is, with the single exception of the fig, the most abundant fruit in the country. In highlands and lowlands alike, by the shores of the Mediterranean and on the banks of the Jordan, in the nooks of Judea, under the heights of Lebanon, in the recesses of Galilee, and in the glades of Gilead the apricot flourishes, and yields a crop of prodigious abundance. Its characteristics meet every condition of the 'tappuach' of Scripture (Cant. ii. 3). Near Damascus, and on the banks of the Barada, we have pitched our tents under its shade, and spread our carpets secure from the rays of the sun (Cant. vii. 8). There can scarcely be a more deliciously-perfumed fruit than the apricot; and what fruit can better fit the epithet of Solomon (Prov. xxv. 11) than this golden fruit, as its branches bend under the weight in their setting of bright yet pale foliage?" Dr. Kitto is found fault with by Dr. Thomson (*Land and Book*, p. 546) for translating "tappuach" by citron, and is himself taken to task by Dr. Tristram for rendering it "apple;" and though Sir C. Warren has vindicated his statements regarding the apples of Ashkelon (*Survey Mem.*, Jer. vol., p. 441), yet the "apple" is not (now at least) as common as the apricot, nor does it so well fit scriptural allusions to the "tappuach."

TOPOGRAPHICAL INDEX.

———o———

NOTE.—Roman letters (I. II. etc.), following references to sections, refer to Maps. *L.* denotes Levitical city.

Abana or **Amana**. *Barada*. 2 Kings v. 12.
'Abarah (§ 10, 24, I.). See Bethabara.
Abarim (§ 26, 58, I.). Mountains of Moab. In Reuben. Num. xxvii. 12, xxxiii. 47, 48; Deut. xxxii. 49.
Abd-el-Maaz. High hill 10 miles south-east of Bozrah in the Hauran.
Abdon (§ 78, II. *L.*). In Asher. *Abdeh*, 3½ miles east of Ez-Zib. Josh. xxi. 30; 1 Chron. vi. 74. Probably also Josh. xix. 28, where it is called Hebron or Abron.
Abel (§ 86). In Judah, at Bethshemesh. 1 Sam. vi. 18. "A stone;" possibly *Deir Aban*.
Abel-beth-Maachah (§ 36, 79, II.), also **Abel-Maim**=*Abel*. In Naphtali. 6½ miles west of Banias. 2 Sam. xx. 14-18; 1 Kings xv. 20; 2 Kings xv. 29; 2 Chron. xvi. 4.
Abel-Ceramim. Judg. xi. 33, marg. In Moab.
Abel-Meholah (§ 19, 76, 82, 114, II.). *'Ain Helweh*, 10 miles south of Bethshean. In Issachar. Judg. vii. 22; 1 Kings iv. 12, xix. 16.
Abel-Mizraim. Probably near Hebron. Gen. l. 11.
Abel-Shittim (§ 19, 26, 30, 45, 56, 57, I.). Plain of *Seïsebân*. In Reuben. Num. xxxiii. 49.
Abez (II.). In Issachar. Either *El-Beida* in the extreme north-west of tribe, or at Bir Tibes, 1 mile north-west of Nain. Judg. xix. 20.
Abila (1). *Abil.* In Decapolis, 12 miles east of Gadara. See Decapolis. Map V.
Abila (2). Chief town of Abilene, 12 miles north-west of Damascus.
Abilene. District in the Antilebanon. Luke iii. 1. Map V.
'Abilin (§ 77). Town on Wâdy 'Abilin, half-way on road between Sepphoris and Acre. The *Wâdy 'Abilin* is the valley of Jephtah-El (Josh. xix. 27), and 'Abilin is possibly Zebulun there named. See Zebulun for another identification.
Abron. See Abdon.
Accho (§ 8, 65, 78, II.). In Asher. Judg. i. 31. Now *Akka* or Accho, whence "Bay of Acre" is named. Called Ptolemais, Acts xxi. 7.
Aceldama. Acts i. 19. *Hak-el-Dumm*, opposite Jerusalem on the south.
Achor, Valley of (§ 12, 58, 63, 68, I.). Josh. vii. 24, 26, xv. 7; Isa. xlv. 10; Hos. ii. 15. Generally identified with the *Wâdy Kelt*, the gorge up which the road ascends from Jericho to Jerusalem.

Achshaph (§ 78, II.). *El-Yasif.* Town of Asher, close to Hhaiffa or Caiffa, with which some identify it. It was a royal city of Canaanites. Josh. xi. 1, xii. 20, xix. 25.

Achzib (in Judah). *Ain Kezbeh*, ½ mile from Beit Nettiff, 3 miles north of Adullam. In Josh. xv. 44, Mic. i. 14, it is named with Mareshah, and is probably Chezib of Gen. xxxviii. 5.

Achzib (§ 78, II.). In Asher. Is *Ez-Zib*, on the shore, 8 miles north of Accho among "the creeks." Judg. v. 17, marg.; Josh. xix. 29; Judg. i. 31.

Acrabbim (§ 68, 99, I. II.). Ma-a-leh Akrabbim, the ascent of scorpions, between south of Dead Sea and Kadesh-Barnea. Num. xxxiv. 4; Josh. xv. 3; Judg. i. 36.

Adadah. Josh. xv. 22. Town of Judah, now *'Ad'adah*, in desert south-east of Beersheba (Conder).

Adam (§ 62, II.). Town on the Jordan. Josh. iii. 6. Placed by some at *Dâmieh* ford where Jabbok falls into Jordan; it was "beside Zaretan," which see, and may have been farther north, though the connection Zaretan and Succoth is favourable to this site.

Adamah (§ 79, II.). Fenced city of Naphtali. Josh. xix. 36. Either *Damieh*, 6 miles west of Sea of Tiberias, or Admah, 5 miles south of it. See next.

Adami (§ 79). Town of Naphtali on plateau south-west of Sea of Galilee. Josh. xix. 33. Near Naklb, Admah or Damieh. See preceding.

Adar. Town in extreme south of Judah. Josh. xv. 3. Called (Num. xxxiv. 4) Hazar (village or enclosure) Addar, and must have lain west of Hezron. Conder (*Palestine Quarterly Statement*, 1881, p. 61) proposes Jebel-Maderah, facing the pass Es-Sufa.

Adasa (§ 99). *'Adasah*, 1 mile east from *El-Gib*, on road from Jerusalem to Bethhoron, over the Wâdy Ed-Dumm (valley of blood). Scene of victory gained by Maccabees. 1 Macc. vii. 45.

Adida = *Haditheh*. A fortress of the Maccabees. See next.

Adithaim (same as Hadid, Neh. vii. 37). Town in north-west of Judah. Now Haditheh, 3 miles east of Lydda (in 1 Macc. xii. 38 it is called Adida). Josh. xv. 36. Note "Gederoth and Gederothaim" in same verse.

Admah (§ 44, 45). One of the cities of the plain. Gen. x. 19. xiv. 2, 8; Deut. xxix. 23; Hos. xi. 8. See *Adam*, with which some would identify it. But it possibly lay on the east of Jordan, and may be traceable in El-'Adeimeh, and the wâdy of same name which flows into Salt Sea, 2 miles east of the mouth of the Jordan. El-'Adeimeh is 2 miles south of Zoar, which see.

Adoraim. Fenced city built by Rehoboam. 2 Chron. xi. 9. Now *Dûra*, 6 miles west from Hebron, and north of Dumah on road from Hebron to Egypt by Beersheba. Maps II. and III.

Adraa (§ 56). Now *Der'a*, in Bashan, 35 miles up valley of Hieromax.

Adullam (§ 54, 88, II. III. V.). Now *'Aîd-el-Mâ*, in valley of Elah. Home of Hirah, Gen. xxxviii. Royal city of Canaanites, Josh. xii. 15. Given to Judah, xv. 35. David's hiding-place, 1 Sam. xxii. 1; 2 Sam. xxiii. 13; 1 Chron. xi. 15. It lies half-way between Sochoh and Keilah, 10 miles north-west of Hebron. 2 Chron. xi. 7; Neh. xi. 30; Mic. i. 15.

Adummim (§ 68, II.). *Tal-at-ed-Dumm*. "The ascent" of the Wâdy Kelt. Perhaps so called from the blood-coloured rock there. It was a landmark on northern boundary of Judah. There is a well-known *Khan* or Jun here on the Jericho road close to mediæval fortress which commanded the pass. Josh. xv. 7, xviii. 17.

Ænon (§ 12, 18, 109, V.). 7 miles north of Salim. (Salim of this place, 2 miles east of Jacob's well.) Now *'Ainûn*="springs" or "many waters." John iii. 23.

Ahlab. Town of Asher, kept by Canaanites. Judg. i. 31. Commonly identified with Giscala of Josephus, and also the Talmudic Gush Halab, now *El-Jish*; but that is in Naphtali, and a good way from territory of Asher. More probably it was on the sea-coast, perhaps *'Adlân*.

Ai (§ 12, 42, 45, 63, 95, II.). Royal city of Canaanites, 2 miles east of Bethel; now most probably *Haiyan*. Called also Hai, Aija, and Aiath. Gen. xii. 8, xiii. 3; Josh. vii. 2, 5, viii. ix. 3, x. 1, 2, xii. 9; Ezra ii. 28; Neh. vii. 32, xi. 31; Isa. x. 28; Jer. xlix. 3. For this El-Tell has been proposed, which lies nearer Bethel; and Khurbet-el-Hai farther down the valley. Avim (Josh. xviii. 23) more probably stands for Bethaven.

Aijalon (1) (§ 12, 64, 71, 72, 80, 87, 95, I. II. III. *L*.), also **Ajalon**. Represented by modern Yálo, in tribe of Dan. Kept by Amorites. Afterwards fortified by Rehoboam. The valley of Ajalon is now Merj-ibn-Omeir. Josh. x. 12, xix. 42, xxi. 24; Judg. i. 35; 1 Sam. xiv. 31; 1 Chron. viii. 13; 2 Chron. vi. 69, xi. 10, xxviii. 18.

Aijalon (2) (§ 77, 82, II.). A town of Zebulun, burial-place of Elon the judge of Israel. Judg. xii. 12. Probably Jallûn, 3 miles north of Kabul.

Ain (§ 70). Num. xxxiv. 11. Neba Auja at the foot of Antilebanon (Keil), or perhaps Merj Ayûn.

Ain Duk (§ 62). A famous spring nearly 4 miles up the valley from Jericho, and 2½ miles from the 'Ain-es-Sultan, or "fountain of Elisha."

Ain Feshkah=*spring of Pisgah* (?). On the north-western shore of Dead Sea. Brackish.

Ain Gadis=*Ain Kadeis*. See Kadesh. No doubt a "sacred" city, but doubtful if it should be identified with a Kadesh of Scripture.

Ain Hajla (§ 68). See Beth-Hogla.

Ain Haud. See En-Shemesh.

Ain Jalud. A spring at the foot of Mount Gilboa, near Jezreel. The name also attaches to the valley which forms the eastern extremity of the plains of Esdraelon. This probably is the fountain of Jezreel (1 Sam. xxix. 11), and may be the well "Harod" (Judg. vii. 1); though Captain Conder would place this latter at Ain-el-Jemm'ain, the "spring of two troops," near Bethshean.

Ain Kadeis (§ 46). See Ain Gadis.

Ain Karim (§ 69, 86, 109). A village with copious spring and Christian church. From its commanding position, it must always have been occupied. It has been identified with Rekem (Josh. xviii. 27), which is named after Mozah, 1½ mile south of which Ain Karim lies; in that case it was, as is otherwise probable, a town of Benjamin. Others have proposed to identify it with the Bethcar of 1 Sam. vii. 11; and see Beth-Haccerem.

Ain Mudauwerah. A spring in the plain of Gennesareth. See on Capernaum, § 113.

Ain Musa=*Wells of Moses* (§ 26). See Ashdoth-Pisgah.

Ain Muweileh (§ 47) or **Moilahhi.** About 50 miles south of Beersheba. Hagar's well, Beer-lahai-roi. Gen. xvi. 14, xxiv. 62, xxv. 11.

Ain Rimmon=*En Rimmon* (§ 70).

Ain Sareh (§ 60). See Sirah.
Ain Shems (§ 72). See Bethshemesh (1).
Ain-es-Sultan (§ 62). The fountain of Jericho. See Ain Dûk.
Ain-et-Tin. Spring at Khan Minyeh.
Ain Tâbghah. Spring to the north of Gennesareth, whose waters were carried by aqueduct into that plain. See Bethsaida. This is "the fountain of Capernaum" (Joseph. *Wars*, iii. 10, 8), which therefore lay south, § 113 (see Wilson's *Rec. of Jeru.*, p. 348).
Ain Zahrah. Spring 3 miles west of Bethshean. See Zaretan.
Ajlûn. A valley, river, and mountain in Gilead.
Akra. See Millo.
Alammelech. Town of Asher. Josh. xix. 26. Probably situated in Wâdy El-Maleh, which joins the Kishon 6 miles from the sea.
Alemeth or **Almon** (*L.*). Now *'Almit*, in Benjamin, on north-east of Mount of Olives. Josh. xxi. 18; 1 Chron. vi. 60. Three and a half miles from Jerusalem. Map V.
Allon (§ 78, II.). Town of Naphtali. Josh. xix. 33. It should perhaps be read Allon-Besanannim. See Zaanaim.
Allon-Bachuth (§ 80). "Oak of weeping." Gen. xxxv. 8. Near Bethel.
Alma. See Ummah.
Almon. See Alemeth.
Almon-Diblathaim or **Beth-Diblathaim.** In Moab. Unknown. "The two discs" may have been sun images. See Conder's *Heth and Moab*, p. 262. Num. xxxiii. 46, 47; Jer. xlviii. 22.
Aloth. 1 Kings iv. 16. This may be a district. Some identify it with *'Alia*, a town of Asher.
Alush. Encampment of Israelites. Site unknown. Num. xxxiii. 13, 14.
Amad. Town of Asher. Traces of its ruins found by Tristram at Un-el-'Amad, in Wâdy El-Malek. See Alammelech.
Amam. In Judah, near Hezron. Probably in Wâdy El-Yemen. Josh. xv. 26.
Amatha. Baths in valley of the Yarmûk or Hieromax.
Amathus. *Amateh*, at the junction of Wâdy Ajlun, Jordan valley, in Decapolis.
Ammah. 2 Sam. ii. 24. "A hill," east of Giah. Not known. It must have lain east of Gibeon.
Amman. A tributary of the Jabbok. See Rabbath-Ammon.
Ammaus. See Hammath.
Amud (Wâdy). Valley descending from Jebel-Jermûk to plain of Gennesareth.
Amwas (§ 72). See Emmaus.
Anab. Josh. xv. 50. 'Anab, west of Debir, and half-way between Sochoh and Eshtemoah; a town of the Anakim. Josh. xi. 21. Taken by Ramses II. Map II.
Anaharath. Town of Issachar, now *En-N'aurah*, in the plain north of Jezreel. Map. II. Josh. xix. 19.
Ananiah. In Benjamin. Neh. xi. 32. Now *Beit Hanina*, close to Gibeon.
Anathoth (§ 95, 116, III. *L.*). Now *'Anata*, 2 miles east of Gibeon, an hour and a half from Jerusalem, beyond Nob. Josh. xxi. 18; 1 Kings ii. 26; 1 Chron. vi. 60; Ezra ii. 23; Neh. vii. 27, xi. 32; Isa. x. 30; Jer. i. 1, xi. 21, 23, xxix. 27, xxxii. 7-9. City of Abiathar and Jeremiah.
Anem. Levitical city in Issachar. 1 Chron. vi. 73. Possibly for *Engannin* (2), named Josh. xix. 21.
Aner. 1 Chron. vi. 70. In Manasseh. Probably *'Anin*, near Taanach.

See Josh. xxi. 25. In 1 Chron. vi. 70 it stands in the place of Taanach, from which 'Anim and Khurbet 'Anin lie 3½ miles distant to the south-west, the latter being 2 miles south-east of former. Map. II.

Anim. Now *El-Ghuwein*, near Eshtemoh. Town of Judah. Josh. xv. 50. (Wilson, *Lands of the Bible.*)

Antipatris (§ 100, 118, 119, V.). On border line between Judæa and Samaria, at foot of a long rugged valley where it joins the plain of Sharon. A strong military town built by the Herods, 42 miles from Jerusalem and 26 miles from Cæsarea, whence a road also ran to Lydda. At the site, now Ras-el-Ain, rise the springs of the Aujeh, the largest springs in Palestine. Acts xxiii. 31. Part of the paved road from Jerusalem to Cæsarea which passed through it yet remains.

Aphek (1). A name frequently recurring, meaning either a "stronghold" or *stream*, as in Ps. cxxvi. 4. The position of Aphek (1) (Josh. xii. 18) is uncertain, possibly Fukna, 6 miles south-east of Jezreel, from order in which it stands, probably (4).

Aphek (2). *Aphekah* (Josh. xv. 53) must have been in neighbourhood of Hebron. Unknown.

Aphek (3). *Aphek* (1 Sam. iv. 1), not far from Ebenezer. It may be represented by the Wâdy Fukin, 6 miles west of Bethlehem on a road up from land of Philistines to valley of Rephaim.

Aphek (4). *Aphek*, where the Philistines pitched (1 Sam. xxix. 1), can scarcely be *Fukna* (see No. 1) on Gilboa, for the Israelites were at Jezreel; it certainly was not far from Shunem. 1 Sam. xxviii. 4. Possibly near, if not at, El-Afuleh, 2 miles west of Shunem.

Aphek (5) (§ 78). *Aphek* or *Aphik*. Josh. xiii. 4, xix. 30; Judg. i. 31. Town in extreme north of Asher, now *Afka* on the Adonis.

Aphek (6). *Aphek* (1 Kings xx. 26, 30; 2 Kings xiii. 17) lay in the "*Mishor*" of Bashan, now *Fik*, on the eastern side of the Lake of Galilee opposite Tiberias, on the high road to Damascus. Wâdy Fik descends 3 or 4 miles to the lake.

Apherema (§ 95, 100). 1 Macc. xi. 34.

Aphrah. Mic. i. 10. Some think this town lay in Philistia, others in Judah. If the former, it may be the Ophrah of 1 Chron. iv. 14, which is unknown; if the latter, it is probably Ophrah of Benjamin.

Ar (§ 59). See Rabbath, in Moab.

Arab. Josh. xv. 52. Now *Er-Rabîyeh*, 8 miles south-west of Hebron.

Arabah (§ 21, 22, 70). Josh. xviii. 18. Distinctively used for the drepressed tract of desert which marks the ancient continuation of the Jordan valley towards the Gulf of Akaba.

Arad. Josh. xii. 14; Judg. i. 16. *Tell 'Arad* on plateau, 20 miles east of Beersheba and 17 miles south of Hebron. Map. II.

Aram = *Syria*. Num. xxiii. 7; 1 Chron. ii. 23. Aram Naharaim = Mesopotamia. Aram Zobah lay near Damascus. Ps. lx. title; 2 Sam. x. 6; also *cf.* Padan-Aram.

Arba. See Kirjath-Arba. See 2 Sam. xxiii. 35.

Arbela. Town of Decapolis, which see. Now *Irbid*. Map IV. 1 Macc. ix. 2.

Archelais. Founded by *King* Archelaus, now El-Buseiliyeh, in Wâdy Farah, 11 miles east of Shechem. Map. V.

Archi (§ 71, II.). On the boundary of Benjamin and Ephraim. 'Ain 'Arik, 6 miles west of Bethel. Josh. xvi. 2; 2 Sam. xv. 32, xvi. 16, xvii. 5, 14; 1 Chron. xxvii. 33.

Ard-el-Buttauf. See Buttauf.
Ard-el-Hamma (§ 17). Plain between Tabor and Sea of Galilee.
Argob (§ 24, 52, 56, 60, 61, 99, II.) = *Trachonitis*. Now *El-Lejah*. Deut. iii. 4, xiii. 14 ; 1 Kings iv. 13.
Arimathæa. Matt. xxvii. 57 ; Mark xv. 43 ; Luke xxiii. 51 ; John xix. 38. Probably Ramathaim. 1 Sam. i. 1 ; 1 Macc. xi. 34. Unknown. The name *Ramah* was common, applied to *single* heights. The peculiar form by which it was known requires twin heights. See Ramah.
Armageddon (§ 76). See Megiddo.
Arnon (§ 26, 28, 55, 56, 59, I. II. V.). Now *Wâdy Mojib*. Southern boundary of Reuben.
Aroer (1) (Judah). 1 Sam. xxx. 28. Haunt of David, 12 miles south-east of Beersheba, now *'Ar'arah*, in Wâdy Ararah. Maps II. and III.
Aroer (2) (Gad). Num. xxxii. 34. Probably 'Aireh on the right bank of Shaib between Beth-Nimrah and Ramoth-Gilead. Josh. xiii. 25 ; 2 Sam. xxiv. 5.
Aroer (3) (Reuben) (§ 28, 59, II.). On the Arnon, and usually so distinguished, city of the Amorites. Deut. ii. 36, iii. 12, iv. 48 ; Josh. xii. 2, xiii. 9, 16 ; Judg. xi. 26, 33 ; 2 Kings x. 33 ; 1 Chron. v. 8 ; Jer. xlviii. 19, and probably Isa. xvii. 2 and 1 Chron. xi. 44.
Arpad or Arphad. Always named with Hamath, which see.
Arrabattene = *Acrabbim*. 1 Macc. v. 3.
Aruboth. 1 Kings iv. 10. One of Solomon's districts, including Sochoh and the land of Hepher, which see.
Arumah (§ 82). Judg. ix. 41. Now *El-'Orma*, 6 miles south-east of Shechem.
Ashan (§ 70). Josh. xv. 42. Levitical city in tribe of Simeon, probably same as Chorashan. It has been placed at 'Aseileh, north-east of Beersheba, and also at Kurbet 'Azanah, 5 miles south of Beit-Jibrin. The former seems the more likely neighbourhood. Josh. xix. 7 ; 1 Chron. iv. 32, vi. 59.
Ashdod or Azotus (§ 83, II.) is Esdûd, 3 miles from sea. It was a city of the Anakim, and one of 5 cities of Philistines, still a large village. Josh. xi. 22, xv. 46, 47 ; 1 Sam. v. 1-7, vi. 17 ; 2 Chron. xxvi. 6 ; Neh. xiii. 23, 24 ; Isa. xx. 1 ; Jer. xxv. 20 ; Amos i. 8, iii. 9 ; Zeph. ii. 4 ; Zech. ix. 6 ; Josh. xiii. 3 ; Neh. iv. 7.
Ashdoth Pisgah. *'Ayûn Mûsa*, p. 35. Deut. iii. 17, iv. 49 ; Josh. xii. 3–xiii. 20.
Asher (§ 110). Frontier town of Manasseh. Josh. xvii. 7. It has been commonly identified with Asirah in the Wâdy Malith, 4 miles north-east of Tubâs, but it could scarcely be so far from Tana, more probably 'Askar or Ischar, which is also called Sychar.
Ashkelon (§ 80, 83, 100, 119, II.). *'Askalân*, p. 174. Judg. i. 18, xiv. 19 ; 1 Sam. vi. 17 ; 2 Sam. i. 20 ; Jer. xxv. 20, xlvii. 5, 7 ; Amos i. 8 ; Zeph. ii. 4, 7 ; Zech. ix. 5.
Ashnah (1) (Josh. xv. 33) has been identified with 'Asalin, close to Zorah.
Ashnah (2) (Josh. xv. 43) may be Idnah, 5 miles south-east of Beit-Jibrin.
Ashtaroth (§ 33, 44, 99, II. *L*.). Most probably same as Ashteroth-Karnaim (*i.e.* two-horned), now *Tell 'Asherah*, 4 miles from Edrei. It was a city of the Rephaim, in Bashan, in tribe of Manasseh. Gen. xiv. 5 ; Deut. i. 4 ; Josh. ix. 10, xii. 4, xiii. 12, 31 ; 1 Chron. vi. 71. It is the Beeshterah or Beer-Astaroth of Josh. xxi. 27.

Ataroth (1) (§ 73, II.). Josh. xvi. 2, 7. Frontier town of Ephraim and Benjamin, named next to Naarath. Conder places it at Tell-el-Irûni, 7 miles north-east of Jericho.

Ataroth (2). 1 Chron. ii. 54. Uncertain whether name of person or town.

Ataroth (3) or **Atroth**. Num. xxxii. 3, 34. Placed by Tristram at ruins on slopes of Jebel-Attarus between Heshbon and Dibon. Map. II.

Ataroth-Adar (§ 71, II.). Frontier town between Ephraim and Benjamin. Josh. xvi. 5, xviii. 13. Now *Ed-Dárieh*, over a mile south-west of Lower Bethhoron. Map. II.

Ataroth-Shophan. Num. xxxii. 35. Probably in same neighbourhood to the north of Ataroth (3). See Shophan.

Athach. 1 Sam. xxx. 30. In the south. Unknown.

Attarus (§ 27, 57, 59). Jebel.

Avim (§ 32). Josh. xviii. 23. Possibly for *Ai* (now Haiyân) or for *Aven* = Bethaven, near Bethel.

Avith. City of Moab. Gen. xxxvi. 35; 1 Chron. i. 46. Unknown.

Azal. Zech. xiv. 5. See Beth-Ezel.

Azekah (§ 64, 88). Josh. x. 10, 11, xv. 35 ; 1 Sam. xvii. 1 ; 2 Chron. xi. 9 ; Neh. xi. 30 ; Jer. xxxiv. 7. Town of Judah. Not improbably Deir-el-Aashek, 8 miles north of Socoh, in Wâdy Sumt.

Azem (§ 70). Josh. xv. 29, xix. 3. *Ezem*. 1 Chron. iv. 29. See under Iim. Probably El-Aujeh, headquarters of Azazimeh Arabs, who may, as some have thought, retain the name (see § 83). Situated two-thirds of the way from Beersheba to Ain-Gadi, where are extensive ruins.

Azmaveh of Ezra ii. 24 is now *Hizmeh*, scarce 2 miles north of Anathoth. Neh. xii. 29.

Azmon. Num. xxxiv. 4, 5. Not known ; must have been in extreme southwest of Simeon. Josh. xv. 4.

Aznoth-Tabor (§ 79). Josh. xix. 34. A landmark on Mount Tabor, meaning "Ears of Tabor."

Azotus (2). 1 Macc. ix. 15. A hill north of Bethel, where is found Bir-ez-Zeit.

Azotus (§ 119, V.) = *Ashdod*.

'Azur. Mountain between Bethel and Shiloh. See Baal-Hazor.

Azzah = *Gaza*. Deut. ii. 23 ; 1 Kings iv. 24 ; Jer. xxv. 20 ; 1 Chron. vii. 28.

Baal. 1 Chron. iv. 33. Town in Simeon. *Khurbet Zebâlah*. Probably same as Baalah. Josh. xv. 29, xix. 3, and Bilhah ; 1 Chron. iv. 29.

Baalah (2) (§ 83, II.) = *Kirjath-Jearim*. 1 Chron. xiii. 6 ; Josh. xv. 9, 10. On boundary of Judah, Benjamin, and Dan.

Baalah (3) (§ 36, 85), (Mount). Close to Ekron on border of Judah. Name may remain in Wâdy El-Baghl, near Sorek. Josh. xv. 11.

Baalath (§ 72). Josh. xix. 44. Town of Dan. Probably Bel-'Ain in the plain of Sharon. 1 Kings ix. 18 ; 2 Chron. viii. 6.

Baalath-Beer. In Simeon. Josh. xix. 8. Identifies it with Ramoth Negeb, and is named, 1 Sam. xxx. 27, among towns friendly to David.

Baal-Gad. Under Mount Hermon. Josh. xi. 17, xii. 7, xiii. 5. Probably the place known as Banias, p. 182.

Baal-Hamon. Song of Sol. viii. 11. Unknown. Hammon, now Hamûn, was in Sidonia, the land of Baal-worship. May the name not be corrected to Baal-Hermon ?

Baal-Hazor (§ 11, 58, 71). 2 Sam. xiii. 23. Beside Ephraim (or Ophrah) at Tell 'Asûr.

Baal-Hermon (§ 23). Judg. iii. 3 ; 1 Chron. v. 23.

Baal-Meon or **Beth-Meon**. Now *M'Ain*, in Moab. A town of Reuben. Num. xxxii. 3, 38 ; Josh. xiii. 17 ; 1 Chron. v. 8 ; Jer. xlviii. 23 ; Ezek. xxv. 9.

Baal-Peor = *Beth Peor*, which see. On the ridge immediately north of the Callirhoe or Zerka M'Ain.

Baal-Perazim. 2 Sam. v. 20 ; 1 Chron. xiv. 11. Near valley of Rephaim. Not known.

Baal-Shalisha. 2 Kings iv. 42. For this *Kefr Thilith* in Ephraim has been suggested (Conder).

Baal-Tamar. Near Gibea. Judg. xx. 33. Placed at *'Attâra*.

Babel (§ 1).

Baca, Valley of—*i.e.* mulberry tree = *Valley of Rephaim*, which see. Probably now El-Bakeia, between Jerusalem and Bethlehem. Ps. lxxxiv. 6.

Bahurim. 2 Sam. xvi. 5. On the eastern slopes of Olivet. (Almon?) 2 Sam. iii. 16, xvi. 5, xvii. 18, xix. 16, xxiii. 31 ; 1 Kings ii. 8 ; 1 Chron. xi. 33.

Bajeth. Isa. xv. 2. Meaning doubtful.

Bamoth (§ 55, 57), and probably also Bamoth-Baal, Moabite city north of the Arnon, afterwards in Reuben. Josh. xiii. 17 ; Num. xxi. 19, 20, xxii. 41 (rendered "high places of Baal").

Banias (§ 14, 15, 20, 27, 115, 1. V.). See Cæsarea-Philippi.

Bashan (§ 7, 24, 32, II.). Also *Batanea* and *Bathaniyeh*.

Bath-Rabbim. At Heshbon. Song vii. 4. Either a city gate, or a gate closing passage to pools in the Wâdy Heshbon, yet clear and beautiful and alive with fish.

Bath-Zacharias. 1 Macc. vi. 32. Now Beit Skâria, south-west from Bethlehem.

Bealoth. Josh. xv. 24. Some take to be Baalath-Beer, which see.

Beer (§ 55). Num. xxi. 16. Must have been near Dibon, p. 68, between the Arnon and Callirhoe, probably the same as Beer-Elim of Isa. xv. 8. *Beer* of Judg. ix. 21 is unknown.

Beer-lahai-roi (§ 47). And see *'Ain Muweileh*.

Beeroth (Wells). In wilderness near Mount Hor. Deut. x. 6 ; Num. xx. 28.

Beeroth (§ 36, 85, 107). City of Hivites. Josh. ix. 7–17, in tribe of Benjamin, xviii. 25 ; 2 Sam. iv. 2, 3, v. 9, xxiii. 37 ; 1 Chron. xi. 39 ; Ezra ii. 25 ; Neh. vii. 29. Now *Bireh*, 2 miles from Bethel on way to Jerusalem. As the usual halting-place on the first night from Jerusalem, the incident of Luke ii. 44 may be placed here.

Beersheba (§ 5, 7, 11, 37, 46, 48, 50, 54, 70, 95, I. II. III. V.). Bîr-es-Seb'a. Gen. xxi. 14–33, xxii. 19, xxvi. 23, 33, xxviii. 10, xlvi. 1, 5 ; Josh. xv. 28, xix. 2 ; Judg. xx. 1 ; 1 Sam. iii. 20, viii. 2 ; 2 Sam. iii. 10, xvii. 11, xxiv. 2, 7, 15 ; 1 Kings iv. 25, xix. 3 ; 2 Kings xii. 1, xxiii. 8 ; 1 Chron. iv. 28, xxi. 2 ; 2 Chron. xix. 4, xxiv. 1, xxx. 5 ; Neh. xi. 27, 30 ; Amos v. 5, viii. 14.

Beeshterah. See Ashteroth.

Bela. Gen. xiv. 2, 8. See Zoar.

Belka (§ 59, II. Mishor) = "Mishor" of Moab.

Belmen. Entrance to the hills of Samaria from the north = Bel-'Ameh. Judith iv. 4.

Beneberak (§ 72). Town of Dan. Josh. xix. 45. Ibn Ibrak in plain of Sharon.

Beon. Num. xxxii. 3. Probably contraction for Beth-baal-Meon and Beth-Meon.
Berachah (§ 98). 2 Chron. xx. 26. Probably represented by Breikût in Wâdy 'Arrub between Bethlehem and Hebron.
Berea. Cf. 1 Macc. ix. 4 = Beeroth.
Bered (§ 46). Uncertain. Gen. xvi. 14 indicates that it lay west of Beer-lahai-roi.
Berothah and **Berothai.** 2 Sam. viii. 8; Ezek. xlvii. 16. Now *Beirût* or *Beyrout.*
Besor. 1 Sam. xxx. 9, 10, 21. Perhaps Wâdy Sheriah, 3 miles from supposed site of Ziklag, which see.
Betah. 2 Sam. viii. 8.
Betane. Judith i. 9. Conder suggests it is Bethany or Beit 'Ainûn.
Beten. Josh. xix. 25. In Asher. Abtûn, N. of Carmel, or B'Aneh, E. of Accho.
Bethabarah (§ 24, 109, V.). John i. 28. The ford of 'Abârah. The LXX. render Beth-Nimrah by Bethabarah.
Bethanabrah. 3 miles north of Beth-Aram.
Bethanath (§ 79, II.). Fenced city of Naphtali. Josh. xix. 38; Judg. i. 33. 'Ainath, 5 miles west of Kedesh.
Bethania (§ 24, 109). Revised Version, John i. 28 = Bashan probably, which see.
Bethanoth. In Judah. Josh. xv. 59. Beit 'Ainûn, 1 mile east of Halhul and near Beth-Zur.
Bethany (§ 12, 109, 116, III. V.). Now El-'Aziriyeh. The town of Lazarus, nearly 2 miles east of Jerusalem on road down to Jericho, over the southern shoulder of Olivet. Matt. xxi. 17, xxvi. 6; Mark xi. 1-12, xiv. 3; Luke x. 38 (?), xix. 29, xxiv. 50; John xi. 1, xii. 1.
Beth-Arabah. Josh. xv. 6, 61, xviii. 22. A town on edge of wilderness of Judah, assigned to both Judah and Benjamin, not far from Jericho.
Beth-Aram (§ 60). Town of Gad. Josh. xiii. 27. Probably same as Num. xxxii. 36. Beth-Haran in district of Jordan Valley, in the middle of Abel-Shittim. Most probably at the Tell-er-Rama at the mouth of the Wâdy Heshbon, 6 miles east of the Jordan. It became Betharamphtha. Herod Antipas changed it to Julias (or Livias). Map II. See Merrill, *East of Jordan*, p. 383, who suggests this as the scene of Matt. xiv. 6-11.
Beth-Arbel. Hos. x. 14. Placed by Tristram at *Irbid* on the Wâdy Hamam near Gennesareth, 2½ miles west from Magdala. Arbela of Decapolis has now same name.
Bethaven (§ 71, 87). Josh. vii. 2, xviii. 12; 1 Sam. xiii. 5, xiv. 23; Hos. iv. 15, v. 8, x. 5. On boundary of Benjamin and Ephraim, possibly meaning the desert north-east of Bethel. It signifies "House of Vanity," or idolatry in contrast to Bethel or "House of God." See Avim.
Bethazmaveth. See Azmaveth. Neh. vii. 28.
Bethbarah (§ 82). Judg. vii. 24. Possibly = Bethabarah, but the history requires apparently a lower ford of the Jordan—that at Succoth.
Beth-Basi = Beth-Hogla.
Beth-Birei (§ 70). Town of Simeon. 1 Chron. iv. 31.
Beth-Car. 1 Sam. vii. 11. Site unknown. Possibly 'Ain Karim. See Beth-Haccerem.
Beth-Dagon (1) (§ 77). Josh. xv. 41. Between Joppa and Lydda, originally given to Judah, afterwards in Dan. Doubtless a shrine of "Dagon" (1 Sam. v. 2), now Beit Dejan, 5 miles from Lydda.

Beth-Dagon (2). In Asher, at mouth of Belus. Josh. xix. 27. Now Tell D'Aûk, 4½ miles south-east of Accho. Map II.

Beth-Diblathaim. See Almon-Diblathaim.

Bethel (§ 11, 42, 48, 51, 53, 58, 62, 64, 71, 74, 81, 86, 96, 100, I. II. III. V.). Now Beitin, p. 55. Gen. xii. 8, xiii. 3, xxviii. 19, xxxi. 13, xxxv. 1-8, 15, 16; Josh. vii. 2, viii. 9, 12, 17, xii. 9, 16, xvi. 1, 2, xviii. 13, 22; Judg. i. 22, 23, iv. 5, xx. 18, 26, 31 (?), xxi. 2 (?), 19; 1 Sam. vii. 16, x. 3, xiii. 2, xxx. 27; 1 Kings xii. 29, 32, 33, xiii. 1–32; 2 Kings ii. 2, 3, 23, x. 29, xvii. 28, xxiii. 4-19; 1 Chron. vii. 28; 2 Chron. xiii. 19; Ezra ii. 28; Neh. vii. 32, xi. 31; Jer. xlviii. 13; Hos. x. 15, xii. 4; Amos iii. 14, iv. 4, v. 5, 6, vii. 10, 13.

Beth-Emek. In Asher. Josh. xix. 27. Now Amkah, 7 miles north-east of Accho. Map II.

Bether (§ 69). Song ii. 17. Probably mountains of Wâdy Bittîr, west from Bethlehem.

Bethesda (§ 92). John v. 2.

Bethezel. Mic. i. 11. Unknown (most probably in the land of the Philistines): called Azal in Zech. xiv. 5.

Beth-Gamul. Jer. xlviii. 23. Placed by Tristram at Um-el-Jemal, east of Gerasa and south-west of Bozra; by Conder at Jemâil, east of Dibon.

Beth-Haccerem. Neh. iii. 14; Jer. vi. 1. Identified by some with Jebel Fureidis or Herodium. A more recent and better suggestion would place the "House of Vineyards" at '*Ain Kârim*, the "Well of Vineyards." Cf. Bethshemesh and 'Ain Shems, and other examples of same change. On the ridge above 'Ain Kârim are cairns which may have been used as beacons of old. One is 40 feet high and 130 feet in diameter, with flat top 40 feet across (*Palestine Quarterly*, 1881, p. 271).

Beth-Haran (§ 60). See Beth-Aram.

Beth-Hogla (§ 68, II. V.). Josh. xv. 6, xviii. 19-21. Now 'Ain Hajlah. Frontier town of Benjamin, 5 miles south-east from Jericho. There is a well, as its present name implies, and some take it for Eneglaim of Ezek. xlvii. 10. Comparison of Josephus, *Ant*. xiii. 1, 5, shows that it is the Bethbasi of 1 Macc. ix. 62.

Bethhoron (§ 71, 72, 95, 99, II. *L.*), Upper and Nether. Now "Beit 'Ur." "El Fôka" and "Et Sahta," scarce 2 miles apart. The former is 10 miles north-west of Jerusalem. Josh. x. 10, 11, xvi. 3, 5, xviii. 13, 14, xxi. 22; 1 Sam. xiii. 18; 1 Kings ix. 17; 1 Chron. vi. 68; 2 Chron. viii. 5, xxv. 13.

Beth-Jesimoth (§ 59, II.). Town of Reuben, at north-east edge of Dead Sea. Possibly Sûcimeh at mouth of Jordan. Num. xxxiii. 49; Josh. xii. 3, xiii. 20; Ezek. xxv. 9.

Beth-Lebaoth (§ 70). Josh. xix. 6. In territory of Simeon, not known.

Bethlehem (1) (§ 11, 27, 58, 69, 106, II. IV. V.), 5 miles south of Jerusalem. Gen. xxxv. 19, xlviii. 7; Judg ..; Ruth; 1 Sam. xvi. 4, xvii. 12-15, xx. 6, 28; 2 Sam. ii. 32, xxiii. 14-24; 1 Chron. xi. 16-26; 2 Chron. xi. 6; Ezra ii. 21; Neh. vii. 26; Jer. xli. 17; Mic. v. 2; Matt. ii. 1-16; Luke ii. 4-15; John vii. 42.

Bethlehem (2) (§ 77, 82). In Zebulon. Josh. xix. 15; Judg. xii. 8, 10. *Beitlahm*, 7 miles west by north of Nazareth.

Beth-Marcaboth (§ 70). Josh. xix. 5. Town of Simeon. 1 Chron. iv. 31. "Place of Chariots" on the road into Egypt, not far from Ziklag. Madmannah is by some supposed to stand for it in Josh. xv. 31.

Beth-Meon. See Baal-Meon, and Beon.
Beth-Nimrah (§ 59, 60, II.). House of Leopards in Gad, now *Nimrim*. Num. xxxii. 3, 36; Josh. xiii. 27; Isa. xv. 6. 10 miles north of Salt Sea.
Beth-Palet. Josh. xv. 27. (Phelet) Neh. xi. 26. Near Beersheba.
Beth-Pazzez. Josh. xix. 21. Town of Issachar.
Beth-Peor (§ 27). Deut. iii. 29, iv. 46, xxxiv. 6; Josh. xiii. 20. (See *Peor*, Num. xxiii. 28).
Bethphage (§ 116). On the Mount of Olives near Bethany. Matt. xxi. 1; Mark xi. 1; Luke xix. 29. It was the limit of a Sabbath day's journey east from Jerusalem, *i.e.* 2000 cubits, and probably then stood where Kefr-et-Tor now stands.
Beth-Rehob. Judg. xviii. 28; 2 Sam. x. 6. Also Rehob. Num. xiii. 21; 2 Sam. x. 8. This must have lain near Laish on road from Hamath. The site of Hunin is suggested by Robinson. See *Rehob* for places to be distinguished.
Bethsaida (1) (§ 112). The way in which this name is in John's Gospel accompanied with a note of distinction, suggests that there were two cities of the name, John i. 44, xii. 21 (cf. ii. 1, xxi. 2); to this Matt. xi. 21, Mark vi. 45, Luke x. 12, refer. It has been placed at 'Ain Tâbghah, a little bay north of Gennesareth; but its position is doubtful.
Bethsaida (2) (§ 112, V.). Distinguished as "Julias," 2 miles up the Jordan from the Sea of Galilee, on eastern side of the ford there. Luke ix. 10, R.V., and probably also Mark viii. 22.
Bethshan (§ 10, 18, 45, 60, 75, 76, 82, 95, 110, 114, II.)=*Bethshean*. Now *Beisân*, on a mound commanding the eastern entrance to the plain of Esdraelon at the crossing of Jordan. Josh. xvii. 11, 16; Judg. i. 27; 1 Sam. xxxi. 10, 12; 2 Sam. xxi. 12; 1 Kings iv. 12; 1 Chron. vii. 29.
Bethshemesh (1) (§ 69, 72, 83, 85, II. *L.*). Now *'Ain Shems*, in Judah. Josh. xv. 10, xxi. 16; 1 Sam. vi. 9-20; 1 Kings iv. 9; 1 Chron. vi. 59; 2 Chron. xxviii. 18.
Bethshemesh (2). 2 Kings xiv. 11, 13, and 2 Chron. xxv. 21, 23. Unknown.
Bethshemesh (3). In Issachar. Josh. xix. 22. Ain-esh-Shemsiyeh, 7½ miles south of Bethshean, at south-east corner of Issachar.
Bethshemesh (4) (§ 79, 88). In Naphtali. Josh. xix. 38; Judg. i. 33. Now *Khurbet Shema*, 3 miles west of Safed.
Beth-Shittah (§ 82). Judg. vii. 22. Tristram suggests with great probability Shutta, half-way between Jezreel and Bethshean.
Beth-Tappuah. Josh. xv. 53. In Judah, to west of Hebron, now Tuffûh (see Tappuah).
Bethul (§ 70). In Simeon. Josh. xix. 4; 1 Chron. iv. 30 (Bethuel). *Beit Leyi* has been proposed, 4 miles south-east of Beit Jibrin (Conder).
Bethulia. Judith iv. 6, v. 21. Now *Mithilia*, 4 miles south-east of Dothan.
Bethzur (§ 99, III. V.). Josh. xv. 58; 2 Chron. xi. 7; Neh. iii. 16. Now *Beit Sur*, 4 miles north of Hebron, famous in Maccabean history.
Betogabra=*Beit Jibrin*. See Gath.
Betomestham. Judith iv. 6. Probably *Massin*, 5 miles south-west of Dothan (Conder).
Betonim. Josh. xiii. 26. Probably in Gad. Butneh, north-east of Beth-Nimrah.

Bezek (1). Judg. i. 4, 5. Capital of Adoni-Bezek, identified with Bezkah, 6 miles south-east of Lydda (Conder).
Bezek (2) (§ 82, 87, 110, II.). Probably Ibzik in Manasseh, on the western hills just opposite Jabesh-Gilead. 1 Sam. xi. 1-8. 13 miles from Shechem on road to Bethshean. Map II.
Bezer (§ 59, *L.*). Deut. iv. 43; Josh. xx. 8, xxi. 36; 1 Chron. vi. 78. In Moab, identified (Palmer) with Kasur-el-Besheir, 2 miles south-west of Dibon.
Bezeth (§ 117) = *Bezethah*. Hill on north-east quarter of Jerusalem.
Bileam. 1 Chron. vi. 70. See Ibleam.
Bilhah. See Baal.
Bir-Eyub (§ 68). In the Kedron Valley. A *well* (not a fountain) south of Siloam, probably for watering the king's gardens.
Bithron. 2 Sam. ii. 29. A district not again named. The rugged hill country between wilderness of Gibeon and the Jordan (cf. Migron).
Bizjothjah. Josh. xv. 28. Near Beersheba.
Bochim (§ 80). Judg. ii. 1-5. A place where Israelites assembled, possibly at Bethel (Gen. xxxv. 8 may indicate same spot).
Bohan. Josh. xv. 6, xviii. 17. A landmark on boundary of Judah near mouth of Wâdy Kelt, placed at Hajr-el-Asbah (Ganneau) with probability.
Bosora = *Bozrah* (2) of Bashan. 1 Macc. v. 26.
Bozez (§ 63, 87). 1 Sam. xiv. 4. Identified with the chalky white cliff on the north of the Wâdy Suweinit. Opposite is the sharp rock *Seneh* on the south side (*Tent Work*, ii. 113).
Bozkath. Josh. xv. 39. Between Lachish and Eglon. 2 Kings xxii. 1. Birthplace of King Josiah's mother. Most probably on high road to Gaza.
Bozrah (1). In Edom. Gen. xxxvi. 33; 1 Chron. i. 44; Isa. xxxiv. 6, lxiii. 1; Jer. xlix. 13, 22; Amos i. 12.
Bozrah (2) (§ 24, 99, II). Now *Buzrah* (Gk. Bostra). Most probably referred to, Jer. xlviii. 24; Mic. ii. 12. A town beside Kerioth in south-east of Hauran. Bosora of Maccabees.
Buttauf (§ 8, 87). Fertile district to the east of Accho, reaching eastward on the northern side of the Nazareth range.

Cabbon. Josh. xv. 40. Judean town in Philistia. Perhaps El-Kubeibah, 3 miles south-west from Beit Jibrin.
Cabul (§ 77, II.). Frontier town of Asher. Josh. xix. 27. Probably referred to 1 Kings ix. 13, "in *Galilee*." It lies 9 miles east by south of Accho, and is now *Kabûl*.
Cæsarea (§ 100, 105, 119, V.). Acts viii. 40, ix. 30, x. 1, 24, xi. 11, xii. 19, xviii. 22, xxi. 8-16, xxiii. 23, 33, xxv. 1-13. On the sea-shore south of Carmel, 32 miles north of Joppa.
Cæsarea-Philippi (§ 14, 115, V.). Now *Banias*, formerly Paneas. Matt. xvi. 13; Mark viii. 27.
Cain (§ 38, 58, II.). Now *Yekin*, on the eastern edge of the Judean hills, 3 miles south-east from Hebron, visible from the mountains of Moab. Josh. xv. 57. It is doubtless referred to by Balaam, Num. xxiv. 22.
Caleb. 1 Sam. xxx. 14. Properly Negeb Caleb. Possibly the position is still marked by Wâdy El-Kulâb, 10 miles south-west from Hebron.
Caleb-Ephratah. 1 Chron. ii. 24 (see preceding). The name came probably

from Caleb's second wife, Ephrath (ver. 19), who may have been of Bethlehem.

Callirhoe (§ 27, 59, 105, 111). Now the *Zerka M'ain*. Anciently this deep gorge was called *Nahaliel*, the valley of God. Num. xxi. 19. The name may be expressive only of its greatness, as "cedars of God," or it may mark a sacred place, possibly the "valley" of Deut. xxxiv. 6.

Callirhoe (§ 59).

Calvary (§ 117). See Gareb.

Camon. Judg. x. 5. In the north of Gilead. Burial-place of Jair. Kiepert gives *Kamm* near Arbela (on Map V.).

Cana (§ 108, V.). John ii. 1, 11, iv. 46, xxi. 2. *Kefr Kenna*, 4 miles north of Nazareth.

Canatha (§ 114, V.). One of the cities in Decapolis.

Capernaum (§ 108, 113, V.). Matt. iv. 13, viii. 5, xi. 23, xvii. 24; Mark i. 21, ii. 1, ix. 33; Luke iv. 23, 31, vii. 1, x. 15; John ii. 12, iv. 46, vi. 17-59. Most probably *Khan Minieh*, where there are yet unexplored traces of ruins. The removal of its stones for building elsewhere, as at Tell Hum, may explain, as in other cases, their absence.

Caphar-Salama of Maccabees. Probably *Selmeh*, near Joppa (Conder).

Carchemish (§ 37).

Carmel (§ 88, III.). Josh. xv. 55; 1 Sam. xv. 12, xxv. 2-40. Town in Southern Judah. Now *Kurmul*, 7 miles south of Hebron.

Carmel, Mount (§ 8, 10, 11, 23, 30, 31, 58, 65, 75, 76, 77, 78, 81, 96, 107, I. II. V.). In tribe of Manasseh. Josh. xii. 22, xix. 26; 1 Kings xviii. 19-42; 2 Kings ii. 25, iv. 25, xix. 23; 2 Chron. xxvi. 10; Song vii. 5; Isa. xxxiii. 9, xxxv. 2, xxxvii. 24; Jer. xlvi. 18, xv. 19; Amos i. 2, ix. 3; Mic. vii. 14; Nah. i. 4.

Casphor. 1 Macc. v. 26. *Casphon*, verse 36. A town in Gilead. Not known.

Cedron (1). John xviii. 1. See Kidron.

Cedron (2). 1 Macc. xv. 39. Town near Jannia. Identified by Warren with Katra.

Charashim. 1 Chron. iv. 14, and Neh. xi. 35. Now *Hirsha*, near Lydda (Conder).

Chephar-ha-Ammonai. Josh. xviii. 24. *Villages of the Ammonites*. In Benjamin.

Chephirah (§ 36). Josh. ix. 17, xviii. 26; Ezra ii. 25; Neh. vii. 29. Town of the Gibeonites, became town of Benjamin, 2 miles west of Ajalon. Now *Kefireh*.

Cherith (§ 61, 97). Brook east of Jordan. 1 Kings xvii. 3, 5.

Chesalon. Name of mountain. Josh. xv. 10. Preserved in Kesla, near Kirjath Jearim. Probably it is the mountain on which Kesla stands, on the north of Wâdy Ismaîn.

Chesil (§ 70, III.). Josh. xv. 30. Town of Simeon = *Bethul* in other lists. Now *Khelasa*, where are extensive ruins a little north of Rehoboth.

Chesulloth (§ 76, II.) = *Xaloth*, V. Josh. xix. 18. In Issachar. Or *Chisloth Tabor*. Josh. xix. 12. Now *Iksâl*, 2 miles south-east of Nazareth.

Chezib. Gen. xxxviii. 5. Canaanite town alloted to Judah. Probably '*Ain Kezbeh*, near Beit Nettif (Conder). Map III.

Chidon, Threshing floor of (1 Chron. xiii. 9) = *Nachon*. 2 Sam. vi. 6. Unknown.

Chinnereth (§ 65, 79, II.). This through *Ginizer* became *Gennesareth*. The

Sea of Galilee is in V. T. called Sea of Chinnereth. Num. xxxiv. 11; Deut. iii. 17; Josh. xi. 2, xii. 3, xiii. 27, xix. 35; 1 Kings xv. 20.

Choba or **Chobai**. Judith iv. 4. *El-Mekhobby*, east of Jenin (Conder). Map V.

Chorashan (1 Sam. xxx. 30), may be the *Ashan* of Josh. xv. 42, etc. Possibly, however, it may be found in Khoreisah, 2½ miles south of Beit Jibrin.

Chorazin (§ 113, V.). Now *Kerâzeh*. Matt. xi. 21; Luke x. 13.

Chun. Town of Syria, pillaged by David. 1 Chron. xviii. 8.

Chuzeba. Judean town. *Kueizîba*, 6 miles north-east from Hebron (Palmer's *Name Lists*). 1 Chron. iv. 22.

Chuzi. Now *Kûzah*, south of Shechem (Conder). Judith vii. 18.

"**Ciccar**"-**kik-kahr** (§ 19). The plain of Jordan. Gen. xiii. 10, 11, 12; Deut. xxxiv. 3; 2 Sam. xviii. 23; 2 Chron. iv. 17; Neh. iii. 22; and Gen. xiii. 14 and 19.

Coreæ. Josephus. North-east of Shiloh. *Kuriyut*. Map V.

Cyamon. Judith vii. 3. *Tell Keimûn*. Commona (Euseb.), on the south of Carmel = *Jokneam*.

Dabareh or **Daberath** (§ 76, II. *L.*). Josh. xix. 12, xxi. 28; 1 Chron. vi. 72. On border of Issachar and Zebulon. Now *Debûrieh*, at the foot of Tabor. Map II.

Dabbasheth. Josh. xix. 11. Frontier town of Zebulon, near Jokneam. Not known.

Dalmanutha (§ 114). Mark viii. 10. The narrative of Matt. xv. R.V. reads *Magadan* for Magdala, and the narrative does not suggest our Lord's going to neighbourhood of Capernaum and Tiberias where Magdala lay. For Dalmanutha, Dr. Thomson (*Land and Book*) suggests Ed-Delhemiyeh, situated at the junction of the Jarmûk with the Jordan. For Magadan, Ewald suggests Megiddon, which see.

Damascus (§ 3, 23, 41, 44, 50, 114, I.). Now *Demesk-esh-Shâm*. Its position is indicated on Physical Map, though it lay outside Palestine.

Dametha (§ 99). 1 Macc. v. 9-34. Now *Dâmeh*, in the centre of the Argob or Lejah, 30 miles north of Bozrah.

Dan (§ 5, 7, 14, 44, 50, 79, 96, II.). So named, Gen. xiv. 14. Also in Deut. xxxiv. 1; Josh. xix. 47; Judg. xviii. 29, xx. 1; 1 Sam. iii. 20; 2 Sam. |iii. 10, xvii. 11, xxiv. 2, 15; 1 Kings iv. 25, xii. 29, 30, xv. 20; 2 Kings x. 29; 1 Chron. xxi. 2; 2 Chron. xvi. 4, xxx. 5; Jer. iv. 15, viii. 16; Ezek. xxvii. 19; Amos viii. 14. Also called *Laish*. Judg. xviii. 7, 14, 27, 29; Isa. x. 30. At one of the fountains of the Jordan the name survives in the branch of Jordan called Leddân.

Dan-Jaan. 2 Sam. xxiv. 6. A town of Asher on the coast north of Achzib (Conder). Map II.

Dannah. Josh. xv. 49. In hill country of Judah. Conder proposes *Idnah*, half-way between Hebron and Beit Jibrin. Possibly, however, *Daneh*, 4½ miles south of Beit Jibrin.

Dead Sea (§ 20-22) = *Salt Sea*.

Debir (1). Josh. xiii. 26. A border town of Gad, named next to Mahanaim. Tristram suggests it is the *Lodebar* of 2 Sam. ix. 4, 5, xvii. 27, and may be *Dibbin* near Gerash, where he found "a fine ancient fountain and other remains."

Debir (2) (§ 64, II. *L.*). Josh. x. 38, 39, xi. 21, xii. 13. xv. 15; Josh. xxi. 15; 1 Chron. vi. 58. 12 miles south-west of Hebron, called also *Kirjah Sannah*, Josh. xv. 49; and *Kirjath Sepher*, Josh. xv. 15, Judg. i. 11, 12. Now *Edh-Dhâheriyeh*. Probably it was a Canaanite oracle, or sacred city.

Debir (3). Josh. xv. 7. A place on border of Judah and Benjamin, near the valley of Achor. The name is yet found in the pass Ed-Debr, on the south of the road from Jerusalem to Jericho, about midway (Palmer's *Name Lists*).

Decapolis (§ 60, 114, V.). The 10 towns from which this district had its name are—*Bethshean, Gadara, Gerasa, Canatha, Abila* (1), *Raphana* or *Raphon, Hippos* or *Susitha, Dion, Pella, Philadelphia* or *Rabbath-Ammon*. Sometimes 'Abila is omitted, and Damascus included. See each name in Index. Ptolemy reckons also *Capitolias*, which Oliphant places at Beit-er-Ras, 10 miles east of Gadara. Matt. iv. 25; Mark v. 20, vii. 31.

Der'a. See Edrei (1).

Diblath. Ezek. vi. 14. "Wilderness of" or "towards Diblathah," apparently in the extreme north of the land. Some suppose it a mistake for Riblah; but Conder points out Dibl in the midst of the land westward from Lake Hûleh.

Dibon (1) (§§ 44, 55, 59, II. V., and also Appendix I.). City of Reuben. Now *Dhibân*. Num. xxi. 30, xxxii. 3, 34; Josh. xiii. 9, 17; Isa. xv. 2; Jer. xlviii. 18, 22.

Dibon (2). Josh. xv. 22; Neh. xi. 25. See Dimonah.

Dibon-Gad. Num. xxxiii. 45, 46. See Dibon (1).

Dilean. Josh. xv. 38. In Philistia, probably not far from Lachish. *Tina*, 5 miles north-west of Umm Lâkis, has been proposed. The name means "gourd" or "cucumber," and as these are abundant in the district, the origin of the name and cause of its loss are apparent.

Dimnah (L.). In Zebulon. Josh. xxi. 35. Possibly *Rimmon*. Cf. 1 Chron. vi. 77.

Dimon. Now *Dimnah*, south of the Arnon. See *Land of Moab*, p. 105. Isa. xv. 9.

Dimonah. Josh. xv. 22. The *Dibon* of Neh. xi. 25, in the south-east of Judah. Now *Ed-Dheib*, "a collection of rude ruins at the head of a wâdy of the same name, 5 miles north of Arad" (Tristram).

Dinhabah. Edomite city. Unknown. Gen. xxxvi. 32; 1 Chron. i. 43.

Dio Cæsarea = *Sepphoris*. Chief city of Galilee in our Lord's time. According to Josephus, it lay 3 miles north of Nazareth. Map V.

Dion. Unknown. See Decapolis.

Dizahab. Deut. i. 1. Not known. Some place it at *Dahab*, near Eziongeber.

Dophkah. Num. xxxiii. 12, 13. In the desert far south. Not identified.

Dor (§§ 65, 72, 74, 75, II. V.) = *Dora*. Situated at the northern end of the plain of Sharon; 7 or 8 miles north of Cæsarea. Now Tantûrah, town of Manasseh; seat of one of Solomon's twelve local governments. Josh. xi. 2, xii. 23, xvii. 11; Judg. i. 27; 1 Kings iv. 11; 1 Chron. vii. 29.

Dothan (§ 53, II.). 10 miles north of the city of Samaria, discovered by Van de Velde. A large mound marks the site of the ancient city, the summit of which is strewn with remains of building material, and of pottery. Gen. xxxvii. 17; 2 Kings vi. 13.

Dragon-Well. Neh. ii. 13.

Dumah. Josh. xv. 52. In Judah. Now *Dômeh*, 10 miles south-west of Hebron. A large ruin, with foundations, rock-cut towers, cisterns, and caves. (Not the Dumah of Isa. xxi. 11, which was in Edom.)

Ebal (§ 11, 41, 58, 73, I.), 3077 feet high. Called now Jebel Eslamîyah. Summit is a level plateau, with remains of rough masonry, probably of ancient enclosures 92 feet square, with walls 20 feet thick, in which are recessed chambers 10 feet square. The design of this drystone building is not known. The mountain has remains of terraces and ancient cisterns to the top. Deut. xi. 29, xxvii. 4, 13 ; Josh. viii. 30, 33.

Eben. 1 Sam. vi. 14. "A great *stone* or Eben." Now Deir Eban, 2 miles east of 'Ain-Shems. This has been identified with Ebenezer since fourth century, but that must be sought much farther to the north-east.

Ebenezer (§ 85, 86). See foregoing. It lay probably near Neby Samwîl, but not identified. 1 Sam. iv. 1, v. 1, vii. 12.

Ebronah. Num. xxxiii. 34, 35. Unknown.

Ed, the Altar of. Apparently on east of Jordan. Position not known. Probably near Jebel 'Osha. Josh. xxii. 34.

Eder (1) or **Edar**, "Tower of." Gen. xxxv. 21. Jerome located it 1000 paces from Bethlehem, but on what ground is unknown. It has not been recovered. Cf. Mic. iv. 8.

Eder (2). Josh. xv. 21. Khurbet 'Adâr, 5 miles south of Gaza.

Edrei (1) (§ 24, 56, II.). Num. xxi. 33 ; Deut. i. 4, iii. 1, 10 ; Josh. xii. 4, xiii. 12, 31. The capital of Og, king of Bashan. Situated on the south-west edge of the district of Argob. The ruins are miles in extent. Greek and Roman buildings have crumbled, but the older homes of the earliest inhabitants remain. As Adraa it was known in early Christian times. It is now called *Edr'a*. It has often been placed at Dera, which is 20 miles to the south-west of its true site.

Edrei (2) (§ 79, II.). Josh. xix. 37. Possibly Y'ater, in Naphtali, 15 miles due west from Lake Hûleh.

Eglaim. Isa. xv. 8. See En-Eglaim.

Eglon (§ 35, 64, II. III.). Ajlân, on a low round hillock, 16 miles north-east of Gaza, and 2 miles from Umm Lâkis, which probably represents Lachish. Josh. x. 3, 5, 23, 34, 36, 37, xii. 12, xv. 39.

Ekrebal. Judith vii. 18. 'Ak-Rabeh = Acrabatta. One of the eleven Toparchies of Judea.

Ekron (§ 8, 69, 72, 80, 85, 100, 119, II. III. V.). Now Akîr (meaning barren), 12 miles north-east of Ashdod ; 200 feet above sea, from which it is 9 miles distant. No traces of antiquity are found. Built probably of unburnt bricks (Guérin); its ruins, as others so constructed, have vanished. There are wells, one of good construction. In time of Crusaders it was called Accaron. Josh. xiii. 3, xv. 11, 45, 46, xix. 43 ; Judg. i. 18 ; 1 Sam. v. 10, vi. 16, 17, vii. 14, xvii. 52 ; 2 Kings i. 2, 3, 6, 16 ; Jer. xxv. 20 ; Amos i. 8 ; Zeph. ii. 4 ; Zech. ix. 5, 7.

Elah (1) (§ 12, 72, I.). This valley, famous as the scene of David's victory over Goliath, is now called Wâdy Es-Sunt. The earlier name was derived from the terebinths growing there; the present from the acacias. There is a famous terebinth still remaining as a representative of the ancient times. 1 Sam. xvii. 2, 19, xxi. 9.

Elath or **Eloth.** At the head of the Gulf of 'Akabah. Deut. ii. 8 ; 1 Kings ix. 26 ; 2 Kings xiv. 22, xvi. 6 ; 2 Chron. viii. 17, xxvi. 2.

Elea'eh (§ 56, 58, 59, II.). Now El-'Al, a mile and a half north of Heshbon. Num. xxxii. 3, 37; Isa. xv. 4, xvi. 9; Jer. xlviii. 34.
Eleasa (§ 99). 1 Macc. ix. 5. Il'asa.
Eleph. Josh. xviii. 28. Now Lifta, a town of Benjamin, 2 miles north-west of Jerusalem.
Eleutheropolis = *Beit Jibrin* or *Betogabra*. By some identified with Gath. Tristram says that the central heap is known as Khurbet Gat; but this is disputed. See Gath. Situated at Mareshah. Map II.
Elkosh. Nah. i. 1. Said by Jerome to be in Galilee; thought by others to be on banks of Tigris. Schwartz reported the Prophet's Grave as shown, 2½ miles north of Tiberias, but this is probably from supposed site of Capernaum.
Elon (§ 72, II.). Josh. xix. 43. Now Beit Ello, 8 miles north-west of Bethel. A town of Dan, situated on high ground.
Elon-beth-Hannan. 1 Kings iv. 9. Probably Beit 'Anân, 9 miles north-west of Jerusalem, on road toward Bethhoron. Map III.
Eltekeh (§ 72, II. *L.*). In Dan. Now Beit Likia, 3 miles north-west of preceding. Josh. xix. 44, xxi. 23.
Eltekon. Josh. xv. 59. Not identified; but from its enumeration with Gedor, Halûl, and Bethanoth (which see) it must have lain on the east of the watershed, 5 or 6 miles north of Hebron.
Eltolad (§ 70). Assigned to Simeon out of Judah. Possibly El-Toula in Wâdy Lussan. Josh. xv. 30, xix. 4; = Tolad, 1 Chron. iv. 29.
Emmaus (1) (§ 17, 79, 118, V.). Luke xxiv. 13.
Emmaus (2) (§ 99, 118) = *Nicopolis*. 1 Macc. iii. 40. Now 'Amwâs. The reading of the Sinaitic MS. of the New Testament would identify this with (1), as it has in Luke xxiv. 13, 160 stadia; but the probability is that this is an alteration to suit known distance of Nicopolis from Jerusalem.
Emmaus (3) (§ 79). Now Hammam = Hammon (2).
Enam (§ 54). Josh. xv. 34. Unknown.
Endor (§ 75, 76, 81, 107, II.). A town of Issachar assigned to Manasseh, over 3 miles south of Tabor, and 2 miles east from Nain, on the range of the Jebel Duhy or Little Hermon, about 7 miles from Gilboa. Josh. xvii. 11; 1 Sam. xxviii. 7; Ps. lxxxiii. 10.
En-Eglaim. Ezek. xlvii. 10. Possibly Eglaim of John xv. 8. Tristram suggests 'Ain Hajla, the ancient Beth-Hogla. See § 68.
Engannin (1) (§ 69, III.). Josh. xv. 34. In tribe of Judah. Now Umm Jina, 1 mile west of Bethshemesh.
Engannin (2) (§ 76, 80, II. *L.*). Josh. xix. 2, xxi. 29. Town of Issachar. Now Jenîn, 7 miles south of Jezreel.
Engedi (§ 19, 21, 22, 27, 35, 38, 44, 58, 88, 98, I. II. III. V.). "The spring of the wild goat," which may still be seen upon the rocks above it. Its earlier name was Hazezon-Tamar, which see. It lies on the west shore of the Salt Sea. Josh. xv. 62; 1 Sam. xxiii. 29, xxiv. 1; 2 Chron. xx. 22; Song i. 14; Ezek. xlvii. 10.
En-Haddah. Josh. xix. 21. Town of Zebulon. Now Kefr Adân, 3 miles north-west of Engannin (2), with which it is named. Identified also with Kefr Outherin of the Talmud on borders of Samaria and Galilee (*Memoirs*, ii. 45). Map II.
En-Hakkore (§ 83). Judg. xv. 19. Very probably so named by Samson as punning on the familiar name. There are many instances of this.

En-Hattannin. See Dragon-Well.

En-Hazor (§ 79, II.). Josh. xix. 37. Fenced city in west of Naphtali (as in § 79), or 'Ain Hazzur, 4½ miles north of Yarûn.

En-Mishpat. Gen. xiv. 7. Another name for Kadesh, *i.e.* probably Kadesh-Barnea.

En-Rimmon. Neh. xi. 29 = *Ain Rimmon.* Josh. xv. 32, xix. 7; Zech. xiv. 10. See Rimmon (2).

En-Rogel (§ 68). This seems most probably the Fountain of the Virgin. Some place it at Ber Eyub, lower down the Kedron Valley, which is not an "'Ain" or well-spring. Josh. xv. 7, xviii. 16; 2 Sam. xvii. 17; 1 Kings i. 9.

En-Shemesh. Josh. xv. 7, xviii. 17. "The Fountain of the Sun" is generally, and with most probability, placed at 'Ain Haud, a fountain a mile from Bethany on the road down to Jericho. Commonly called "the Apostle's Fountain."

En-Tappuah (§ 73). Josh. xvii. 7. A spring at the head of the Wâdy Kânah. See Tappuah (2).

Ephes-Dammim (§ 88). In the valley of Elah. Means "the Boundary of Blood." We have perhaps a trace in the modern Beit Fasid, or "House of Bleeding," near Shocoh (*Tent Work*, ii. p. 160). 1 Sam. xvii. 1; 1 Chron. xi. 13, marg.

Ephraim (1) (§ 23, 35, 81, 82, 95). "Mountains of" and "Mount Ephraim."

Ephraim (2) (§ 95, 115) = *Ophrah* (1). 2 Sam. xiii. 23; 2 Chron. xiii. 19; John xi. 54. See Ophrah.

Ephratah or Ephrath (§ 43, 53, 94, II. III. V.) = *Bethlehem.* Gen. xxxv. 16, 19, xlviii. 7; Ruth iv. 11; Ps. cxxxii. 6; Mic. v. 2.

Ephron (1) (§ 69). Josh. xv. 9. "Mount" on border of Judah and Benjamin. Not identified. Probably south-west of Bethlehem.

Ephron (2). 1 Macc. v. 46. Not known. A fortress in Gaulonitis, probably on the Hieromax.

Esdraelon (§ 7, 8, 10, 19, 53, 65, 75, I.). See Jezreel (2). Valley or plain of Jezreel. Josh. xvii. 16; Judg. vi. 33; Hos. i. 5.

Esek. Gen. xxvi. 20. Not known.

Eshcol (§ 34, 55). 'Ain Kashkaleh, at the north end of the town of Hebron (Van de Velde). Num. xiii. 23, 24, xxxii. 9; Deut. i. 24.

Eshean. Josh. xv. 52. From position in *Name List* here, must have been near Hebron. Unknown.

Eshtaol (§ 72, 83). Now Eshû'a, a mile and half east of Surah, with which it is always named. Josh. xv. 33, xix. 41; Judg. xiii. 25, xvi. 31, xviii. 2, 8, 11.

Eshtemoa (*L.*). Now Es Semû'a, 9 miles south of Hebron. Josh. xv. 50, xxi. 14; 1 Sam. xxx. 28; 1 Chron. vi. 57.

Esora. Judith iv. 4. 'Asireh, 2 miles north of Shechem.

Etam (1) (§ 83, II. III.). A rock where Samson hid. Judg. xv. 8, 11. Properly "the cleft;" a remarkable cave at Beit 'Atab has been identified with it.

Etam (2) (§ 69, 92, II.). 2 Chron. xi. 6. Between 2 and 3 miles south of Bethlehem. In the position of the ancient Nephtoah, now marked by 'Ain 'Atân.

Etam (3). Town of Simeon. 1 Chron. iv. 32. Possibly Aitûn, 12 miles west by south of Hebron. Map II.

Ether (§ 70). Probably El-'Atr, near Beit Jibrin (*Mem.* iii. 261), on northwest. This seems to stand for Tochen of 1 Chron. iv. 32. The marg. reading of 1 Chron. iv. 32 substitutes it for Etam. Josh. xv. 42, xix. 7.
Ezel. 1 Sam. xx. 19. "The stone." Unknown.
Ezem. See Azem, and note, § 83, on names of tribes and their dwelling-places.

Ferata (§ 75, 82) = *Ophrah.*
Fountain-gate. At south-east corner of Jerusalem, near or leading to Siloam.

Gaash. A mountain which gave its name to the valleys about it, in Ephraim. The name suggests volcanic origin = earthquake. It was near Timnath Serath. Josh. xxiv. 30; Judg. ii. 9; 2 Sam. xxiii. 30; 1 Chron. xi. 32.
Gaba. The same as Geba, which see. Josh. xviii. 24; Ezra ii. 26; Neh. vii. 30, xi. 31.
Gadara (§ 18, 114, V.). Mark v. 1; Luke viii. 26, viii. 37. Now *Umm Keis.*
Galeed (§ 51). A play upon the name Gilead. Position unknown. Gen. xxxi. 47, 48.
Galem (§ 69). In LXX. Josh. xv.; lying south of Jerusalem, not to be confounded with Gallim, which must have been to the north.
Galgala. 1 Macc. ix. 2. Probably Gilgal (2), now *Jiljilia*, which see.
Gallim (§ 95). Unknown; but from the passage in Isaiah it must have been just north of Jerusalem (one reading substitutes Gallim for Galem in the list inserted in LXX. after Josh. xv. 59, and some suggest, therefore, Beit-Yâla at Bethlehem), which, however, will not suit. Isa. x. 30; 1 Sam. xxv. 44; Isa. x. 30.
Gamala. See Decapolis, now *Kulât-el-Husn.* On the eastern side of the Sea of Galilee, about 10 miles north of Gadara.
Gareb. Jer. xxxi. 39. Identified by Ewald with Golgotha, by Gesenius with Bezetha; which are reconcilable if it be remembered that Bezetha was divided by a quarry, § 117. Others, as Keil, take the word to have the meaning originally of scratching, and then to be applied to lepers, and they place Gareb on the west (where the lepers still live), and identify it with the mount at the head of the valley of Rephaim. Josh. xv. 8, xviii. 16.
Gath (§ 72, 88, 119, II. III.). Most probably at Tell-es-Sâfi (also under Beit Jibrin). Josh. xi. 22; 1 Sam. v. 8, vi. 17, vii. 14, xvii. 4, 23, 52, xxi. 10, 12, xxvii. 2-4, 11; 2 Sam. i. 20, xv. 18, xxi. 20, 22; 1 Kings ii. 39-41; 2 Kings xii. 17; 1 Chron. vii. 21, viii. 13, xviii. 1, xx. 6, 8; 2 Chron. xi. 8, xxvi. 6; Ps. lvi. title; Amos vi. 2; Mic. i. 10.
Gath-Hepher or **Gittah-Hepher** (§ 77, II.). Josh. xix. 13; 2 Kings xiv. 25. Birthplace of Jonah identified with El-Meshhed. "The monument," *i.e.* of Neby Yûnas, or Prophet Jonah, 3 miles north of Nazareth, where the rabbinical tradition places it; it is in Zebulon.
Gath-Rimmon (1) (§ 72, II. III. *L.*). Josh. xix. 45, xxi. 24; 1 Chron. vi. 69. In tribe of Dan, meaning High-Gath, probably Tell-es-Safi, § 88.
Gath-Rimmon (2). Josh. xxi. 25. Possibly a mistake. See 1 Chron. vi. 70, where Bileam stands for it.
Gaulanites (§ 61, 114, V.). Now *Jaulan.* A district on east of Sea of Galilee.

Merrill seems to think that the name remains in Wady 'Allan, which he makes its southern boundary. See Golan.

Gaza (1) (§ 8, 34, 46, 64, 80, 83, 119, I. II. III. V.) Philistine town, now *Guzzeh*. Gen. x. 19; Josh. x. 41, xi. 22, xv. 47; Judg. i. 18, vi. 4, xvi. 1, 21; 1 Sam. vi. 17; 2 Kings xviii. 8; Jer. xlvii. 1, 5; Amos i. 6, 7; Zeph. ii. 4; Zech. ix. 5; Acts viii. 26.

Gaza (2). 1 Chron. vii. 28. Possibly instead of Gaza "'Ayyah" should be read; it lay apparently near Shechem, and might be Khurbet Heiyeh, 4 miles south-east of it.

Gazara or Gazer=*Gezer*. 2 Sam. v. 25; 1 Chron. xiv. 16; 1 Macc. xviii. 52.

Geba (1) (§ 87, 95, II. L.). A town and surrounding district. Now *Jeb'a* and *Sahel Jeb'a* (*i.e.* "plain of Jeba") on the edge of the Wâdy Suweinit, 5 miles north of Jerusalem. Jeba was a Levitical city. See Gaba. The name is still written sometimes Jeba' and sometimes Jeba'h (*Palestine Quarterly*, 1881, p. 89). Josh. xxi. 17; 1 Sam. xiii. 3; 2 Sam. v. 25; 1 Kings xv. 22; 2 Kings xxiii. 8; 1 Chron. vi. 60, viii. 6; 2 Chron. xvi. 6; Neh. xi. 31, xii. 29; Isa. x. 29; Zech. xiv. 10.

Geba (2). Geba of horsemen mentioned by Josephus is not to be confounded with preceding; it lies 12 miles north of Cæsarea, still bearing same name (*Wars*, ii. 18, 1, iii. 3, 1).

Gebal (§ 36). Josh. xiii. 5; 1 Kings v. 18, marg.; Ezek. xxvii. 9. Known as Byblos by the Greeks. Now *Jibeil*. A city devoted to the worship of Adonis, and celebrated for its science and skill in handicrafts. Its inhabitants were called Giblites (Ewald's *History of Israel*, iii. 226, and *Heth and Moab*, pp. 76, 77).

Gebim. Isa. x. 31. See Gibeah.

Geder. Josh. xii. 13=*Gedor*. Royal city of Canaanites.

Gederah (1). Josh. xv. 36. Placed by Conder at Jedireh, 10 miles south-east of Lydda. Tristram identifies it with Ghuderah, 2 miles south-east of Ekron, which is not, however, on Survey Map.

Gederah (2). Town of Benjamin. 1 Chron. xii. 4. Now Jedireh, 1 mile north-east of Gibeon.

Gederoth. Possibly Katrah, 4 miles south-west of Ekron (Warren)=*Cedron* of Maccabees. This may be the place given in Onomasticon for Gederah. Josh. xv. 41; 2 Chron. xxviii. 18.

Gederothaim. Josh. xv. 36. Doubtful if distinct from Gederah. It may be an appellative to distinguish the *twin* cities from others of same name ="sheepfold."

Gedor. Now Jedâr, 7 miles north of Hebron. Josh. xv. 58; 1 Chron. iv. 39, xii. 7.

Gehenna. See Hinnom.

Geliloth. Josh. xviii. 17. Opposite Adummim on the boundary of Judah and Benjamin.

Gennesaret (§ 17, 65, 79). Matt. xiv. 34; Mark vi. 53; Luke v. 1. From the more ancient Chinnereth, which see.

Gerar (§ 46, 50, 98, 100, I. II. V.). Now *Umm-el-Jerrâr*, 6 miles south of Gaza. Gen. x. 19, xx. 1, 2, xxvi. 1, 6, 17, 20, 26; 2 Chron. xiv. 13, 14.

Gerasa (§ 60, 114, I.). Matt. viii. 28; Mark v. 1. In R. V. the reading in Matt. viii. 28 is Gadarenes. Probably the extensive district about Gadara. The Gadaritis of Josephus and Strabo included Gerasa.

Gergesa. See preceding.
Gerizim (§ 11, 27, 41, 48, 58, 73, 74, 82, 105, 110, I.). Deut. xi. 29, xxvii. 12; Josh. viii. 33; Judg. ix. 7; John iv. 20, 21
Geshur (1) (§ 24, 61, II.). Josh. xii. 5, xiii. 11, 13; 2 Sam. iii. 3, 13, 37, 38, xiv. 23, 32, xv. 8; 1 Chron. ii. 23, iii. 2. District in north of Bashan.
Geshur (2) (§ 24, 32). Geshurites dwelt also on the southern border of Philistia. Deut. iii. 14; Josh. xiii. 2; 1 Sam. xxvii. 8.
Gethsemane (§ 116). Matt. xxvi. 36; Mark xiv. 32.
Gezer (§ 64, 71, II. *L*.). A royal city of Canaanites. Josh. x. 33, xii. 12, xvi. 3, 10, xxi. 21; Judg. i. 29; 1 Kings ix. 15, 16, 17; 1 Chron. vi. 67, vii. 28, xx. 4.
Giah. 2 Sam. ii. 24. Means "the ravine." Probably the Wâdy Suweinit or one of its tributaries, as it lay east of Gibeon towards Jordan. See Ammah.
Gibbethon (§ 72, *L*.). A town of Dan, most probably identified with Kibbiah, 6 or 7 miles north by east of Lydda. Josh. xix. 44, xxi. 23; 1 Kings xv. 27, xvi. 15, 17.
Gibeah (1) (§ 83, 87, 88, 95, III.). Known as Gibeah of Saul. Distinguished in Isa. x. 29 from Geba. It lay north of Jerusalem and south of Geba. It was placed by Robinson at Tell-el-Ful, west of Neby Samwil. The name is so common = hill, that probably there were several. Gebim (Isa. x. 31) may be intended to group several in one. In 1 Sam. xiv. 2, 5, Gibeah seems to be distinguished from Gibeah of Benjamin, and in ver. 16 seems to be equivalent to Geba. Judg. xix. 12–16, xx. 4, 5, 9, 10, 13, 14, 15, 19, 20, 21, 25, 29, 30, 31, 33 (Geba), 34, 36, 37, 43; 1 Sam. x. 26, xi. 4, xiii. 2, 15, 16, xiv. 2 (?), 5 (?), 16, xv. 34, xxii. 6, xxiii. 19, xxvi. 1; 2 Sam. vi. 3, 4, xxi. 6, xxiii. 29; 1 Chron. xi. 31; 2 Chron. xiii. 2 (?); Isa. x. 29; Hos. v. 8, ix. 9, x. 9.
Gibeah (2). Josh. xv. 57. Now Jeba, 8 miles west by south of Bethlehem.
Gibeah (3). Josh. xviii. 28. Now Jebia, 10 miles north-west of Jerusalem.
Gibeah (4) (§ 87). 1 Sam. x. 5. "Hill of God," A.V. ("Gibeah Naelohim," Heb.). This from 1 Sam. xiii. 3 appears the same as "Geba." If Neby Samwîl were not probably Mizpeh, though this is not certain, one would naturally fasten on it as the hill. Cf. Ps. lviii. 15, "A hill of God is the hill of Bashan."
Gibeah (5). Hill of Phinehas. Possibly Jibia, 7 miles west of Tell 'Azûr. Awertah is the traditional site. This Jibia some take to be the Gaba of Josh. xviii. 24.
Gibeah (6). 2 Sam. vi. 3, 4. A hill at Kirjath Jearim. See 1 Sam. ix. 14.
Note.—The expression "Gibeah in the field" (Judg. xx. 31) is peculiar. Just north of Tell-el-Ful, the north road from Jerusalem divides, one branch going on to Bethel, the other turning eastward towards Geba, which is therefore the Gibeah here meant. Ai is similarly described (Josh. viii. 24). As there is no level at Ai, even like the Sahel Geba, it is hardly possible to avoid the conclusion that the designation had become the proper name of a district; as in "the field of Sophim," and the plural "Siddim." This would explain the use of the word in 1 Sam. xx. 5, 11, 24, 35; see also Neh. xi. 29. It may be noticed that the LXX. translation is the phrase of Mark xv. 21, xvi. 12, where it seems to be used as indicating a well-understood direction from Jerusalem (§ 118).

Gibeon (§ 36, 63, 64, 71, 86, 95, II. III. *L.*). Now *El-Gib*, on the north of Neby Samwil. Josh. ix. 3, 17, x. 1, 2-6, 10, 12, 41, xi. 19, xviii. 25, xxi. 17; 2 Sam. ii. 12, 13, 16, 24, iii. 30, xx. 8; 1 Kings iii. 4, 5, ix. 2; 1 Chron. viii. 29, ix. 35, xiv. 16, xvi. 39, xxi. 29; 2 Chron. i. 3, 13; Neh. iii. 7, vii. 25; Isa. xxviii. 21; Jer. xxviii. 1, xli. 12, 16.

Gidom (§ 84). Judg. xx. 45. Unknown. Possibly named from the massacre here. It means "the cutting down," as Gideon = "the cutter down."

Gihon (1), Upper = The "Virgin's Fountain" so called = *Enrogel*, distinguished from

Gihon (2), the lower "opening," which may have been the issue of the waters of the Siloam tunnel. 1 Kings i. 33, 45; 2 Chron. xxxii. 30, xxxiii. 14.

Gilboa, Mountains of (§ 10, 11, 27, 40, 76, 82, 96, 107, I.). See Gilead (2). 1 Sam. xxviii. 4, xxxi. 1, 8; 2 Sam. i. 6, 21, xxi. 12; 1 Chron. x. 1, 8.

Gilead (1) (§ 18, 25, 59, II.). Name of a district allotted to Gad.

Gilead (2) (§ 7, 10, 25, 29, 35, 51, 58, 82, II.). Judg. vii. 3. Probably a part of Mount Gilboa. The name remains in Wâdy Jalûd.

Gilgal (1) (§ 62, 63, 64, 81, 86, 97, III.). In the plain of Jordan 3 miles east of Jericho. Now *Tell Jiljulieh*. In *Joshua* of this same series, p. 47, a different view is taken in regard to "Gilgal" mentioned Josh. ix. and x. The argument against confounding Gilgal in the plain of Jordan with that Gilgal from which Elijah "went down" to Bethel (2 Kings ii. 1) is conclusive, certainly. But equally fatal to the supposition that the Gilgal of Josh. ix. and x. was Jiljilia is the statement that "Joshua ascended from Gilgal," . . . "going up from Gilgal all night" (x. 6-9) (cf. 1 Sam. x. 6, xv. 12). The difficulty arises from the account of the going to Shechem in chap. viii. 30-35; but this seems told by anticipation. Deut. xi. 30; Josh. iv. 19, 20, v. 9, 10, ix. 6, x. 6, 7, 9, 15, 43, xiv. 6, xv. 7; Judg. ii. 1, iii. 19; 1 Sam. vii. 16, x. 8, xi. 14, 15, xiii. 4, 7, 8, 12, 15, xv. 12, 21, 33; 2 Sam. xix. 15, xix. 40; Neh. xii. 29; Hos. iv. 15, ix. 15, xii. 11; Amos iv. 4, v. 5; Mic. vi. 5.

Gilgal (2) (§ 74, 97). 2 Kings ii. 1, iv. 38. Now *Jiljilia*.

Gilgal (3) (§ 74). Josh. xii. 23. Probably Jiljulieh, 14 miles north-east of Joppa.

Giloh. For this Kurbet Jâla has been suggested, 7 miles north of Hebron, and 2 miles west of Jerusalem road. Josh. xv. 51. And Gilonite. 2 Sam. xv. 12, xxiii. 34.

Gimzo. 2 Chron. xxviii. 18. *Jimzu*, 3 miles south-east of Lydda.

Girgashites (§ 36).

Giscala (§ 79) = *Eljish*, 11 miles west of south end of Lake Hûleh.

Gittah-Hepher (§ 77, II.) = *Gath-Hepher*. Josh. xix. 13.

Gittaim. Unknown. It is doubtful if the two texts added refer to the same place. 2 Sam. iv. 3; Neh. xi. 33.

Goath. Jer. xxxi. 39. Unknown.

Gob. 2 Sam. xxi. 18, 19. "The pit" probably near Gezer. See 1 Chron. xx. 4, where Gezer stands for it.

Golan (§ 60, 61, II. V. *L.*). City of refuge in Manasseh east of Jordan. The chief city of the district which bore the name. Not known. Deut. iv. 43; Josh. xx. 8, xxi. 27; 1 Chron. vi. 71.

Golgotha (§ 117). See Calvary. Matt. xxvii. 33; Mark xv. 22; John xix. 17.

Gomorrah (§ 45). Gen. x. 19, xiii. 10, xiv. 2, 8, 10, 11, xviii. 20, xix. 24, 28; Deut. xxix. 23, xxxii. 32; Isa. i. 9, 10, xiii. 19; Jer. xxiii. 14,

xlix. 18, l. 40; Amos iv. 11; Zeph. ii. 9; Matt. x. 15; Mark vi. 11; Rom. ix. 29; 2 Pet. ii. 6; Jude 7.
Gophna. Now *Jufna*. See Ophni.
Goshen (1) (§ 64). Josh. x. 41, xi. 16. A district in Judah. Unknown.
Goshen (2). Josh. xv. 51. Town in Judah. From the towns with which it is named (see Holon and Giloh) it probably lay north of Hebron.
Gudgodah. Deut. x. 7. Or Hor-Hagidgad, Num. xxxiii. 32. Unknown.
Gur. 2 Kings ix. 27. "Going up of." Near Ibleam. Not known.
Gur-Baal (§ 98). 2 Chron. xxvi. 7. *Tell-el-Ghur*.

Hachilah (§ 88, III.). *El-Kôlah*, 8 miles south-east of Hebron. 1 Sam. xxiii. 19, xxvi. 3.
Hadadrimmon (§ 76, 98). Zech. xii. 11. Probably Rummânch, 7 miles north-west of Jezreel, on southern edge of plain of Esdraelon close to Taanach.
Hadashah. Josh. xv. 37. Lay in Philistia probably not far from Ashkelon; but is not known. Few of the towns in the same group have been identified. The Talmud mentions a town of this name as the smallest in Judea—possibly K.-el-'Addeiseh, 3 miles north-east of Hebron; not therefore the same.
Hadattah. See Hazor-Hadattah.
Hadid = *Adithaim*. Ezra ii. 33; Neh. vii. 37, xi. 34.
Halak. Josh. xi. 17. A mount in Edom, in Seir. Unknown.
Halhul. Josh. xv. 58. *Halhûl*, about 4 miles north of Hebron.
Hali. Josh. xix. 25. Perhaps 'Alia, 13 miles north-east of Accho.
Ham (§ 33). Gen. xiv. 5. Possibly Rabbath-Ammon, which lay between Ashteroth-Karnaim in Bashan and Kirjathaim in Moab.
Hamath (§ 13, 36, 55). On the north boundary of the land, a district in the upper part of the plain of Cœle Syria, watered by the Orontes. Num. xiii. 21, xxxiv. 8; Judg. iii. 3; 2 Sam. viii. 9; 1 Kings viii. 65; 2 Kings xiv. 25, 28, xvii. 24, 30, xviii. 34, xix. 13, xxiii. 33, xxv. 21; 1 Chron. xiii. 5, xviii. 3, 9; 2 Chron. vii. 8, viii. 4; Isa. x. 9, xi. 11, xxxvi. 19, xxxvii. 13; Jer. xxxix. 5, xlix. 23, lii. 9, 27; Ezek. xlvii. 16, 17, 20, xlviii. 1; Amos vi. 2, 14; Zech. ix. 2.
Hammath (§ 17, 79, II.). Josh. xix. 35. See Hammon (2).
Hammon (1) (§ 78, II.). Josh. xix. 28. Possibly Umm-el-'Amud en Mediterranean, 10 miles south of Tyre (Conder), or Hamûn (Tristram). It was a purely Phœnician city consecrated to Hammon (*Heth and Moab*, p. 86).
Hammon (2) (§ 79, *L.*). 1 Chron. vi. 76. In Naphtali. Probably Hammoth-Dor, and Hamath, Josh. xix. 35. Now Hammâm, 1½ mile south of Tiberias, called by Josephus, Emmaus. The name signifies "hot baths."
Hammoth-Dor. Josh. xxi. 32. See Hammon (2).
Hananeel, Tower of. On the north of the temple. Probably afterwards included in the citadel Baris, or Antonia. Neh. iii. 1, xii. 39; Jer. xxxi. 38; Zech. xiv. 10.
Hannathon (§ 79, II.). Josh. xix. 14. Now *Kefr 'Anân*, 5 miles south-west of Safed.
Haphraim. Josh. xix. 19. Rather Hapharaim. Most probably El-Fanlych, 6 miles north-west of Lejjûn.
Hareth (§ 88, III.). 1 Sam. xxii. 5. Now *Kharâs*, 2 or 3 miles east of Keilah.

Harod (§ 82). Judg. vii. 1. Spring in plain of Esdraelon. Probably 'Ain-el-Jem'ain, the well of the two companies, 4 miles west of Bethshean (Conder). Others place it at the fountain of Jezreel,—surely too near Midianite camp.

Harosheth (§ 81, 107). Judg. iv. 2, 13, 16. Now *El-Harāthiyeh* (Thomson), on the north bank of the Kishon, 8 miles from its mouth.

Haruph. 1 Chron. xii. 5 and Neh. vii. 24 (?). *Khurbet Kharûf*, 2 miles west of Keilah.

Hassenaah. Neh. iii. 3. Probably = Senaah.

Hattin (§ 37, 65, 79, 113). Mountain with two summits known as the horns of Hattin.

Hauran (§ 17, 18, 24). Ezek. xlvii. 16, 18. Now *Haurân*.

Havoth-Jair = "The villages of Jair" in Argob. Num. xxxii. 41; Deut. iii. 14; Josh. xiii. 30; Judg. x. 4; 1 Chron. ii. 23.

Hazar-Addar. Num. xxxiv. 4. See Adar.

Hazar-Enan. On the northern boundary of Israel, probably near Lebon or Lebweh in the plain of Cœle Syria. Num. xxxiv. 9, 10; Ezek. xlvii. 17, xlviii. 1.

Hazar-Gaddah. Josh. xv. 27. Unknown, on the south-east border of Simeon. Possibly Hadâdah at head of ravine leading up from Engedi, 8 or 9 miles east of Hebron, which Tristram proposes for Hadattah (*Land of Israel*, p. 360).

Hazar-Hatticon. Ezek. xlvii. 16. Unknown.

Hazar-Shual (§ 70). Probably in Wâdy S'aweh Kurbet at Tell S'aweh, 11 or 12 miles north-east of Beersheba. Josh. xv. 28, xix. 3; 1 Chron. iv. 28; Neh. xi. 27.

Hazar-Susah (§ 70). Josh. xix. 5; 1 Chron. iv. 31. "Susim" is by some supposed to be the Sansannah of Josh. xv. 31, and placed at Simsim, 9 miles north-east of Gaza. Tristram places it at Beit Susin, on the caravan road to Egypt, some 5 miles south-west of Gerar; which is more probably correct, as its identity with Sansannah is very doubtful.

Hazerim. Deut. ii. 23. = Enclosures or villages of the Avim, who dwelt in the south of Canaan unto Gaza, and whom the Caphtorim expelled. This generic name of their cities explains its frequent recurrence in this district. See note after Hazor.

Hazezon-Tamar (§ 21). Early name of Engedi. Tamar = Palm. Gen. xiv. 7; 2 Chron. xx. 2.

Hazor (1) (§ 65, 79, II. V.). Josh. xi. 1, 10, 11, 13, xii. 19, xix. 36; Judg. iv. 2, 17; 1 Sam. xii. 9; 2 Kings xv. 29. Town of Naphtali near Kadesh.

Hazor (2). Josh. xv. 23. A city of Simeon. Unknown in extreme south.

Hazor (3). Josh. xv. 25. = Kerioth Hezron of same verse.

Hazor (4). Josh. xv. 25. Hazor-Hadattah = New Hazar. Not known.

Hazor (5) (§ 71). Town of Benjamin. Neh. xi. 33; 1 Kings ix. 15. Now Hazzur, 4 miles north by west of Jerusalem.

Hazor-Addah. Num. xxxiv. 4. A town on southern boundary of Simeon. See Adar.

Hazor-Hadattah = "New Hazor," probably. Josh. xv. 25. Tristram proposes Hadâdah, which see under Hazar-Gaddah.

Note.—As observed under Hazerim, the name is very common in the southern district of the land, and specially in the south-east. El-Hudeirah, "the little enclosure," and Wâdy Hudair, "valley of little enclosures," are found 12 miles south-east of Hebron and 7 miles north of Arad, possibly preserving the position of some. Conder, *Palestine Quarterly*, 1883, p. 181, suggests that the name Hazor applied to circles which had a sacred origin. This is possible, but the name seems too widely used, unless we should suppose that in early times the Avim made an enclosure, as the Patriarchs built an altar, wherever they settled. More probably the "*Hazor*" marked the settled villages among a nomadic population.

Hebron (1) (§ 6, 11, 22, 27, 31, 34, 35, 37, 43, 49, 50, 53, 55, 64, 65, 69, 70, 80, 88, 98, I. II. III. V. L.). The name quoted before was Kirjath-Arba. Gen. xiii. 18, xxiii. 2, 19, xxxv. 27, xxxvii. 14; Num. xiii. 22; Josh. x. 3, 5, 23, 36, 39, xi. 21, xii. 10, xiv. 13-15, xv. 13, 54, xx. 7, xxi. 11, 13; Judg. i. 10, 20, xvi. 3; 1 Sam. xxx. 31; 2 Sam. ii. 1, 2, 3, 11, 32, iii. 2, 5, 19, 20, 22, 27, iv. 1, 8, 12, v. 1, 3, 5, 13, xv. 7, 9, 10; 1 Kings ii. 11; 1 Chron. iii. 1, 3, 4, vi. 55, 57, xi. 1, 3, xii. 23, 38, xxix. 27; 2 Chron. xi. 10.

Hebron (2) (*L.*). Josh. xix. 28, most likely for 'Abron or Abdon, xxi. 30. City in Asher. Now 'Abdeh, 10 miles north-east of Acre.

Helbah. Judg. i. 31. In territory assigned to Asher. Tristram says its name lingers on the border of the Anwaby, which falls into the sea 2 or 3 miles north of Sidon.

Helbon. Ezek. xxvii. 18. In the mountains near Damascus. Now Helbôn.

Heleph (§ 79, II.). Josh. xix. 33. Beit Lif, 16 miles east of head of Lake Hûleh. In Naphtali.

Helkath (*L.*). Josh. xix. 25, xxi. 31. In Asher. Perhaps Yerka, 9 miles north-east of Accho.

Helkath-Hazzurim. 2 Sam. ii. 16. "The field of strong men," identified with Wâdy El-Askar, "the valley of the soldiery," a broad, smooth valley at Gibeon.

Hepher. Josh. xii. 17 and 1 Kings iv. 10. It is not known. It lay in the west, either in Philistia or Sharon probably, and may have had its name from "Cheper"=the setting sun.

Heres. Judg. i. 35. In the district of Ajalon. Possibly Ibn Harith, 10 miles west of Bethel. See Mount Heres.

Hermon (§ 7, 10, 12, 23, 27, 29, 31, 36, 58, 76, 107). Deut. iii. 8, 9, iv. 48; Josh. xi. 3, 17, xii. 1, 5, xiii. 5, 11; 1 Chron. v. 23; Ps. lxxxix. 12, cxxxiii. 3; Song iv. 8.

Herodium, or "the Frank mountain," a conical hill 3 to 4 miles south-east of Bethlehem. Now Jebel Fureidis.

Heshbon (§ 25, 26, 45, 56, 57, 58, 59, 60, I. II. V. L.). The Wâdy Heshbon formed the northern boundary of Reuben. Num. xxi. 25-34, xxxii. 3, 37; Deut. i. 4, ii. 24, 26, 30, iii. 2, 6, iv. 46, xxix. 7; Josh. ix. 10, xii. 2, 5, xiii. 10-27, xxi. 39; Judg. xi. 19, 26; 1 Chron. vi. 81; Neh. ix. 22; Song vii. 4; Isa. xv. 4, xvi. 8, 9; Jer. xlviii. 2, 34, 45, xlix. 3.

Heshmon. Josh. xv. 27. Unknown. It has been proposed to place it 3 miles west of Tell-el-Milh at El-Meshash, but it is doubtful.

Hethlon. Ezek. xlvii. 15, xlviii. 1. Unknown. It lay near Zedad, now Sadâd in Cœle Syria.

Hezron. Josh. xv. 3, 25. A place on south border of tribe of Simeon. Identified (Conder) with mountain Hadireh. See Maps I. and II.

Hilen = *Holon* (1). 1 Chron. vi. 58.

Hinnom, Valley of. Josh. xv. 8, xviii. 16; 2 Kings xxiii. 10; 2 Chron. xxviii. 3, xxxiii. 6; Neh. xi. 30; Jer. vii. 31, 32, xix. 2, 6, xxxii. 35.

Hippos or Susitha (the meaning is the same in Greek and Hebrew). Town of Decapolis, not known, described in *Onomasticon* as near Pella and Gadara.

Holon (1) (*L.*). Josh. xv. 51, xxi. 15. Most probably Beit 'Aula, 7 miles north-west of Hebron.

Holon (2). In Moab, unknown. Jer. xlviii. 21. Compare Josh. xiii. 18.

Hor (1) (§ 7, 58). Mountain in Edom. Now Jebel Neby Harûn. Num. xx. 22, 23, 25, 27, xxi. 4; Deut. xxxii. 50.

Hor (2) (§ 9). Mountain in the north. Num. xxxiv. 7, 8.

Horeb. The mount of God lay 250 miles south of Beersheba. Ex. iii. 1, xvii. 6, xxxiii. 6; Deut. i. 2, 6, 19, iv. 10, 15, v. 2, ix. 8, xviii. 16, xxix. 1; 1 Kings viii. 9, xix. 8; 2 Chron. v. 10; Ps. cvi. 19; Mal. iv. 4.

Horem (§ 79, II.). Josh. xix. 38. Fenced city of Naphtali. Probably Hârah (Conder).

Hor-Hagidgad = *Gudgodah*. Num. xxxiii. 32, 33.

Hormah (§ 70, 80). Also called Lephath. It must have lain south of Arad. It is identified with Sebaita, 30 miles south of Beersheba, by many; but lay in all probability much nearer the south end of the Salt Sea, and south-east of Arad. Num. xiv. 45, xxi. 3; Deut. i. 44; Josh. xii. 14, xv. 30, xix. 4; Judg. i. 17; 1 Sam. xxx. 30; 1 Chron. iv. 30.

Horonaim. Not known, but situated in the north of Moab by Heshbon. Tristram regards it as a trace of the Horites; and compare the two Bethhorons. On dual form of Moabite towns, see § 28. Conder, *Heth and Moab*, p. 403, says: Possibly Wâdy Ghûeir (with ancient road). The Hebrew and Arabic have the same meaning, with a slight change of guttural. Isa. xv. 5; Jer. xlviii. 3, 5, 34.

Hosah (§ 78, II.). Josh. xix. 29. A town in Asher. Possibly El-Ezziat, 7 miles south of Tyre.

Hukkok (1) (§ 79, II.). Josh. xix. 34. Naphtali. Now *Yâkûk*.

Hukkok (2) (*L.*). 1 Chron. vi. 75. In Asher. Not recovered (stands for Helkath of Josh. xix. 25).

Huleh. See Merom.

Humtah. Josh. xv. 54. From towns with which it is named, probably close to Hebron on the north.

Ibleam (§ 98, *L.*) = *Bileam*. Uncertain. Either Bel'ameh, 1 mile south of Jenin (Engannim) or Yemma, 4 miles west of Kerak, or most probably Jelameh, midway between Jenin and Jezreel. See Gath-Rimmon (2). Josh. xvii. 11; Judg. i. 27; 2 Kings ix. 27.

Idalah. Josh. xix. 15. "Later name was Hirii (Tal. Jer. Megillah, now El-Huwarah," Conder, *Handbook*, pp. 268, 415). 1 mile south of Bethlehem in Zebulon. If Carmel, or the north side of it, belonged to Zebulon, as Josephus seems to say, Edala might be Ed Dâlieh on Carmel.

Iim (§ 70). Josh. xv. 29. Joined by Wilton with Azem (p. 181). It means crooked, as Aujeh does in Arabic. Proposed to be placed at El-Aujeh.

Ijon (§ 79, II.). Situated in the Merj Ayun by the Hashbany branch of the Jordan. Possibly as Conder proposes, Khiyam. 1 Kings xv. 20; 2 Kings xv. 29; 2 Chron. xvi. 4.

Iron (§ 79). Josh. xix. 38. Yârûn in Naphtali.

Irpiel. Josh. xviii. 27. Town of Benjamin, unknown. Conder proposes Râfât, 1½ mile north of Gibeon.
Irshemesh (§ 72). Josh. xix. 41. City of the sun = *Bethshemesh*. Now '*Ain Shems*.
Issachar (§ 76).
Ithnan. Josh. xv. 23. Not identified.
'Ittah-Kazin (§ 77). Josh. xix. 13. See Kazin. Possibly there is a confusion in the text of Gittah-Hepher and 'Ittah-Kazin, unless both mark a distinct name; or we may take it = Gath-Hepher and 'Ith-Kazin.
Iturea (§ 60, V.). Luke iii. 1.

Jaazer (*L.*). Possibly Sâr, 10 miles north of Heshbon. Conder suggests Beit Zer'ah or Zar'a as the Zara of Josephus (*Heth and Moab*, p. 140), 4 miles north-east of Heshbon. See Jazer. Num. xxi. 32, xxxii. 1, 3, 35; Josh. xiii. 25, xxi. 39; 2 Sam. xxiv. 5; 1 Chron. vi. 81, xxvi. 31; Isa. xvi. 8, 9; Jer. xlviii. 32.
Jabbok, The brook (§ 18, 23, 24, 25, 51, 52, 56, 60, I. II. V.). Now Wâdy Zerka. Gen. xxxii. 22; Num. xxi. 24; Deut. ii. 37, iii. 16; Josh. xii. 2; Judg. xi. 13-22.
Jabesh. See next.
Jabesh-Gilead or **Jabesh** (§ 60, 87, II.). Judg. xxi. 8-14; 1 Sam. xi. 1, 9, 10, xxxi. 11, 12, 13; 2 Sam. ii. 4, 5, xxi. 12; 1 Chron. x. 11.
Jabez. 1 Chron. ii. 55. A town of Judah, probably near Zorah, within 2 miles of which is Deir Abu Kabûs.
Jabneel (1) (§ 69, 99, 119, II.). Josh. xv. 11. Now Yebnah. The Jamnia of Maccabean times, 13 miles south from Joppa. See Jabneh.
Jabneel (2). Josh. xix. 33. According to the Talmud, Yama is now Yemma, 4 miles west of Kerak.
Jabneh = *Jabneel* (1). 2 Chron. xxvi. 6.
Jagur. Josh. xv. 21. In the extreme south-east border of Israel. Unknown.
Jahaz or **Jahazah** (§ 56, *L.*). Scene of Israel's victory over Sihon. Num. xxi. 23; Josh. xiii. 18, xxi. 36; Judg. xi. 20; 1 Chron. vi. 78; Isa. xv. 4; Jer. xlviii. 21, 34.
Jahzah = *Jahaz.* 1 Chron. vi. 78.
Jair (§ 61) = *Havoth-Jair.* Josh. xiii. 30; 1 Chron. ii. 23.
Janoah (§ 73, 79, II.). 2 Kings xv. 29. Possibly Yanûh, 6 or 7 miles east of Tyre (Conder).
Janohah. Josh. xvi. 6, 7. On the border of Ephraim, 7 miles south-east of Shechem.
Janum. Josh. xv. 53. Probably N'aîm, 3 miles east of Hebron.
Japhia (§ 77, II.). Josh. xix. 12. Yâfa, a mile and a half south of Nazareth.
Japhleti (§ 71). Josh. xvi. 3. Unknown.
Japho = *Joppa.* Josh. xix. 46.
Jarmuth (1) (§ 8, 35, 64, 114, I.) = *Yarmûk.* Josh. x. 3, 5, 23, xii. 11, xv. 35; Neh. xi. 29. Now *Yarmûk*, 3 or 4 miles south of Bethshemesh.
Jarmuth (2) (*L.*). Josh. xxi. 29. In Issachar. Unknown. Probably Remeth of Josh. xix. 21, and Ramoth, 1 Chron. vi. 73, which see.
Jattir (*L.*). Now '*Attir*, 13 miles south by west of Hebron. Josh. xv. 48, xxi. 14; 1 Sam. xxx. 27; 1 Chron. vi. 57.

Jazer (§ 56, 99). See Jaazer, also Y'azer.
Jebus (§ 84). See Jerusalem. Josh. xviii. 16, 28; Judg. xix. 10, 11; 1 Chron. xi. 4, 5.
Jehoshaphat, Valley of. Joel iii. 2, 12. This name is often given to the Kidron valley, but the meaning is doubtful.
Jehud (§ 72, II.). Josh. xix. 45. Now *El-Yehûdiyeh*, 5 miles north of Lydda.
Jekabzeel = *Kabzeel*.
Jericho (§ 12, 19, 26, 30, 42, 45, 58, 62, 68, 71, 73, 74, 80, 82, 105, II. III. V.), "the city of palm trees," lies at the level of 820 ft. below the sea. The 'Ain-es-Sultan—Elisha's fountain—probably marks the site of the ancient city. Num. xxii. 1, xxvi. 3, 63, xxxi. 12, 33, 48-50, xxxiv. 15, xxxv. 1, xxxvi. 13; Deut. xxxii. 49, xxxiv. 1, 3; Josh. ii. 1-3, iii. 16, iv. 13, 19, v. 10, 13, vi. 1, 2, 25, 26, vii. 2, viii. 2, ix. 3, x. 1, 28, 30, xii. 9, xiii. 32, xvi. 1, 7, xviii. 12, 21, xx. 8, xxiv. 11; 2 Sam. x. 5; 1 Kings xvi. 34; 2 Kings ii. 4, 5, 15, 18, xxv. 5; 1 Chron. vi. 78, xix. 5; 2 Chron. xxviii. 15; Ezra ii. 34; Neh. iii. 2, vii. 36; Jer. xxxix. 5, lii. 8; Matt. xx. 29; Mark x. 46; Luke x. 30, xviii. 35, xix. 1; Heb. xi. 30.
Jeruel. 2 Chron. xx. 16. Part of the Judean wilderness west of Hazziz (§ 22).
Jerusalem (68, 69, 71, 80, 89-93, I. II. III. IV. V.). Josh. x. 1; Judg. i. 7, 8, 21; 1 Sam. xvii. 54; 1 Chron. iii. 4; 2 Chron. i. 4, etc. See Concordance.
Jeshanah. 2 Chron. xiii. 19. Now *'Ain Sinia*, 3 or 4 miles north by west of Bethel (see *Name Lists*, p. 224).
Jeshimon (§ 12, 68, 98, II.). The wilderness of Judah, stretching along the western side of the Dead Sea. Num. xxi. 20, xxiii. 28; 1 Sam. xxiii. 19, 24, xxvi. 1, 3; Isa. xliii. 19, 20 (?). The same word wilderness is used also, Deut. xxxii. 10, Ps. lxviii. 7, lxxviii. 40, cvi. 14, cxvii. 4, but it does not there seem to be the name of the Judean wilderness.
Jeshua. Neh. xi. 26. Conder suggests S'awi. See under Hazor Shual. Named also in next verse.
Jethlah (§ 72, II.). Josh. xix. 42. In LXX. Silatha. 7 miles east of Lydda is Shilta, which probably represents it. Conder puts it at Beit Tul, 3 miles off Yalo (or Ajalon), named before it.
Jezreel (1). Josh. xv. 56; 1 Sam. xxv. 43, xxvii. 3, xxx. 5; 2 Sam. ii. 2, iii. 2; 1 Chron. iii. 1. Town in south of Judah. Unknown.
Jezreel (2) (§ 18, 19, 40, 58, 76, 82, 96, 107, I. II.). Town of Issachar, on western extremity of Gilboa. Josh. xix. 18; 1 Sam. xxix. 1, 11; 2 Sam. ii. 9, iv. 4; 1 Kings iv. 12, xviii. 45, 46, xxi. 1, 4, 6, 7, 15, 16, 23; 2 Kings viii. 29, ix. 10, 37, x. 1, 6, 7, 11; 2 Chron. xxii. 6.
Jezreel (3). Hos. i. 4, 11, ii. 22. A prophetic designation of northern kingdom, with allusion to Ahab's capital.
Jezreel, Valley of. Josh. xvii. 16; Judg. vi. 33; Hos. i. 5 = *Esdraelon*.
Jiphtah. Josh. xv. 43. Unknown.
Jiphthah-El (§ 77). Josh. xix. 14, 27.
Jogbehah (§ 52, 82, II.). Num. xxxii. 35; Judg. viii. 11. In Gilead. Kiepert places it at Djubêhât, which Conder (*Heth and Moab*) writes Jubeihah, 7 miles north-west of Rabbath-Ammon.
Jokdeam. Josh. xv. 56. Unknown. It lay south of Hebron.
Jokneam (1) (§ 76, 77, II. L.) Tell Keimûm, border city of Zebulon, 12 miles from the sea, under Carmel. Josh. xii. 22, xix. 11, xxi. 34.

Jokneam (2). 1 Kings iv. 12. Apparently in the Jordan valley. Not identified. See Kibzaim.
Jokmeam (3) (*L.*). In Ephraim. 1 Chron. vi. 68. Unknown. See Kibzaim.
Joktheel (1). Josh. xv. 38. In Philistia, belonging to Judah. Unknown. Tristram proposes Beit Jerja, north-west of Umm Lakis, and Conder, Kutlâneh, south-east of Ekron.
Joktheel (2). 2 Kings xiv. 7. A city of Edom. Selah, now *Petra*.
Joppa (§ 8, 72, 119, I. II. III. V.) = *Japho* of Josh. xix. 46. Now *Yáfa*. 2 Chron. ii. 16; Ezra iii. 7; Jonah i. 3; Acts ix. 36, 38, 42, 43, x. 5, 8, 23, 32, xi. 5, 13.
Jordan (§ 13). Gen. xiii. 10. ... Zech. xi. 3; Matt. iii. 5–13, iv. 15–25; Mark i. 5. Now the *Nahr-esh-Sheriah*.
Jotbah. 2 Kings xxi. 19. Not known.
Judah (§ 68, 69).
Judah on Jordan. Josh. xix. 34. Several suggestions have been offered for this. See *Handbook on Joshua* in same series, p. 104. The most probable solution is that it should be "*Hurah*" = the Ghor or hollow of Jordan. See *Palestine Quarterly*, 1883, p. 183.
Judea (§ 100, *L.*). Ezra v. 8; Dan. v. 13; Matt. ii. 1, 5, 22, iii. 1, 5, iv. 25, xix. 1, xxiv. 16.
Juttah (§ 88, *L.*). Josh. xv. 55, xxi. 16. In Judah. Now *Juttah*, 5½ miles south of Hebron. Still a large village whose inhabitants are rich in sheep and cattle.

Kabzeel. Tristram notes traces of ruins at the mouth of the Wâdy Kuseib at the south end of the Salt Sea at the beginning of the ascent of Acrabbim. It must have been hereabout. Josh. xv. 21; 2 Sam. xxiii. 20; 1 Chron. xi. 22; Neh. xi. 25.
Kadesh (1). Possibly the name of a district of the wilderness (Ps. xxix. 8) as well as of a town or towns within it. For position on the eastern edge near Edom (Num. xx. 16), see Map II. By others it is placed 40 miles west at 'Ain Kadeis. Gen. xiv. 7, xvi. 14, xx. 1; Num. xiii. 26, xx. 1, 14, 16, 22, xxvii. 14, xxxiii. 36, 37; Deut. i. 46, xxxii. 51; Judg. xi. 16, 17; Ezek. xlvii. 19, xlviii. 28; Ps. xxix. 8. See Kadesh-Barnea. The name means "*sacred* city."
Kadesh-Barnea (§ 44, 46, 55, 64, II.). On Kadesh and Kadesh-Barnea, see p. 60. In Josh. x. 41 it seems to mark an extreme easterly position, as Gaza an extreme westerly. Num. xxxii. 8, xxxiv. 4; Deut. i. 2, 19, ii. 14, ix. 23; Josh. x. 41, xiv. 6, 7, xv. 3.
Kanah (1) (§ 12, 73, 74, I. II.). Josh. xvi. 8, xvii. 9. The brook, now *Kânah*. It formed the north boundary of Ephraim and Dan.
Kanah (2) (§ 78, II.). Josh. xix. 28. A town in Asher, now *Kânah*, 7½ miles south-east of Tyre.
Karkaa. Josh. xv. 3. On the south-west of Israel's territory. Not known.
Karkor. Judg. viii. 10. East of Jordan. Unknown.
Kartah (*L.*). Josh. xxi. 34. In Zebulun. Unknown.
Kartan (*L.*). Josh. xxi. 32. In Naphtali. Not known. Possibly = Kirjathaim.
Kattath. Josh. xix. 15. Town in Asher. Unknown. Probably not far from Nazareth.
Kazin (§ 77). In Zebulon. May have been one (or both) the places which bear the name Kezaz within 2 miles of each other, 10 miles north of Seffurieh.

Kedemoth (*L.*). Deut. ii. 26 ; Josh. xiii. 18, xxi. 37 ; 1 Chron. vi. 79. A town in Reuben, on extreme south-east of that tribe.

Kedesh (1) (§ 15, 37, 79, II. V. *L.*). Josh. xii. 22, xix. 37. Probably also Josh. xx. 7, xxi. 32 ; 2 Kings xv. 29. A city of refuge.

Kedesh (2) (§ 79, 80). In Naphtali. Town of Barak. Now called *Kadish*, within 2 or 3 miles of south end of the Sea of Galilee. Judg. iv. 6, 9, 10, 11. See Zaanaim named in last reference.

Kedesh (3). In Issachar. 1 Chron. vi. 72. Kudeis, 7 miles west of Jezreel.

Kedesh (4). On southern boundary of Palestine. Josh. xv. 23. This, if not Kadesh-Barnea, is probably 'Ain Kadis, which many take for it.

Keilah (§ 88, I. II. III.). Town in hills of Judah. Kilah, 6½ miles east of Beit Jibrin. Josh. xv. 44 ; 1 Sam. xxiii. 1-8, 10-13 ; Neh. iii. 17, 18.

Kenath (§ 52). Num. xxxii. 42 ; 1 Chron. ii. 23. Now *Kunawât*=Greek *Canatha*.

Kerak (1) (§ 59, II.)=*Kir*.

Kerak (2) (§ 114, V.)=*Tarichææ*.

Kerioth (1). Josh. xv. 25. Now *Kureitein*, meaning, as Kerioth, "two fortresses," 4½ miles north of Arad. Some render Iscariot, "Man of Kerioth."

Kerioth (2)=*Ar of Moab*. Amos ii. 2. See Keil on Jer. xlviii. 24, 41.

Keziz (Josh. xviii. 21) or **Emek Keziz**, on border of Benjamin, east of Jerusalem. Not known. See note in *Handbook on Joshua*, p. 95. The name Kaziz is not on Survey Map.

Kibzaim (*L.*). Josh. xxi. 22. Apparently same as Jokmeam of Ephraim (3).

Kidron (68, 89, IV.). 2 Sam. xv. 23 ; 1 Kings ii. 37, xv. 13 ; 2 Kings xxiii. 4, 6, 12 ; 2 Chron. xv. 16, xxix. 16, xxx. 14 ; Jer. xxxi. 40 ; Isa. xviii. 1. Now *Wâdy En-Nâr*.

Kinah. Josh. xv. 22. Unknown.

King's Dale=*Shaveh*. Gen. xiv. 17 ; 2 Sam. xviii. 18.

King's Pool. Probably=Old Pool. Map IV. Neh. ii. 14 ; Isa. vii. 3, xxii. 11.

Kir or **Kirharesh** (§ 59, II.). In Moab. Now *Kerak*. 2 Kings iii. 25 ; Isa. xv. 1, xvi. 7, 11 ; Jer. xlviii. 31, 36.

Kirjath. Josh. xviii. 28. Most probably El-Kuryeh. Called also Kuryet-el-Enab, 7 miles west from Jerusalem.

Kirjathaim (1) (§ 44, 59, 94, II.). Num. xxxii. 37 ; Josh. xiii. 19 ; Jer. xlviii. 1, 23 ; Ezek. xxv. 9. Now *El-Kureiyat*. In Reuben.

Kirjathaim (2) (*L.*). 1 Chron. vi. 26. In Naphtali. Unknown. Probably Kartan of Josh. xxi. 32.

Kirjath-Arba (§ 33, 49, I. II. III. V.)=*Hebron*. Gen. xxiii. 2 ; Josh. xiv. 15, xv. 54, xx. 7 ; Judg. i. 10 ; Neh. xi. 25.

Kirjath-Arim=*Kirjath-Jearim*. Ezra ii. 25 ; Neh. vii. 29, marg.

Kirjath-Baal=*Kirjath-Jearim*. Josh. xv. 60, xviii. 14.

Kirjath-Jearim (§ 36, 69, 71, 72, 85, II.). This has often, since Robinson, been placed at Khuryet-el-Enab, which in no way suits requirements of the history. These led to the suggestion of Khurbet 'Erma as the site of this city — a suggestion endorsed by Conder, to whom is due the recovery of the names of the mount and city of Jearim in 'Erma. See *Palestine Quarterly*, 1878, pp. 196-199 ; reprinted in *Memoirs*, III. pp. 50-52, also pp. 43-50. See Mahaneh-Dan, Chesalon, Mount Seir, and Bethshemesh, in regard to which its direction is given ; also Ps. cxxxii. 6, where the road to the city "of the woods," *i.e.* Kirjath-Jearim, is described as passing Bethlehem. Khurbet 'Erma is on the line between Rachel's

sepulchre and Bethshemesh, between which the boundary of Judah ran. Josh. ix. 17, xv. 9, 60, xviii. 14, 15; Judg. xviii. 12; 1 Sam. vi. 21, vii. 1, 2; 1 Chron. xiii. 5, 6; 2 Chron. i. 4; Ezra ii. 25; Neh. vii. 29; Jer. xxvi. 20.
Kirjath-Huzoth (§ 57). Num. xxii. 39.
Kirjath-Sannah (§ 64). Josh. xv. 49, and next.
Kirjath-Sepher (§ 37, 64) = *Debir* (2). Now *Edh Dhâheriyah*. Josh. xix. 15, 16; Judg. i. 11, 12.
Kishion (*L.*). Josh. xix. 20, xxi. 28. In Issachar. Uncertain, possibly Kedesh (3).
Kishon (§ 8, 10, 31, 76, 81, I. II.). The river now called *Nahr-el-Mokatta*. Judg. iv. 7, 13, v. 21; 1 Kings xviii. 40; Ps. lxxxiii. 9.
Kithlish or **Cithlish**. Josh. xv. 40. Near Eglon, perhaps Kashkaliyeh close to Khurbet-el-Lahm, which represents town named with it. LXX. reads Maachos, which may be Khurbet-el-Makhas, 8 miles south by west of Beit Jibrin.
Kitron. Judg. i. 30. According to Talmud = Sepphoris or Seffurich, 3½ miles north of Nazareth.

Laban. Deut. i. 1. Generally identified with Libnah of Num. xxxiii. 22.
Lachish (§ 35, 64). An important city of the Canaanites, not identified. See Smith's *Bible Dictionary* and Kitto's *Cyclopædia of Bible Literature*, where valuable notes will be found by Mr. Grove and Dr. Porter. Josh. x. 3, x. 5-35, xii. 11, xv. 39; 2 Kings xiv. 19, xviii. 14, 17, xix. 8; 2 Chron. xi. 9, xxv. 27, xxxii. 9; Neh. xi. 30; Isa. xxxvi. 2, xxxvii. 8; Jer. xxxiv. 7; Mic. i. 13.
Lahmam. Josh. xv. 40. Written variously Lachmas and Lehemas. Probably K.-el-Lahm, 3 miles south of Beit Jibrin.
Laish (1) (§ 44, 95). Called Leshem. Josh. xix. 47. Afterwards called Dan. Now *Tell-el-Kâdy* = *Heb*. Dan, "a judge." The name may remain in Lazazeh, 4 miles south-west of Tell-el-Kâdy. Judg. xviii. 7, 14, 27, 29.
Laish (2). 1 Sam. xxv. 44; Isa. x. 30. In both places named with Gallim, also lost. They must have been close to Jerusalem on the north.
Lakum (§ 79). Josh. xix. 33. In Naphtali, in its south-east border near Jordan. Probably Kefr Kama, 4 miles north-east of Tâbor.
Lasha. Gen. x. 19. Doubtful. If the description could be taken as going round the land from Sidon, southward to Gaza, eastward to cities of the plain, and north by Jordan valley, Lasha would be Laish (1).
Lasharon. Josh. xii. 18. Sârôna, 5 miles east by north of Tabor, is given by Palmer (*Name Lists*) as a proper name—Lashuron. "The houses are rudely built on two hillocks, which lie round a valley watered by a spring . . . the whole of ancient appearance" (Guérin, *Memoirs*, I. p. 414).
Lebaoth = *Beth Lebaoth*. Josh. xv. 32.
Lebonah (II.). Judg. xxi. 12. Lubban, 3 miles west of Shiloh.
Lehi (§ 83). Judg. xv. 9, 14-19. Apparently a district; it means "a cheek" or "jaw," and may be the Wâdy Ismaîn and En-Hakkore.
Leshem = *Laish*. Josh. xix. 47.
Libnah (§ 64, *L.*). Royal Canaanite city in Judah situated between Makkedah and Lachish in Philistia. Probably Tell-es-Safi, whose "white chalk cliffs" are so conspicuous. Libnah means white. It was called *Alba specula*; and its present name has the same significance. Possibly Gath

was the city on the hill, or beside it. Josh. x. 29–39, xii. 15, xv. 42, xxi. 13; 2 Kings viii. 22, xix. 8, xxiii. 31, xxiv. 18; 1 Chron. vi. 57; 2 Chron. xxi. 10; Isa. xxxvii. 8; Jer. lii. 1.

Lod=*Lydda*. Now *Ludd*, 11 miles south-east from Joppa. 1 Chron. viii. 12; Ezra ii. 33; Neh. vii. 37, xi. 35; Acts ix. 32, 35, 38.

Lodebar. 2 Sam. ix. 4, 5, xvii. 27. Most likely=*Debir* (1). Josh. xiii. 26. Now *Dibbin*, near Gerash.

Luhith (§ 45, 59), "Ascent of." Isa. xv. 5; Jer. xlviii. 5. Tal'at-el-Heith (Conder, *Heth and Moab*, p. 140), south of Nebo.

Luz (1)=*Bethel*. Possibly the earlier name remains in 'Ain-el-Lôzeh, 3 miles west. As the district round a city and its villages (lit. "daughters") bore the name of the city when that was changed, the original name might cling to the villages, wells, etc. This would explain several other cases as well as this, where old names are found in the neighbourhood of old sites. Gen. xxviii. 19, xxxv. 6, xlviii. 3; Josh. xvi. 2, xviii. 13; Judg. i. 23.

Luz (2). Judg. i. 26. Conder suggests Lûeizeh (or Luweiziyeh?), 2 miles north-west of Tell-el-Kâdy, but this is hardly far enough north.

Lydda (§ 37, 72, 80, 99, 100, 119, III. V.). See Lod.

Maachah (§ 24, 61, II.). A district on the eastern side of Jordan, beyond the waters of Merom. 2 Sam. x. 6, 8; 1 Chron. xix. 6, 7. Maacathites are mentioned in Deut. iii. 14; Josh. xii. 5, xiii. 11, 13; 2 Sam. xxiii. 34; 2 Kings xxv. 23; 1 Chron. iv. 19; Jer. xl. 8.

Maaleh-Akrabbim = "The ascent of Acrabbim," which see.

Maarath. Josh. xv. 59. Probably Beit Ummar, 6 or 7 miles north of Hebron.

Machpelah, Cave of (§ 49). Gen. xxiii. 9, 17, 19, xxv. 9, xlix. 30, l. 13.

Madian=*Midian*. Acts vii. 29.

Madmannah. Josh. xv. 31 and 1 Chron. ii. 49. See Beth Marcaboth. Now *Umm Deimneh*, 12 miles north-east of Beersheba.

Madmen. Jer. xlviii. 2. In Moab. Possibly M'Deineh, north-east of Dibon.

Madmenah (§ 95). Isa. x. 31. Close to Jerusalem on the north. Unknown.

Madon (§ 65, 79). Josh. xi. 1, xii. 19. Now *Madin*, close to Hattin, a royal city of northern Canaanites.

Magadan (§ 114). Matt. xv. 39, R.V.

Magdala (§ 17, 113, 114, V.). Matt. xv. 39, A.V.

Mahanaim (§ 51, 56, 94, *L*.). Meaning two camps. Gen. xxxii. 2; Josh. xiii. 26, 30, xxi. 38; 2 Sam. ii. 8, 12, 29, xvii. 24, 27, xix. 32; 1 Kings ii. 8, iv. 14; 1 Chron. vi. 80.

Mahaneh-Dan (§ 83). Judg. xviii. 12. "The camp of Dan" lay "behind," *i.e.* west of Kirjath-Jearim and between Zorah and Eshtaol, which exactly corresponds with little plain 2 miles east of Bethshemesh.

Makaz. 1 Kings iv. 9. There is a possible site in Khurbet Makkûs, 5 miles south of Ashdod. The name "ruin of the tolls and taxes" (*Name Lists*) would agree with its being a customs town in one of Solomon's districts.

Maked or Maged. 1 Macc. v. 26, 36. In Gilead. Not known.

Makkedah, Cave of (§ 64, 69, II.). Now *El-Moghâr*. Josh. x. 10, 16, 17, 21, 28, 29, xii. 16, xv. 41.

Maktesh. Zeph. i. 11. "A hollow" at Jerusalem (Tyropœon?). Cf. Judg. xv. 19.

Mamre, Plain or Oak of (§ 43, 44, 48, 53). Gen. xiii. 18, xviii. 1, xxiii. 17, 19, xxv. 9, xxxv. 27, xlix. 30, l. 13.
Manahath. 1 Chron. viii. 6. Possibly Malhah, 3 miles south-west of Jerusalem (Conder).
Maon (1) (§ 88, 98, III.). Now *M'Ain*, 8 miles south of Hebron. Josh. xv. 55 ; 1 Sam. xxv. 2. "Wilderness of," 1 Sam. xxiii. 24, 25.
Maralah. Josh. xix. 11. Uncertain. It lay near Nazareth. Possibly M'Alul (Conder).
Mareshah (§ 98, II.). Now *Mer'ash*, half a mile south of Beit Jibrin. Josh. xv. 44 ; 2 Chron. xi. 8, xiv. 9, 10, 20, 37 ; Mic. i. 15.
Maroth. Mic. i. 12. Ewald suggests it to be a later form of Maarath, which see.
Mashal (*L.*). 1 Chron. vi. 74. Town in Asher. Possibly K. Muslih, 6 miles north-east of Acre. It may be also the Misheal of Joshua, which see. There is a Wâdy M'Aisleh to the east, in which the name may be also preserved.
Masrekah. Unknown. Gen. xxxvi. 36 ; 1 Chron. i. 47.
Mattanah (§ 55). Num. xxi. 18, 19. Must have lain south of the Callirhoe, the next station.
Meah. Neh. iii. 1, xii. 39. A tower immediately on the north of the temple.
Mearah. Josh. xiii. 4. Means "a cave," placed by Conder at Mogheiriyeh, north of Sidon.
Medeba (§ 59, II.). In Reuben, now *Madeba*, 12 miles east from north end of Salt Sea. Num. xxi. 30 ; Josh. xiii. 9, 16 ; 1 Chron. xix. 7 ; Isa. xv. 2.
Megiddo (§ 37, 76, 95, 98). Placed by Robinson at El-Lejjun ; by Thomson at Tell-el-Mutasellim, 1 mile north-west ; and by Conder at Mujedda, 4 miles south-west of Bethshean. Josh. xii. 21, xvii. 11 ; Judg. i. 27, v. 19 ; 1 Kings iv. 12, ix. 15 ; 2 Kings ix. 27, xxiii. 29, 30 ; 1 Chron. vii. 29 ; 2 Chron. xxxv. 22 ; Zech. xii. 11.
Mejarkon (§ 72). Josh. xix. 46. The "river" identified by Conder with the Nahr-el-'Auja, which rises at Antipatris. He also notes that the turbid character of the stream still suits its old name—"yellow water."
Mekonah. Neh. xi. 28. Now *Mekenna*, 5½ miles south of Ekron (Conder).
Meonenim, Oak of. Judg. ix. 37. Probably same as in verse 6, or that named in Gen. xxxv. 4, which may have been the same, or on the same spot.
Mephaath or **Mophaath** (*L.*). In Moab. Unknown. Josh. xiii. 18, xxi. 37 ; 1 Chron. vi. 79 ; Jer. xlviii. 21.
Meribah, or perhaps Umm-Riba, lay near Kadesh-Barnea. Unknown.
Merom, Waters of (§ 9, 15, 30, 65, 78, I. II.) = *Lake Hûleh*. Josh. xi. 5, 7.
Meronoth. Unknown. 1 Chron. xxvii. 30 ; Neh. iii. 7. Conder suggests Marrina in Hebron mountains.
Meroz (§ 81). Judg. v. 23. Probably El-Murussas, 5 miles north of Bethshean.
Michmash (§ 63, 87, 95, II.). In Benjamin. Now *Mukhmas*, 4 miles south-east of Bethel. 1 Sam. xiii. 2, 5, 11, 16, 23, xiv. 5, 31 ; Ezra ii. 27 ; Neh. vii. 31, xi. 31 ; Isa. x. 28.
Michmethah. Josh. xvi. 6, xvii. 7. Probably the great plain of Mukhnah, east of Shechem.
Middin. Josh. xv. 61. Probably Khurbet Mird, 10 miles east from Bethlehem, "in the wilderness."
Migdalel (§ 79, II.). Josh. xix. 38. Mujeidel, 10 miles east of Tyre.

Migdal-Gad. Josh. xv. 37. Probably Mejdel, 2½ miles inland from Ashkelon. Mejâdil, 13 miles north of Beersheba, seems too far south.

Migron (§ 84, 95) = Precipice. 1 Sam. xiv. 2; Isa. x. 28. Burj Beitin at Bethel is also called Burj Makhrûn.

Millo (1). Citadel (?) of Shechem. Judg. ix. 6, 20.

Millo (2). Fortification in Jerusalem. 2 Sam. v. 9; 1 Kings ix. 15, 24, xi. 27; 1 Chron. xi. 8; 2 Chron. xxxii. 5. Beth-Millo (2 Kings xii. 20) seems the fuller name.

Minnith (§ 59). Judg. xi. 33; Ezek. xxvii. 17. In Moab. Of a site Menjah, east of Heshbon, Tristram failed to find traces. Conder (*Heth and Moab*) suggests Minyeh, to the south of Nebo. Tristram points to the "vineyards" about Dibon.

Miphkad. Neh. iii. 31. A gate of Jerusalem (cf. Ezek. xliii. 21, Heb.).

Misheal. Josh. xix. 26, xxi. 30. Probably the same as Mashal of 1 Chron. vi. 74, which see.

Misrephoth-Maim. Josh. xi. 8, xiii. 6. Identified with Sarafend = *Sarepta.* See Map II.

Mizpah (1) (§ 51, II.) Gen. xxxi. 49; Judg. x. 17, xi. 11, 29, 34. = *Maspha* (1 Macc. v. 35) and the *Ramoth Mizpeh* (Josh. xiii. 26). See Oliphant, *Land of Gilead*, pp. 209-216.

Mizpah (2) (§ 26). In Moab. 1 Sam. xxii. 3.

Mizpah (3) (§ 56). Josh. xi. 3, 8. As these texts show, this lay close to Hermon on its south-eastern slope.

Mizpah (4). Josh. xv. 38. In Philistia. Not known. Possibly Neh. iii. 19. Mizpeh in Neh. iii. 15 seems a district. Perhaps = "Land of Zuph."

Mizpah (5) (§ 86, 95). North of Jerusalem. Josh. xviii. 26; Judg. xx. 1, 3, xxi. 1, 5, 8; 1 Sam. vii. 5, 6, 7, 11, 12, 16, x. 17; 1 Kings xv. 22; 2 Kings xxv. 23, 25; 2 Chron. xvi. 6; Neh. iii. 7; Jer. xl. 6, 8, 10, 12, 13, 15, xli. 1-16; Hos. v. 1. Maspha (1 Macc. iii. 46) and Sapha of Josephus (*Antiquities*, xi. 8, 5). The site of this Mizpah has been much discussed. Neby Samwîl was fixed on by Robinson. Others have proposed Scopus, which has the same meaning. Soba also, some miles west of Jerusalem, has been suggested. Conder thinks this Mizpah was the same as Nob (*Handbook*, p. 277). See Appendix I.

Mizpah (6). A Mizpah, doubtless, is found also in Umm Suffah less than a mile north of Jibia (Gibeah 5). "Perhaps Kirjathhaim Misphat of Samaritan chronicle" (*Memoirs of Survey*, ii. 291).

Molada (§ 70) = *Malatha*, LXX. Josh. xv. 26, xix. 2; 1 Chron. iv. 28; Neh. xi. 26.

Moreh (1), Plain of (§ 41, 50). Gen. xii. 6. By others rendered the "Oak of Moreh."

Moreh (2), Hill of (§ 10, 76, 82). Judg. vii. 1. Probably part of Jebel-Duhy range. Deut. xi. 30.

Moresheth-Gath. Mic. i. 14. "The betrothed of Gath." See Maresha.

Moriah (1), Land of (§ 48). Gen. xxii. 2. Unknown.

Moriah (2) (§ 101). Site of the temple. 2 Chron. iii. 1.

Mount Abarim (1.). The range of the Moabite mountains. Num. xxvii. 12; xxxiii. 47, 48; Deut. xxxii. 49.

Mount of the Amalekites = *Pirathon*, which see. Judg. xii. 15.

Mount Baalah. Josh. xv. 11. The name remains in Wady El-Baghl, which joins the Wâdy Surâr from the north, 5 miles west of Bethshemesh.

Mount Baal-Hermon. Judg. iii. 3.

Mount Bethel. Josh. xvi. 1 ; 1 Sam. xiii. 2. Site of Bethel. Burj Beitin?
Mount Carmel. See Carmel.
Mount of Corruption (2 Kings xxiii. 13), or Destruction, now Mount of Offence.
Mount Ephraim (§ 35). To be distinguished from following. Josh. xvii. 15, xix. 50, xx. 7, xxi. 21, xxiv. 30, 33 ; Judg. ii. 9, iii. 27, iv. 5, vii. 24, x. 1, xvii. 1, 8, xviii. 2, 13, xix. 1, 16, 18 ; 1 Sam. i. 1, ix. 4, xiv. 22 ; 2 Sam. xx. 21 ; 1 Kings iv. 8, xii. 25 ; 2 Kings v. 22 ; 1 Chron. vi. 67 ; 2 Chron. xiii. 4, xv. 8, xix. 4 ; Jer. iv. 15, xxxi. 6, l. 19.
Mount Ephron. Josh. xv. 9.
Mount Halak. Josh. xi. 17, xii. 7. Unknown. In Edom.
Mount Heres. Judg. i. 35. In Ajalon. Perhaps Harith, 10 miles east of Lydda, in the district of the Beni Harith. The name of the Amorites lingers in Khurbet and Wâdy Amurieh, 2 or 3 miles south of Shiloh, and in Amurieh, 5 miles west. The latter is but 5 miles south-east of Haris, the burial-place of Joshua, and 3 or 4 miles north-east of Ajul, the ancient Ajalon of this text.
Mount Hermon (§ 23). Deut. iii. 8 ; Josh. xi. 17, xii. 1, 5, xiii. 5, 11 ; 1 Chron. v. 23.
Mount Hor (1) (§ 58). In Edom.
Mount Hor (2) (§ 9). In the north.
Mount Jearim. Josh. xv. 10. "Mount," "which is also Chesallon."
Mount Lebanon (§ 7, 9). Judg. iii. 3. See Concordance.
Mount Nebo (§ 59). See Nebo.
Mount Olivet or Olives (§ 26, 58, 86). 2 Sam. xv. 30 ; Zech. xiv. 4 ; Matt. xxi. 1, xxiv. 3, xxvi. 30 ; Mark xi. 1, xiii. 3, xiv. 26 ; Luke xix. 29, 37, xxi. 37, xxii. 39 ; John viii. 1.
Mount Perazim. Isa. xxviii. 21. The allusion is to 2 Sam. v. 20. Possibly the name is to be recognised in Khurbet Faraj on the south-east of Neby Samwîl.
Mountain of Samaria (§ 96) = *Hill of Shomer*. Jer. xxxi. 5 ; Amos iii. 9, iv. 1, vi. 1.
Mount Seir (1) and (2) (§ 32) = *Seir* (1) and (2).
Mount Zemaraim. 2 Chron. xiii. 4. Marked by Tal'at-es-Sumra = going up of Zemaraim, which see.
Mount Zion = *Zion*. 2 Kings xix. 31 ; Ps. ii. 6, xlviii. 2, 11, lxxiv. 2, lxxviii. 68, cxxv. 1, cxxxiii. 3 ; Isa. iv. 5, viii. 18, x. 12, 32, xvi. 1, xviii. 7, xxiv. 23, xxix. 8, xxxi. 4, xxxvii. 32 ; Lam. v. 18 ; Joel ii. 32 ; Obad. xvii. 21 ; Mic. iv. 7.
Mozah. Josh. xviii. 26. Beit Mizza, 5 miles north-west of Jerusalem.

Naamah (§ 69). Josh. xv. 4. Now *Nâ'aneh*, 3 miles east by north of Ekron.
Naaran (§ 73, 75, 100, II.) = *Naarath*. Josh. xvi. 7 ; 1 Chron. vii. 28. On border of Benjamin and Ephraim, near Jordan, north of Jericho.
Nahallal (§ 27, 77, II. L.) = *Nahaliel*. As its name is said in Talmud to have been Mahlûl, Ain Mahil, 3½ miles west of Nazareth, has been suggested. Josh. xix. 15, xxi. 35 ; Judg. i. 30.
Nain (§ 76, 107, 108, V.). Luke vii. 11.
Naioth (§ 88). 1 Sam. xix. 18, 19, 22, xx. 1. = "homes" or "dwellings." Probably the colleges of the prophets in Ramah. The plural is explained by 2 Kings iv. 38-43, which records 100 men as living at Gilgal. See Sechu.

O

Nazareth (§ 9, 65, 77, 78, 107, I. V.). It is remarkable that this place is not named in the Old Testament (Matt. ii. 23 refers to no express Scripture, though possibly to the use of the word Nezer as applied to Messiah, from which possibly the town also had its name). Matt. ii. 33, iv. 13, xxi. 11, xxvi. 71; Mark i. 9, 24, x. 47, xiv. 67, xvi. 6; Luke i. 26, ii. 4, 39, 51, iv. 16, 34, xviii. 37, xxiv. 19; John i. 45, 46, etc.

Neah (§ 77). Josh. xix. 13. In Zebulun. Not known.

Neapolis (§ 74). Now *Nâblus = Shechem.*

Neballat. Neh. xi. 34. 4 miles north-east of Lydda. Now *Beit Nebâla,* in territory of Dan. Seems to have been occupied after captivity by Benjamites.

Nebo (1), Mount (§ 26, 27, 45, 57, 58, 59, 86, I.). Num. xxxii. 3, 38, xxxiii. 47; Deut. xxxii. 49, xxxiv. 1; 1 Chron. v. 8; Isa. xv. 2; Jer. xlviii. 1, 22.

Nebo (2). Town probably in Judah. *Nebo*, or possibly "the other Nebo," Ezra ii. 29; Neh. vii. 33. Either Nûba, 1 mile north of Aijalon (1), or as likely it is Nob (as in Neh. xi. 32).

Negeb (§ 11, 46, 70, 100, II.). The south or dry country. Often rendered the south.

Neiel (§ 77). Josh. xix. 27. Probably Y'anîn, within 2 miles of Kâbûl, which follows in this list.

Nekeb (§ 79, II.). Josh. xix. 33. Is identified with *Seiyâdeh*, its Talmudic name being Ziadetha. Tristram mentions a Nakib in this neighbourhood not on Survey Map, which is noticed (*Palestine Quarterly*, 1876, p. 150) as near Ed-Dameh.

Nephthalim (§ 79) = *Naphtali.*

Nephtoah (§ 69, II.). Josh. xv. 9, xviii. 15. Near Bethlehem. Identified in Talmud with *Etam* (2) and =

Netophah. 2 Sam. xxiii. 28, 29; 2 Kings xxv. 23; 1 Chron. ii. 54, ix. 16, xi. 30, xxvii. 13, 15; Ezra ii. 22; Neh. vii. 26, xii. 28; Jer. xl. 8.

Nezib. Josh. xv. 43. In Judah. Now *Beit Nusîb*, 6 miles east of Beit Jibrin. K. Beit Nasîf, 1½ mile south-east of it, may also preserve the name.

Nibshan. Josh. xv. 62. In the wilderness of Judah. Unknown.

Nimrah = *Beth Nimrah.* Num. xxxii. 3, 36; Josh. xiii. 27.

Nimrim (§ 59). Isa. xv. 6; Jer. xlviii. 34. Now *Nemeirah*, in the highlands over the Ghor-en-N'meirah. See *Land of Israel*, ed. 1882, p. 334, and *note*. Others identify the waters of Nimrim with the preceding.

Nob (§ 85, 88, 95, III.). The site of Nob is doubtful. Conder proposes to identify it with Mizpeh (5) (*Palestine Quarterly Statement*, 1875, p. 34-41). On Neby Samwîl are indications of a levelled space such as the tabernacle would require. See on Shiloh. 1 Sam. xxi. 1, xxii. 9, 11, 19; Neh. xi. 32; Isa. x. 32.

Nobah (§ 52). Num. xxxii. 42; Judg. viii. 11. On the east of Gilead. Unknown.

Ono (1). In the plain of Sharon is *Kefr 'Ana*, 5 miles to the north of Lydda. 1 Chron. viii. 12; Ezra ii. 33; Neh. vi. 2, vii. 37, xi. 35.

Ophel (§ 68). See Map IV. The southern part of the eastmost of the mountains of Jerusalem. 2 Chron. xxvii. 3, xxxiii. 14; Neh. iii. 26, 27, xi. 21.

Ophni. Josh. xviii. 24. Afterwards *Gophna* (Josephus), now *Jûfna*, 3 miles north-west of Bethel.

Ophrah (1) (§ 95, 115)=*Ephraim* (2). Its inclusion in Benjamin confirms line of boundary drawn by Tell 'Azûr. Placed at Taiyibeh=*Ephron*. 2 Chron. xiii. 19, 4 miles north-east of Bethel. Josh. xviii. 23 ; 1 Sam. xiii. 17.
Ophrah (2) (§ 75, 82)=*Ferata*. Of the Abiezrites. Now *Feráta* (Conder), formerly called "Ophra," 6 miles south-west of Shechem. Judg. vi. 11, 24, viii. 27, 32, ix. 5.
Oreb (§ 82). Judg. vii. 25 ; Isa. x. 26. Probably 'Osh-el-Ghurâb (*Palestine Quarterly*, 1877, p. 22), a prominent peak 3 miles north of Jericho.

Parah. Josh. xviii. 23. Now *Fârah*, about 6 miles north-east of Jerusalem on Wâdy Fârah, a branch of the Wâdy Kelt. It was in Benjamin.
Parbar. 1 Chron. xxvi. 18. Probably part of Jerusalem=suburb of, 2 Kings xxiii. 11.
Pella (§ 60, 114, II.). A town of Decapolis to which the Christians fled before destruction of Jerusalem.
Peniel or Penuel (§ 25, 52, 82, 109). Gen. xxxii. 30, 31 ; Judg. viii. 8, 9, 17 ; 1 Kings xii. 25.
Peor (§ 57)=*Baal-Peor*. Cliff of Peor was over against Jeshimon, looking towards it over the Salt Sea. Num. xxv. 18, xxxi. 16 ; Josh. xxii. 17.
Perez-Uzzah. 2 Sam. vi. 8 ; 1 Chron. xiii. 11. Unknown.
Pirathon (§ 82), Judg. xii. 15,=*Pharathoni*, 1 Macc. ix. 50. Now *Fer'ôn*, 15 miles west of Shechem (Conder). The home of Abdon the judge.
Pisgah (§ 26, 55, 57, 97, and *Heth and Moab*, p. 129)=*Siâghah*, 2 miles westward from Nebo. Num. xxi. 20, xxiii. 14 ; Deut. iii. 17, 27, iv. 49, xxxiv. 1.
Pool of Siloam. See Siloam.
Pool, "Old." May be the same as following, Isa. xxii. 11 ; but it is more likely "lower pool" of verse 9.
Pool, "King's." Probably the pool lower down the valley from Siloam. Here the king's gardens were, and near the gate of the fountain. Neh. ii. 14.

Rabbah. Josh. xv. 60. Named with Kirjath-Jearim. Possibly Rubba, 6 miles north-east of Beit Jibrin (Conder).
Rabbath-Ammon (§ 25, 33, 59, 92, 94, 114, II.). B.C. 285 called *Philadelphia*. Deut. iii. 11 ; 2 Sam. xi. 1, xii. 26–29, xvii. 27 ; 1 Chron. xx. 1 ; Jer. xlix. 2, 3 ; Ezek. xxi. 20, xxv. 5 ; Amos i. 14.
Rabbath-Moab. 8 miles north of *Kerak*. Now *Rabba*. Josh. xiii. 25.
Rabbith. Josh. xix. 20. Now *Râba*, 7 miles south-east of Jenin.
Rachal. 1 Sam. xxx. 29. Unknown. LXX. have Carmel=Kurmul, south of Hebron.
Rakkath (§ 79, 111, II.). Josh. xix. 35. The ancient name of *Tiberias*, surviving till 4th century A.D.
Rakkon (§ 72). Josh. xix. 46. Recovered by survey in *Tell-er-Rakkeit*, 6 miles north of Jaffa on the sea-shore.
Rama. Matt. ii. 18. An application of Old Testament prophecy not implying necessarily that there was a Rama at Bethlehem any more than verse 23 requires us to seek the name of Nazareth in the Old Prophets.
Ramah (1)=*Ramallah*, near Geba (Isa. x. 29), and *Beeroth* (El-Bireh). Josh. xviii. 25, and
Ramah (2) (§ 81, 95)=*Er-Ram*, 4 miles nearer Jerusalem southward. Josh.

xviii. 25; Judg. iv. 5; Ezra ii. 26; Neh. vii. 30; Isa. x. 29; Hos. v. 8—all refer to the former of these. It is doubtful to which the following refer: Judg. xix. 13; Neh. xi. 33; Jer. xxxi. 15, xl. 1; 1 Sam. xxii. 6, which may not be the name of a town.

Ramah (3) (§ 85). Ramathaim Zophim seems intended in the following. It lay in Mount Ephraim. 1 Sam. i. 1, 19, ii. 11, vii. 17, viii. 4, xv. 34, xvi. 13, xix. 18, 19, 22, 23, xx. 1, xxv. 1, xxviii. 3. The name Ramah does not occur in 1 Sam. vii., and its intrusion by Josephus has caused great confusion. Ewald thinks Samuel's Rama was a very small town (*History of Israel*, Eng. ed., iii. p. 19, note).

Ramah (4). Ramoth-Gilead is in 2 Kings viii. 29, and 2 Chron. xxii. 6 called simply Rama.

Ramah (5) (§ 78). Town in Asher. Josh. xix. 29. Possibly Rameh close to Tyre on the south-east.

Ramah (6) (§ 79). Town in Naphtali, Josh. xix. 36, 7½ miles to south-west of Safed.

Ramath. Josh. xix. 8. *Ramath Negeb.* In Simeon. 1 Sam. xxx. 27. Probably = Baalach-Beer. Unknown.

Ramath-Lehi. Judg. xv. 17. See § 83. Ramah may be here a district.

Ramath-Mizpeh (§ 60) = *Rimthe* or Remtheh, 25 miles east of Sea of Galilee. Josh. xiii. 26.

Ramathaim-Zophim (§ 85) = *Rama* (3). 1 Sam. i. 1.

Ramoth-Gilead (1) (§ 29, 51, 60, 96, II. *L.*). Deut. iv. 43; Josh. xx. 8, xxi. 38; 1 Kings iv. 13, xxii. 3-29; 2 Kings viii. 28, ix. 1, 4, 14; 1 Chron. vi. 80; 2 Chron. xviii. 2-28, xxii. 5. See *Land of Gilead*, p. 209 ff.

Ramoth (2) (*L.*). 1 Chron. vi. 73. In Issachar. Conder places it at Râmeh, which is 5½ miles north-west of Samaria, which seems rather far south.

Ramoth (South). 1 Sam. xxx. 27.

Raphon or **Raphana.** 1 Macc. v. 37. Rafeh, 3 miles west of Edrei (Rev. S. Merrill).

Rechah. 1 Chron. iv. 12. Unknown.

Rehob (1) (§ 55). Num. xiii. 21. Apparently Beth-Rehob, which see.

Rehob (2) (*L.*). Josh. xix. 28. Town in Asher. Unknown.

Rehob (3). Josh. xix. 28, 30, 31; Judg. i. 31; 2 Sam. x. 8; 1 Chron. xi. 75.

Rehoboth (§ 50, 68, III.). Well dug by Isaac. Gen. xxvi. 22. Now *Ruheibeh* (Palmer), 20 miles south of Beersheba. Map III.

Rekem (§ 69). Josh. xviii. 27. Commonly, but improbably, identified with 'Ain Kârim.

Remeth. Josh. xix. 21. Probably = *Ramoth* (2).

Remmon. Josh. xix. 7 = *En-Rimmon.* See Rimmon (2).

Remmon-Methoar. Josh. xix. 13, *i.e.* Rimmon, reaching out or curving towards, Neah. Now *Rummaneh*, 6 miles north from Nazareth, 1 mile west of which is Rumeh in Zebulun, a Levitical city. 1 Chron. vi. 77.

Rephaim, Plain of (§ 33, 68, 94). Now *El-Bukeia*, west and south-west of Jerusalem. Josh. xv. 8, xviii. 16; 2 Sam. v. 18, 22, xxiii. 13; 1 Chron. xi. 15, xiv. 9; Isa. xvii. 5.

Riblah (§ 37, 78, 98). Far north in Cœle Syria, 35 miles beyond Baalbek, on the Orontes. Num. xxxiv. 11; 2 Kings xxiii. 33, xxv. 6-21; Jer. xxxix. 5, 6, lii. 9-27.

Rimmon (1). Rimmon Parez. Num. xxxiv. 19, 20. Unknown.

Rimmon (2) or **'Ain Rimmon** (§ 70, *L.*). Josh. xv. 32, xix. 7; 1 Chron.

iv. 32. 10 miles north-east of Beersheba. Now *Umm-er-Rumâmîn*, close to which are famous springs, as 'Ain Kôleh and Bir Khuweilfeh = the well of the water-drawers. Cf. Zech. xiv. 10, and 2 Kings xxiii. 8.
Rimmon (3) (§ 84, II.). The rock to which the Benjamites fled. Judg. xx. 45, 47, xxi. 13. Placed at Rimmon, 3½ miles east of Bethel. Possibly it should be at Rummaneh, 6 miles east from Bethel, where is a ruin and wâdy of that name. This might be Saul's camp, 1 Sam. xiv. 2, when *Pomegranate* should be the proper name = Rimmon in the uppermost part of Gibeah.
Rimmon (4). Rimmon-Methoar, which see.
Rimmon (5). See Hadad-Rimmon.
Rogelim. 2 Sam. xvii. 27, xix. 31. Unknown.
Rumah. 2 Kings xxiii. 36. Possibly Khurbet Rûmeh, 3 miles north of Seffurieh, though no indication of position is given.

Safed. Jewish town, supposed by some to be referred to Matt. v. 14.
Salchah or **Salcah.** In Bashan. Now *Salkhâd*, 10 miles east of Bozrah. Map I. Deut. iii. 10; Josh. xii. 5, xiii. 11; 1 Chron. v. 11.
Salem. Most probably = *Jerusalem*. Gen. xiv. 18; Ps. lxxvi. 2; Heb. vii. 1, 2.
Salim (§ 109, V.) = *Shalem*. John iii. 23.
Salmon (§ 82) = *Zalmon*. Ps. lxviii. 14.
Samaria (1), Town of (§ 10, 11, 53, 75, 96, 100, 105, I. II. V.). In Old Testament. Originally the hill of Shomer. Now *Sebaste*. 1 Kings xvi. 24-32, xviii. 2, xx. 1-43, xxi. 18, xxii. 10-51, etc.
Samaria (2), District of. In New Testament, except Acts viii. 5 (probably).
Eansannah. Josh. xv. 31. Generally regarded as = *Hazarsusah*. Josh. xix. 5.
Sarepta (§ 8, 65, 78, V.) = *Zarephath*. Luke iv. 26.
Saron = *Sharon*. Acts ix. 35.
Saphir. Mic. i. 11, *i.e.* the beautiful city. The direction in which it lay is uncertain, but most probably (from mention of Gath) we may take the place meant to be now represented by several ruins bearing the name Suâfir, 4 and 5 miles south-east of Ashdod.
Sarid (§ 76). Josh. xix. 10, 12. On the borders of Zebulun and Issachar. Conder, on the strength of various readings in LXX. and Syriac, proposes the probable correction of "d" for "r," a frequent error, and suggests Tell Shadûd, 4 miles south-west of Nazareth.
Scopus of Josephus, most likely the northmost height of Olivet range (*Palestine Quarterly Statement*, 1874, p. 111).
Scythopolis (§ 75, 82, 110, 114, V.) = *Bethshan*.
Secechah. Josh. xv. 16. Perhaps Khurbet Zakukah, 7 miles south of Jerusalem.
Sechu. 1 Sam. xix. 22. This occurs as a proper name in Kurbet-esh-Shukf, 6 miles north-west of Jiljiliah, the Gilgal of 2 Kings, where was the school of the Prophet. Some would render the passage "the well of the threshing-floor on the crag;" but Sechu is more likely a proper name, as its occurrence on the map shows. It is in *Survey Memoirs*, iii. pp. 52 and 126, identified with Khurbet Suweikeh, 1½ mile south of Beeroth, which rather seems to mark another Socoh, but certainly suits the story if Ram Allah be Ramah of Samuel, as is probable. Possibly, as some think, it was a district.

Seir (1) (§ 32, 44, 70). In Edom. Gen. xiv. 6, etc.
Seir (2) (§ 81). On the boundary of Judah and Dan. Josh. xv. 10. Now *Siagh*, 2 miles east of Bethshemesh, and lying between it and Khurbet 'Erma. Possibly the name is connected with the superstitions of Bethshemesh and Baalah, close to which it lay (see *Heth and Moab*, pp. 240 and 354 ff.).
Seirath (§ 80). Judg. iii. 26.
Sela-hammah-Lekoth (§ 88). 1 Sam. xxiii. 28. "The cliff" in the Wâdy Malâky.
Sela = *Petra*. 2 Kings xiv. 7 ; Isa. xvi. 1.
Senaah. Unknown. It seems to have been called Magdal Senna, possibly a watch-tower on the Wâdy Suweinit (near the following). See 1 Sam. xiv. 16; Ezra ii. 35; Neh. vii. 38, and probably = *Hassenaah*, Neh. iii. 3.
Seneh (§ 63, 87). 1 Sam. xiv. 4. A rock opposite Bozez on the south side of the Wâdy Suweinit. Scene of Jonathan's exploit. See illustration, *Tent Work*, vol. ii. p. 113.
Senir = *Hermon*. Possibly it marked one part of the Antilebanon range. Deut. iii. 9; 1 Chron. v. 23; Cant. iv. 8; Ezek. xxvii. 5.
Sepphoris or **Seffurieh** (§ 77) = *Dio Cæsarea*.
Shaalabbin (§ 72). Josh. xix. 42. Same as succeeding.
Shaalbim (§ 87). Judg. i. 35 ; 1 Kings iv. 9. Now *Selbit*, 3 miles north-west of Ajalon (Yalo) next named in Dan.
Shaalbon. 2 Sam. xxiii. 32; 1 Chron. xi. 33 = preceding.
Shaaraim (1). Josh. xv. 36; 1 Sam. xvii. 52. The position required by both passages is a site in the north-east of the plain of Philistines on the border of the Shephelah. The name means "the two gates." Most probably identified as Tell Sakariya and Sakariya, a mile north on the other side of the valley of Elah, § 88. Situated 3 miles north-west of Socoh and 5 miles south-east of Azekah on a line between them.
Shaaraim (2). 1 Chron. iv. 31. In Simeon = *Sharuhen*.
Shahazimah. Josh. xix. 22. In Issachar, properly Shahatsim = heights to the east of Tabor. Unknown.
Shalem (§ 41, 73, II. V.). Gen. xxxiii. 18 = *Salim*, 4 miles east of Shechem, a small village, but evidently ancient, having rock-cut tombs and cisterns (*Memoirs*, ii. p. 230). See also § 104. The valley of Shalem is mentioned in Judg. iv. 14.
Shalim (§ 87). 1 Sam. ix. 4. Seems to be "the land of the jackals," but this is uncertain. Ewald suggests it is an abbreviation of Shaalbim (which see). Shalisha lay on the one side of it and the land of Benjamin and Zuph on the other. Shalisha is identified with Baal-Shalisha, and seems preserved in Kefr Thilth (which corresponds with *Onomasticon*). The land of Shalisha probably lay on the west of Ephraim and northern part of Dan, where the names Thilth, Selita, and Shilta still indicate the district. In some MSS. Sarissa is found, which may be preserved in Sirisa (Beth-Sarisa of *Onomasticon*), 4 miles south of Thilth.
Shalisha (§ 87). 1 Sam. ix. 4. See preceding.
Shamir (1). Josh. xv. 48. Sômerah, 13 miles south-west of Hebron near Debir (Conder) or possibly Samah.
Shamir (2). Judg. x. 1, 2. In Mount Ephraim. Unknown.
Sharon (1), Plain of (§ 3, 8, 72, 74, 76, 100, V.). 1 Chron. xxvii. 29 ; Cant. ii. 1 ; Isa. xxxiii. 9, xxxv. 2, lxv. 10. Saron in New Testament.

Sharon (2). 1 Chron. v. 16. A place east of Jordan. Possibly the north part of the Mishor or plain (which is not improbably derived from same root) in the land of Gad.

Sharuhen (§ 70). Josh. xix. 6 stands apparently for Shilhim of Josh. xv. 32 (which see); 1 Chron. iv. 31 has Shaaraim (a dual form). This name is preserved in Tell-esh-Sheriah (in Wâdy Sheriah), 16 miles south-east from Gaza. See Shilhim.

Shaveh (§ 44). Gen. xiv. 7 and 2 Sam. xviii. 18. Unknown, but near Jerusalem (Josephus, *Ant*. vii. 10, 3).

Shaveh Kariathaim. Gen. xiv. 5. = The Plain of Kiriathaim, which see.

Sheba (§ 70). Josh. xix. 2. Now *Tell-es-Seba*, about 3 miles east of Beersheba.

Shebah. Gen. xxvi. 33. Probably the Wâdy Sheba in which the preceding and Beersheba lie.

Shebam. Num. xxxii. 3. See Sibmah.

Shebarim. Josh. vii. 5. Possibly at Deir Shebbab, 1 mile north-east of Bethel, where are extensive ruins.

Shechem (§ 11, 12, 18, 36, 41, 48, 50, 53, 66, 73, 74, 75, 82, 96, 100, 110, I. II. III. *L.*). Now *Nâblus* for *Neapolis*, in the valley between Ebal (on north) and Gerizim on the south. It was the central "city of refuge," west of Jordan. Gen. xii. 6, xxxiii. 18, xxxv. 4, xxxvii. 12-14; Josh. xvii. 7, xx. 7, xxi. 21, xxiv. 1, 25, 32; Judg. viii. 31, ix. 1-57, xxi. 19; 1 Kings xii. 1, 25; 1 Chron. vi. 67, vii. 28; 2 Chron. x. 1, Ps. lx. 6, cviii. 7; Jer. xli. 5; Acts vii. 16.

Shema. Josh. xv. 26. In LXX. Sebmaa. Now *Rujum* (*i.e.* mound of) Selameh (*Land of Israel*, p. 361), 6 miles south by east of Hebron.

Shen (§ 83, 86). 1 Sam. vii. 12, or Ha-Shen, *i.e.* "the tooth." LXX. read Yashan; 3 miles west of Jerusalem is Deir Yesin, 1½ mile north of Ain Karim, which represents Bethcar. Shen may mean sharp rock, as in describing Seneh and Bozez. Chap. xiv. 4, 5. See Lehi.

Shenir (§ 23) = *Senir*. Song iv. 8.

Shepham. Num. xxxiv. 10. On the boundary of the land of Israel to the north-east. Unknown.

Shibmah = *Sibmah*.

Shicron. Josh. xv. 11. At the west end of the northern boundary of Judah, not far from Ekron.

Shihon. Josh. xix. 19. Now *Ayûn-esh-Sh'aîn*, 3 miles north-west of Mount Tabor.

Shihor-Libnath (§ 8, 77), meaning glass river = *Belus*. Josh. xix. 26. The Wâdy Shaghûr and the Wâdy Belus, which it joins, may preserve both names between them.

Shilhim. Josh. xv. 32. Probably Silhân, 6 miles south-east of Gaza. See Sharuhen.

Shiloah = *Siloam*. Isa. viii. 6. The name probably means "aqueduct."

Shiloh (§ 11, 66, 74, 80, 83, 100, II.). Now *Seilûn*, 9½ miles north of Bethel. Josh. xviii. 1-10, xix. 51, xxi. 2, xxii. 9, 12; Judg. xviii. 31, xxi. 12-21; 1 Sam. i. 3-24, ii. 14, iii. 21, iv. 3-12, xiv. 3; 1 Kings ii. 27, xiv. 2-4; Ps. lxxviii. 60; Jer. vii. 12, 14, xxvi. 6, 9, xli. 5.

Shimron (§ 65, 77, II.). Josh. xi. 1, xix. 5. Now *Simûnieh*, 5 miles west of Nazareth.

Shimron-Meron. Josh. xii. 20. Now *Meirôn*, 3 or 4 miles west of Safed.

Shittim = *Abel Shittim*. Num. xxv. 1, xxxiii. 49; Josh. ii. 1, iii. 1; Joel iii. 18; Mic. vi. 5.

Shophan (§ 59). Num. xxxii. 35. May be same as field of "Zophim" (cf. Num. xxiii. 14), which see, or Safût beside Jogbehah (Maps of Kiepert and Merrill).

Shual. 1 Sam. xiii. 17. Near Ophrah of Benjamin. See Ophrah 2.

Shunem (§ 76, 96, 107, II.). Now *Sûlem*, 3½ miles north of Jezreel. Josh. xix. 8; 1 Sam. xxviii. 4; 1 Kings i. 3, 15, ii. 17, 21, 22; 2 Kings iv. 1, 8, 12, 25, 36; and possibly Cant. vi. 13.

Shur (§ 46) = *Wall.* Gen. xvi. 7, xx. 1, xxv. 18; Ex. xv. 22; 1 Sam. xv. 7, xxvii. 8.

Sibmah, also **Shibmah** and **Shebam,** close to Heshbon (§ 59). Num. xxxii. 3, 38; Josh. xiii. 19; Isa. xvi. 8, 9; Jer. xlviii. 32. The name has not been recovered, but on the hill above Sûmia, where Conder thinks it may be, are "several large wine-presses and ruined vineyard towers" (*Palestine Quarterly Statement*, 1882, p. 9).

Sichem = *Shechem.* Gen. xii. 6.

Siddim, "Vale of" (= *Sodom*). Gen. xiv. 3, 8, 10. The meaning is uncertain. Some take it for plural of Sâdeh = field (see Gibeah in the fields). Conder draws attention to the Arabic *Sidd*, "which is used in a peculiar sense by the Arabs of the Jordan Valley, as meaning cliffs or banks of marl, such as exist along the southern edge of the plains of Jericho, the ordinary meaning being a 'dam' or obstruction" (*Tent Work*, vol. ii. p. 17).

Sidon (§ 65, 78, 115, 120) = *Zidon.*

Silla (§ 93). 2 Kings xii. 20. Possibly connected with *M'Sillah*, "the causeway" (1 Chron. xxvi. 16, 18), "terraces" (2 Chron. ix. 11), and "highway" (2 Kings xviii. 17; Isa. vii. 3).

Siloah-Siloam, Pool of (§ 68). Fed by aqueduct. Isa. viii. 6. A village *Silwân* is perched on the rock on the other side of the Kidron. The name is found on both sides of the valley. Luke xiii. 4; John ix. 7, 11; Neh. iii. 15; Isa. viii. 6.

Sion (1) = *Zion* in New Testament.

Sion (2) (§ 23) = *Hermon.* Deut. iv. 48 and probably Ps. cxxxiii. 3.

Siphmoth. 1 Sam. xxx. 28; 1 Chron. xxvii. 27. Unknown. It lay in the extreme south from Hebron.

Sirah, Well of (§ 88). 1 mile north of Hebron. Now *'Ain Sâreh*. 2 Sam. iii. 26.

Sitnah (§ 50). Gen. xxvi. 21. Is placed by Palmer at Shutneh, a very little to west of Rehoboth.

Socoh (1) (§ 88). Town of Judah in the Shephelah. Josh. xv. 35. Identified with Shuweikeh fully 2 miles north-west of Adullam. The present form is a diminutive for *Shaukeh*, and see next. Few names are more variously written. 1 Sam. xvii. 1; 1 Kings iv. 10; 2 Chron. xi. 7, xxviii. 18.

Socoh (2). In Judah, now *Shuweikeh*, 10 miles S.W. of Hebron. Josh. xv. 48.

Sodom (§ 45, 57). One of the cities of the plain, possibly named from Siddim, which see. Gen. x. 19, xiii. 10, 12, 13, xiv. 2-22, xviii. 16-26, xix. 1-28; Deut. xxix. 23, xxxii. 32; Isa. i. 9, 10, iii. 9, xiii. 19; Jer. xxiii. 14, xlix. 18, l. 40; Lam. iv. 6; Ezek. xvi. 46-56; Amos iv. 11; Zeph. ii. 9; Matt. x. 15, xi. 23, 24; Mark vi. 11; Luke x. 12, xvii. 29; Rom. ix. 29; 2 Pet. ii. 6; Jude 7.

Sorek, Valley of (§ 12, 54, 64, 69, 72, 83, I.). Judg. xvi. 4. Now *Wâdy Surâr.* The stream is formed by the gathering of several wadies, east of Bethshemesh, and flows by Makkedah and Jabneel, or Jamnia, falling into the sea 8 or 9 miles south of Joppa. The site of the town is marked by Khurbet Surik, 2 miles of Zoreah.

Succoth (1) (§ 18, 19, 52, 62, 82, 109, I. II.). Gen. xxxiii. 17 ; Josh. xiii. 27; Judg. viii. 5–16 ; 1 Kings vii. 46 ; 2 Chron. iv. 17; Ps. lx. 6, cviii. 7. Most probably Tar'ala at the mouth of the Jabbok ("*east of Jordan*," Merrill, pp. 385–388).

Suphah (§ 28). Num. xxi. 14, marg. Not the Yam Suph=*Red Sea*, but a place on the south of Moab. Possibly Wâdy Safieh.

Sur. 2 Kings xi. 6. Gate of temple in 2 Chron. xxiii. 5 called apparently Ha-Yesôd, *i.e.* of the Foundation. *Sur*=rock.

Sychar (§ 73, 109, V.). John iv. 5. Now *Ischar* or *'Askar* on the south slope of Ebal, within 1 mile of Jacob's well, on the north.

Sychem (Acts vii. 16)=*Shechem*, as in R.V.

Taanach (§ 75, 76, 95, II. *L.*). A famous fortified town Taanac in the Egyptian records of Thothmes III., still called Tannuk, 7 miles west by south from Jezreel. Josh. xii. 21, xvii. 11, xxi. 25 ; Judg. i. 27, v. 19; 1 Kings iv. 12 ; 1 Chron. vii. 29.

Taanath-Shiloh (§ 73, II.). Josh. xvi. 6. On the boundary of Ephraim, now *T'ana*.

Tabbath (§ 82). Judg. vii. 22. Named in flight of Midianites; for this Tubukhat-Fahil, a bold terrace on the east of Jordan upon which Pella stands, has been, with probability, suggested.

Tabor, Mount (1) (§ 9, 10, 58, 75, 76, 77, 78, 81, 110). Now known as *Jebel-et-Tôr*. A town on it seems meant in Josh. xix. 22 ; Judg. iv. 6, 12, 14, viii. 18 ; Ps. lxxxix. 12 ; Jer. xlvi. 18 ; Hos. v. 1.

Tabor (2) (I.). City in Zebulun, given to Levites. Possibly=*Chisloth-Tabor*, which see. 1 Chron. vi. 77.

Tabor (3). Plain of Tabor. 1 Sam. x. 3. Rather Elon Tabor, or the terebinth of Tabor. Unknown. It lay between Rachel's sepulchre and Gibeah of Saul, but could not be so far north as Bethel, where the Oak of Deborah stood (Gen. xxxv. 8), with which some have identified it.

Tadmor. 1 Kings ix. 18; 2 Chron. viii. 4. In the wilderness, afterwards Palmyra.

Tahtim-Hodshi. 2 Sam. xxiv. 6. There is manifestly some error in the text. The most probable suggestion is that it should be "below the Sea of Kadesh," *i.e.* the waters of Merom.

Tamar. Ezek. xlvii. 19, xlviii. 28. Probably not Engedi, which was also called Hazezon Tamar (seeing it is named in xlvii. 10); it more likely lay south of the Dead Sea.

Tanach=*Taanach*.

Tappuah (1). Josh. xv. 34, and probably xii. 17. Unknown.

Tappuah (2). Josh. xvi. 8, xvii. 8. The town belonged to Ephraim, "the district" to Manasseh=*En Tappuah*, which see. Possibly, as has been suggested, it is represented by 'Atûf on the Wâdy Far'ah, 11 miles east by north of Shechem, in which case it lay out of the bounds of Ephraim proper, as traced on the Map. Captain Conder places it on Map (which see) near Yasûf. As the name applied to a district, the identification is doubtful. Appendix, Note IV.

Taralah. Josh. xviii. 27. A town of Benjamin, near Jerusalem. Unknown.

Taricheæ (§ 114, V.)=*Kerak* (2), which see.

Tekoah (§ 69). Tekua, 5 miles south of Bethlehem, possibly not a walled

218   INDEX.

town, but a village in the centre of a purely pastoral district. 2 Sam. xiv. 2, 4, 9 ; 2 Chron. xi. 6, xx. 20 ; Jer. vi. 1 ; Amos i. 1.

Telaim. 1 Sam. xv. 4. *Telem*, Josh. xv. 24, in far south. Tristram suggests Dhullam, the headquarters of the Dhullaim Arabs.

Thebez (§ 82, II.) = *Thebes*. Judg. ix. 50 ; 2 Sam. xi. 21. Now *Tubas*. The oil and corn of Tubas are held in high esteem ; it is still a large village.

Thimnath (§ 72). Josh. xix. 43. (Thamnatha-Pharathon of 1 Macc. ix. 50). Now *Tibneh*, 12 miles north-east of Lydda.

Tiberias (§ 17, 79, 108, 111, V.). John vi. 1, 23, xxi. 1. Formerly called Rakkath. Rebuilt by Herod Antipas, and named after Tiberius Cæsar.

Timnah (1) (§ 69, 83, II.). Josh. xv. 10. Is now *Tibnah*, 3 miles west by south of Bethshemesh and 4 miles south-west of Zorah. As Zorah is 1150 feet, and Tibnah 740 feet above sea, Samson went down to it, and the Philistines of the plain came up to it. Judg. xiv. 1, 2, 5, xv. 6 ; 2 Chron. xxviii. 18.

Timnah (2) (§ 54, II.). Josh. xv. 57. Probably Tibna, 9 miles west of Bethlehem and 4 miles north-east of Adullam, from which, therefore, Judah "went up" to it. Gen. xxxviii. 12, 13, 14. The exactitude of Scripture history is strikingly illustrated by such expressions.

Timnath-Heres or **Timnath Serah** (§ 74, II.). Josh. xix. 50, xxiv. 30 ; Judg. ii. 9. For this two sites have been proposed—(1) Tibneh = *Thimnath*, Josh. xix. 43 ; proposed by Dr. Eli Smith in 1843 ; Guerin advocates it ; Grove in Smith's *Bib. Dict.* favours it. (2) Kefr Haris, in favour of which tradition is distinct.

Tiphsah (1) (§ 97). 2 Kings xv. 16. For this Conder suggests, with much probability, Tafseh, 6 miles south-west of Shechem—certainly not the Tiphsah of 1 Kings iv. 24, which lay on the Euphrates.

Tirzah (§ 75, 82, 96, 110, II.). 11 miles north-east of Shechem, "in a secluded and fertile open valley with good soil and arable land" (*Sur. Mem.*). The ancient road from Shechem to Bethshean passes through it. This is a better identification than Robinson's at Tulluza (Conder). Josh. xii. 24 ; 1 Kings xiv. 17, xv. 21, 33, xvi. 6–23 ; 2 Kings xv. 14, 16 ; Cant. vi. 4.

Tishbeh. Tobit i. 2 mentions a Thisbe on the south of Kadesh, which some think to have been the birthplace of Elijah the Tishbite. Others look to Tisieh, south of Bozrah, suggested by Robinson (iii. 153), which is not suitable. The name is exceedingly obscure, and it is even doubted if it refer to a place at all ; but, on the whole, it is most likely there was a place of the name ; but that Elijah's town was that of Tobit i. 2, it is impossible to say.

Tob (§ 24, II.). Judg. xi. 3, 5. The name seems to be still preserved 12 miles to the south-east of the Sea of Galilee. *Taiyibeh* is the exact Arabic equivalent for Tob, *i.e.* "good."

Tochen. 1 Chron. iv. 32. In the territory of Simeon in the far south. Not known. See Ether, for which it may have been substituted in later list.

Tolad = *Eltolad.* 1 Chron. iv. 29.

Tophel. Deut. i. 1. *Tufileh* on western side of Edomite mountains.

Topheth or **Tophet.** 2 Kings xxiii. 10 ; Isa. xxxiii. 3 ; Jer. vii. 31, 32, xix. 6, 11–14.

Tower = *Migdal.* As "Tower of David," "the furnaces," "Hananeel," and

"Meah' at Jerusalem. Migdal Edar, Gen. xxxv. 21, can hardly be the Migdal Edar of Mic. iv. 8. See Edar.

Trachonitis (§ 56, 114, V.). Luke iii. 1.

Tyre (§ 8, 13, 33, 40, 78, 115, I. II. V.). For a full account of Tyre with plans, see *Memoirs of Survey App.*, vol. iii. 424 ff. Josh. xix. 29; 2 Sam. v. 11, xxiv. 17; 1 Kings v. 1, xvii. 13, etc.; Matt. xi. 21, 22, xv. 21; Mark iii. 8, vii. 24; Acts xxi. 3-7, etc. See under Zidon.

Ummah. Josh. xix. 30. Possibly 'Alma (Conder) in Asher, not far from Es-Zib, the Achzib of this passage.

Uzzen Sherah. 1 Chron. vii. 24. The "ear" or "corner" (Gesenius) of Sherah, who built it (compare Aznoth-Tabor, Josh. xix. 34), to be recognised in *Beit Sîra*, 2 miles west by south of the lower Bethhoron.

Waters of Merom (§ 15, 16, I. II.) = *Lake Hûleh*. Josh. xi. 5, 7.
Wilderness of Judah = *Jeshimon*.
Wood of Ziph should be *Choresh Ziph*.

Yarmuk (§ 60) = *Jarmûk* = *Jarmuth*.
Y'azer (§ 56) = *Jazer*.

Zaanaim (§ 78, 81) = *Zaananim*, Judg. iv. 11; Josh. xix. 33. It should be read with Allon, and probably as Allon, the oak of Bezaanaim, which Conder places at Bessûm, 5 miles north-east of Tabor. See *Joshua* by Dr. Douglas, p. 103.

Zaanan. Mic. i. 11. Uncertain if the same as Zenan.

Zair. 2 Kings viii. 21. The position of this place is uncertain. It probably lay beyond the bounds of Israel. Zûeirah, on the south-west shores of the Dead Sea, preserves the name most nearly: there is an "upper" and a "lower" in the wâdy of that name (*Land of Israel*, p. 344 ff.). De Saulcy proposed this site for Zoar, while Ewald and others have thought Zair might be Zoar! There is a fortress of crusading or even of older times on the south side of the valley.

Zalmon or **Salmon**, "Mount" (§ 82). Judg. ix. 48; Ps. lxviii. 14. Immediately south of Gerizim.

Zanoah (1). Josh. xv. 34. Now *Zanû'ah*, 2½ miles south of Bethshemesh. To this Neh. iii. 13 seems to refer, as Neh. xi. 30 certainly does, being joined with Adullam, 4½ miles to the south. (See Smith's *Bible Dictionary*.)

Zanoah (2). Josh. xv. 56. At Khurbet or Deir Zanâta, 4 miles south-east of Debir (Professor Palmer's *Name Lists*).

Zaphon. Josh. xiii. 27. Town in Gilead, belonged to Gad. Conder identifies it with Amâteh, between Gadara and the Sea of Galilee, since Talmud identifies Zaphon with the Aamathus of Josephus. Probably we should read "to Zaphon" for northward. Judg. xii. 1.

Zareah = *Zorah*. Neh. xi. 29; and 1 Chron. ii. 53.

Zared, Valley of = *Zered*. Num. xxi. 12; Deut. ii. 13, 14. At the south-east of the Salt Sea. Robinson suggests Wâdy El-Ahsy, the boundary between Moab and Edom. The meaning of the word = *osiers* has suggested to others the Wâdy Safsaf, *i.e.* willows; but this seems named distinctly (see Zuphah). Possibly it was Wâdy Siddiyeh, part of Wâdy Ahsay or the Seil Gerahi, flowing into it.

Zarephath = *Sarepta*. 1 Kings xvii. 9, 10; Obad. 20; Luke iv. 26. It was called originally Mizephoth-Maim. Now *Surafend*.

Zaretan or **Zarthan** (§ 19, 60, 75, 76). Josh. iii. 16; 1 Kings iv. 12, vii. 46. A town in the neighbourhood of Bethshitta and Bethshean. Probably Zellûl-esh-Zahrah and 'Ain-es-Zahrah, 3 miles west of the latter, mark the site. The district of the same name stretched from below Jezreel to Abel Meholah as far as Succoth. See Zererah.

Zareth-Shahar (§ 59). Josh. xiii. 19. Zara, on the shore of the Salt Sea, below the entrance of the Callirhoe.

Zeboim (1) (§ 45, 87). One of the cities of the plain (or ciccar) of Jordan. Gen. x. 19, xiv. 2, 8; Deut. xxix. 23; Hos. xi. 8.

Zeboim (2) (§ 71). A valley in Benjamin. 1 Sam. xiii. 18; Neh. xi. 34. Very probably the two are connected. Zeboim of Gen., being possibly near Jericho.

Zebulun (§ 77). Josh. xix. 27. Van de Velde proposes 'Abilin on the valley of the same name, and others founding on a statement of Josephus (*Wars*, ii. 18, 9), that Cestius marched to Zebulun, a strong city of Galilee, which was called "the city of men," have proposed Sha'ab, which means "nation." The matter is quite indeterminable.

Zedad. Num. xxxiv. 8; Ezek. xlvii. 15. On the extreme north of the land, now *Sadâd*, fully 25 miles east of Riblah, and 70 miles north-east of Damascus.

Zelah or rather **Tzel'a.** A town of Benjamin, not known. There David laid the bones of Saul and Jonathan in the family sepulchre. Josh. xviii. 28; 2 Sam. xxi. 14. Tsalla is mentioned in the *Lists* at Karnak, which exactly represents Tzel'a. Possibly it is represented by Salâh, ½ mile south of Birch. See Palmer's *Name Lists*, pp. 278, 310(?), and 326.

Zelzah. 1 Sam. x. 2. Not to be confounded with preceding. It seems to have been at Rachel's sepulchre.

Zemaraim (1). Town of Benjamin, represented by two ruins, as the name requires. Kh.-es-Sûmrah, 4 miles north of Jericho. Josh. xviii. 22.

Zemaraim (2), Mount. 2 Chron. xiii. 4. Probably the Tal'at-es-Sumra (*i.e.* the ascent of Sumra) marks the place.

Zenan. Josh. xv. 37. Possibly the same as Zaanan. Mic. i. 11. Unknown.

Zephath (§ 70, 80). Judg. i. 17. At Hormah. Some identify it with Sebaita, 25 miles due south of Beersheba; but it was much more likely farther east, near the Mukb-es-Sufa.

Zephathah, Valley of (§ 98). 2 Chron. xiv. 10. At Mareshah, which see. The name Zephathah seems to remain in Safieh, 2½ miles north-east of Mareshah.

Zer. Josh. xix. 35. A fenced city of Naphtali. Unknown. Kerak (2)?

Zereda. 1 Kings xi. 26. The birthplace of Jeroboam, now *Surdah*, most probably a village about 2 miles north-west from Bethel.

Zeredethah. 2 Chron. iv. 17. It is Zarthan in 1 Kings vii. 46.

Zererath (§ 82). Judg. vii. 22. Mentioned after Bethshittah in tracing the flight of the Midianites, and seems identical with the preceding. It is almost certain that Zarthan and Zarthanah, Zererath and Zaredatha are all one; and it is possible we should read Zeredath in Judg. vii. 22, the interchange of "d" and "r" being a common one. See Zaretan.

Ziddim (§ 79, II.). Josh. xix. 35. Called in Jerusalem Talmud Kefr Chittai, and so probably identified with Hattin.

Zidon (§ 8, 33, 36, 40, 78). "Great *Zidon*" or Sidon. Gen. x. 19, xlix. 13;

Josh. xi. 8, xix. 28; Judg. i. 31, x. 6, xviii. 28; 2 Sam. xxiv. 6; 1 Kings xvii. 9; Ezra iii. 7; Isa. xxiii. 2, 4, 12; Jer. xxv. 22, xxvii. 3, xlvii. 4; Ezek. xxvii. 8, xxviii. 21, 22; Joel iii. 4; Zech. ix. 2; Matt. xi. 21, 22, xv. 21; Mark iii. 8, vii. 24, 31; Luke iv. 26, vi. 17, x. 13, 14; Acts xii. 20, xxvii. 3.

Ziklag (§ 70, 88). Many positions have been assigned to it. It lay far south. Josh. xv. 31, xix. 5; 1 Sam. xxvii. 6, xxx. 1, 14, 26; 2 Sam. i. 1, iv. 10; 1 Chron. iv. 30, xii. 1, 20; Neh. xi. 28.

Zin, "The Wilderness of" (§ 21), lay on south of Israel's inheritance. Num. xiii. 21, xx. 1, xxvii. 14, xxxiii. 36, xxxiv. 3, 4; Deut. xxxii. 51; Josh. xv. i. 3.

Zion = *Sion*. 2 Sam. v. 7; 1 Kings viii. 1; 2 Kings xix. 21, 31; 1 Chron. xi. 5; 2 Chron. v. 2, etc. See Concordance.

Zior. Josh. xv. 54. Now *Si'aîr*, 4½ miles north-east of Hebron (Palmer's *Name Lists*, p. 408).

Ziph (1). Josh. xv. 24. Unknown. Probably near Telem, which see.

Ziph (2) (§ 88). Josh. xv. 55. Now *Tell Zif*, 4 miles south of Hebron. 1 Sam. xxiii. 14, 15, 24, xxvi. 2; 2 Chron. xi. 8.

Ziphron. Num. xxxiv. 9. On the northern boundary, named next to Zedad.

Ziz (§ 22, 44, 58, 98, I. II.). 2 Chron. xx. 16. The name appears in Hazezon Tamar, and in the district on the plateau above still known as Hasâsch.

Zoan (§ 33). Num. xiii. 22; Ps. lxxviii. 12, 43; Isa. xix. 11, 13, xxx. 4; Ezek. xxx. 14.

Zoar (§ 45). Originally called Bela. Now identified with Tell-es-Shaghûr (Zoar meaning small, which in Arabic is Saghîr). It lies at the foot of the Wâdy Heshbon. Gen. xiii. 10, xiv. 2, 8, xix. 22, 23, 30; Deut. xxxiv. 3; Isa. xv. 5; Jer. xlviii. 34.

Zobah. A region in Syria, beyond Palestine, on the north-east, called Aram Zobah. 1 Sam. xiv. 47; 2 Sam. viii. 3, 5, 12, x. 6, 8, xxiii. 36; 1 Kings xi. 23, 24; 1 Chron. xviii. 3, 5, 9, xix. 6; 2 Chron. viii. 3; Ps. lx. tit.

Zoheleth (§ 68, 89, IV.). A stone near Enrogel. 1 Kings i. 9.

Zophim (§ 26, 27). Num. xxiii. 14. Recovered by Eastern Palestine Survey at "Tal'at-es-Sufa," the ascent leading up to the ridge of Nebo from the north.

Zoreah (§ 72, 83, II.). Also Zareah and Zorah, a town given to Dan, now *Zura'h*, scarce 2 miles west of Eshtaol. Josh. xv. 33, xix. 41; Judg. xiii. 2, 25, xvi. 31, xviii. 2, 8, 11; 2 Chron. xi. 10; Neh. xi. 29.

Zuph, The Land of (§ 85). 1 Sam. ix. 5. Many conjectures have been made as to this place. Most probably it lay south-west or west of Rachel's sepulchre (cf. x. 2).

'A most useful series of Handbooks. With such helps as these, to be an inefficient teacher is to be blameworthy.'—Rev. C. H. SPURGEON.

BIBLE CLASS PRIMERS.

Edited by Rev. Professor SALMOND, D.D.

In paper covers, 6d. each; free by post, 7d. In cloth, 8d. each; free by post, 9d.

Life of the Apostle Peter.
By Rev. Professor SALMOND, D.D.
'A work which only an accomplished scholar could have produced.'—*Christian Leader.*

Outlines of Early Church History.
By Rev. HENRY WALLIS SMITH, D.D.
'An admirable sketch of early Church history.'—*Baptist.*

Life of David. 12th Thousand.
By the late Rev. PETER THOMSON, M.A.
'I think it is excellent indeed, and have seen nothing of the kind so good.'—Rev. STANLEY LEATHES, D.D.

Life of Moses. 20th Thousand.
By Rev. JAMES IVERACH, M.A.
'Accurately done, clear, mature, and scholarly.'—*Christian.*

Life of Paul. 10th Thousand.
By PATON J. GLOAG, D.D.
'This little book could not well be surpassed.'—*Daily Review.*

Life and Reign of Solomon. 10th Thousand.
By Rev. RAYNER WINTERBOTHAM, M.A., LL.B.
'Every teacher should have it.'—Rev. C. H. SPURGEON.

The History of the Reformation. 6th Thousand.
By Rev. Professor WITHEROW.
'A vast amount of information set forth in a clear and concise manner.'—*United Presbyterian Magazine.*

The Kings of Israel. 5th Thousand.
By Rev. W. WALKER, M.A.
'A masterpiece of lucid condensation.'—*Christian Leader.*

The Kings of Judah. 5th Thousand.
By Rev. Professor GIVEN, Ph.D.
'Admirably arranged; the style is sufficiently simple and clear to be quite within the compass of young people.'—*British Messenger.*

Joshua and the Conquest. 5th Thousand.
By Rev. Professor CROSKERY.
'This carefully written manual will be much appreciated.'—*Daily Review.*

Bible Words and Phrases, Explained and Illustrated.
By Rev. CHARLES MICHIE, M.A. 18mo, cloth, 1s.
'Will be found interesting and instructive, and of the greatest value to young students and teachers.'—*Athenæum.*

For List of Works in preparation, *see next page.*

BIBLE CLASS PRIMERS.

EDITED BY REV. PROFESSOR SALMOND, D.D.

Each Primer is a complete text-book on its subject, arranged in sections, with Maps, and Questions for Examination.

This Series is intended to provide text-books abreast of the scholarship of the day; but so moderate in size and price as to fit them for general use among young people under religious instruction at week-day and Sunday schools, and in Bible classes. It is meant not to conflict with such a series as 'The Handbooks for Bible Classes and Private Students,' but to serve as a preparation for it. The Volumes will be written by competent scholars, known for their interest in the young, and belonging to the various branches of the Church of the Reformation.

IN PREPARATION.

Historical Geography of the Holy Land. [*Soon.*
By Rev. R. S. MACPHAIL, M.A., Liverpool.

Scottish Church History. [*Soon.*
By Rev. G. JOHNSTONE, B.D., Liverpool.

The Life of Our Lord. [*Soon.*
By Rev. Professor SALMOND, D.D.

The Lord's Supper.
By Rev. J. MARSHALL LANG, D.D., Barony Church, Glasgow.

The Planting of the Church.
By Rev. Professor LINDSAY, D.D., Glasgow.

The History of Missions.
By Rev. JOHN ROBSON, D.D., Aberdeen, and Rev. W. FLEMING STEVENSON, D.D., Dublin.

History of New Testament Times.
By Rev. Principal FAIRBAIRN, D.D., Airedale College, Bradford.

Abraham and the Patriarchal Age.
By the Rev. Professor A. B. BRUCE, D.D., Glasgow.

Life and Times of Joseph.
By the Rev. JAMES DODDS, D.D., Edinburgh.

The Period of the Judges.
By the Rev. Professor PATERSON, M.A., Edinburgh.

The Exile and the Return.
By the Rev. Professor A. B. DAVIDSON, LL.D., Edinburgh.

The Prophets of the Eighth Century.
By the Rev. W. ROBERTSON SMITH, LL.D.

The Tabernacle and the Temple.
By JAMES BURGESS, LL.D., F.R.G.S.

Historical Connection between the Old and New Testaments.
By the Rev. Professor J. GIBB, M.A., London.

The Gospel Parables.
By the Rev. Professor SOMERVILLE, M.A., Rothesay.

www.ingramcontent.com/pod-product-compliance
Lightning Source LLC
Chambersburg PA
CBHW021813230426
43669CB00008B/734